Praise for the first edition of *Effective C++*:

Effective C++
Second Edition

Addison-Wesley Professional Computing Series

Brian W. Kernighan, Consulting Editor

Please see our web site (http://www.awl.com/cseng/series/professionalcomputing) for more information on these titles.

Effective C++
Second Edition

50 Specific Ways to Improve Your Programs and Designs

Scott Meyers

▲
▼▼

ADDISON–WESLEY

Boston • San Francisco • New York • Toronto • Montreal
London • Munich • Paris • Madrid
Capetown • Sidney • Tokyo • Singapore • Mexico City

Many of the designations used by manufacturers and sellers to distinguish their products are claimed as trademarks. Where those designations appear in this book, and we were aware of a trademark claim, the designations have been printed in initial capital letters or in all capitals.

The author and publisher have taken care in the preparation of this book, but make no expressed or implied warranty of any kind and assume no responsibility for errors or omissions. No liability is assumed for incidental or consequential damages in connection with or arising out of the use of the information or programs contained herein.

The publisher offers discounts on this book when ordered in quantity for special sales. For more information, please contact:

Pearson Education Corporate Sales Division
One Lake Street
Upper Saddle River, NJ 07458
(800) 382-3419
corpsales@pearsontechgroup.com

Visit AW on the Web: www.awl.com/cseng/

Library of Congress Cataloging-in-Publication Data
Meyers, Scott (Scott Douglas)
    Effective C++: 50 specific ways to improve your programs and designs / Scott Meyers.—2nd ed.
       p. cm.
    Includes index.
    ISBN 0-201-92488-9
    1. C++ (Computer program language). I. Title.
    QA76.73.C153M48 1997
    005.13'3—dc21
                                        97–24041
                                           CIP

Text printed on recycled and acid-free paper.
ISBN 0201924889
10 1112131415 MA 03 02 01 00
10th Printing November 2000

For Nancy,
without whom nothing
would be much worth doing.

Wisdom and beauty form a very rare combination.

– Petronius Arbiter
Satyricon, XCIV

Contents

Classes and Functions: Design and Declaration   77

Classes and Functions: Implementation   123

Contents

Preface

This book is a direct outgrowth of my experiences teaching C++ to professional programmers. I've found that most students, after a week of intensive instruction, feel comfortable with the basic constructs of the language, but they tend to be less sanguine about their ability to put the constructs together in an effective manner. Thus began my attempt to formulate short, specific, easy-to-remember guidelines for effective software development in C++: a summary of the things experienced C++ programmers almost always do or almost always avoid doing.

I was originally interested in rules that could be enforced by some kind of lint-like program. To that end, I led research into the development of tools to examine C++ source code for violations of user-specified conditions.[†] Unfortunately, the research ended before a complete prototype could be developed. Fortunately, several commercial C++-checking products are now available.

Though my initial interest was in programming rules that could be automatically enforced, I soon realized the limitations of that approach. The majority of guidelines used by good C++ programmers are too difficult to formalize or have too many important exceptions to be blindly enforced by a program. I was thus led to the notion of something less precise than a computer program, but still more focused and to-the-point than a general C++ textbook. The result you now hold in your hands: a book containing 50 specific suggestions on how to improve your C++ programs and designs.

In this book, you'll find advice on what you should do, and why, and what you should not do, and why not. Fundamentally, of course, the whys are more important than the whats, but it's a lot more conve-

---

† You can find an overview of the research at the *Effective C++* World Wide Web site: http://www.awl.com/cp/ec++.html.

nient to refer to a list of guidelines than to memorize a textbook or two.

Unlike most books on C++, my presentation here is not organized around particular language features. That is, I don't talk about constructors in one place, about virtual functions in another, about inheritance in a third, etc. Instead, each discussion in the book is tailored to the guideline it accompanies, and my coverage of the various aspects of a particular language feature may be dispersed throughout the book.

The advantage of this approach is that it better reflects the complexity of the software systems for which C++ is often chosen, systems in which understanding individual language features is not enough. For example, experienced C++ developers know that understanding inline functions and understanding virtual destructors does *not* necessarily mean you understand inline virtual destructors. Such battle-scarred developers recognize that comprehending the *interactions* between the features in C++ is of the greatest possible importance in using the language effectively. The organization of this book reflects that fundamental truth.

The disadvantage of this design is that you may have to look in more than one place to find everything I have to say about a particular C++ construct. To minimize the inconvenience of this approach, I have sprinkled cross-references liberally throughout the text, and a comprehensive index is provided at the end of the book.

In preparing this second edition, my ambition to improve the book has been tempered by fear. Tens of thousands of programmers embraced the first edition of *Effective C++*, and I didn't want to destroy whatever characteristics attracted them to it. However, in the six years since I wrote the book, C++ has changed, the C++ library has changed (see Item 49), my understanding of C++ has changed, and accepted usage of C++ has changed. That's a lot of change, and it was important to me that the technical material in *Effective C++* be revised to reflect those changes. I'd done what I could by updating individual pages between printings, but books and software are frighteningly similar — there comes a time when localized enhancements fail to suffice, and the only recourse is a system-wide rewrite. This book is the result of that rewrite: *Effective C++*, Version 2.0.

Those familiar with the first edition may be interested to know that every Item in the book has been reworked. I believe the overall structure of the book remains sound, however, so little there has changed. Of the 50 original Items, I retained 48, though I tinkered with the wording of a few Item titles (in addition to revising the accompanying discussions). The retired Items (i.e., those replaced with completely new material) are numbers 32 and 49, though much of the information that used to be in Item 32 somehow found its way into the revamped Item 1. I swapped the order of Items 41 and 42, because that made it easier to present the revised material they contain. Finally, I reversed the direction of my inheritance arrows. They now follow the almost-universal convention of pointing from derived classes to base classes. This is the same convention I followed in my 1996 book, *More Effective C++*, an overview of which you can find on pages 237–238 of this volume.

The set of guidelines in this book is far from exhaustive, but coming up with good rules — ones that are applicable to almost all applications almost all the time — is harder than it looks. Perhaps you know of additional guidelines, of more ways in which to program effectively in C++. If so, I would be delighted to hear about them.

On the other hand, you may feel that some of the Items in this book are inappropriate as general advice; that there is a better way to accomplish a task examined in the book; or that one or more of the technical discussions is unclear, incomplete, or misleading. I encourage you to let me know about these things, too.

Donald Knuth has a long history of offering a small reward to people who notify him of errors in his books. The quest for a perfect book is laudable in any case, but in view of the number of bug-ridden C++ books that have been rushed to market, I feel especially strongly compelled to follow Knuth's example. Therefore, for each error in this book that is reported to me — be it technical, grammatical, typographical, or otherwise — I will, in future printings, gladly add to the acknowledgments the name of the first person to bring that error to my attention.

Send your suggested guidelines, your comments, your criticisms, and — sigh — your bug reports to:

Scott Meyers
c/o Publisher, Corporate and Professional Publishing
Addison Wesley Longman, Inc.
1 Jacob Way
Reading, MA 01867
U. S. A.

Alternatively, you may send electronic mail to `ec++@awl.com`.

I maintain a list of changes to this book since its first printing, including bug-fixes, clarifications, and technical updates. This list is available at the *Effective C++* World Wide Web site, `http://www.awl.com/cp/ec++.html`. If you would like a copy of this list, but you lack access to the World Wide Web, please send a request to one of the addresses above, and I will see that the list is sent to you.

If you'd like to be notified when I make changes to this book, consider joining my mailing list. For details, consult `http://www.aristeia.com/MailingList/index.html`.

SCOTT DOUGLAS MEYERS

STAFFORD, OREGON
JULY 1997

Acknowledgments

Some three decades have elapsed since Kathy Reed taught me what a computer was and how to program one, so I suppose this is really all her fault. In 1989, Donald French asked me to develop C++ training materials for the Institute for Advanced Professional Studies, so perhaps he should shoulder some blame. The students in my class at Stratus Computer the week of June 3, 1991, were not the first to suggest I write a book summarizing the pearls of alleged wisdom that tumble forth when I teach, but they were the ones who finally convinced me to do it, so they bear some of the responsibility. I'm grateful to them all.

Many of the Items and examples in this book have no particular source, at least not one I can remember. Instead, they grew out of a combination of my own experiences using and teaching C++, those of my colleagues, and opinions expressed by contributors to the Usenet C++ newsgroups. Many examples that are now standard in the C++ teaching community — notably strings — can be traced back to the initial edition of Bjarne Stroustrup's *The C++ Programming Language* (Addison-Wesley, 1986). Several of the Items found here (e.g., Item 17) can also be found in that seminal work.

Item 8 includes an implementation idea from Steve Clamage's May 1993 *C++ Report* article, "Implementing new and delete." Item 9 was motivated by commentary in *The Annotated C++ Reference Manual* (see Item 50), and Items 10 and 13 were suggested by John Shewchuk. The implementation of operator new in Item 10 is based on presentations in the second edition of Stroustrup's *The C++ Programming Language* (Addison-Wesley, 1991) and Jim Coplien's *Advanced C++: Programming Styles and Idioms* (Addison-Wesley, 1992). Dietmar Kühl pointed out the undefined behavior I describe in Item 14. Doug Lea provided the aliasing examples at the end of Item 17. The idea of using 0L for NULL in Item 25 came from Jack Reeves's March 1996 *C++ Report* article, "Coping with Exceptions." Several members of various Usenet C++ newsgroups helped refine that Item's class for implementing NULL-based pointer conversions via member templates. A newsgroup posting by Steve Clamage tempered my enthusiasm for references to functions in Item 28. Item 33 incorporates observations from Tom Cargill's *C++ Programming Style* (Addison-Wesley, 1992), Martin Carroll's and Margaret Ellis's *Designing and Coding Reusable C++* (Addison-Wesley, 1995), *Taligent's Guide to Designing Programs* (Addison-Wesley, 1994), Rob Murray's *C++ Strategies and Tactics* (Addison-Wesley, 1993), as well as information from publications and newsgroup postings by Steve Clamage. The material in Item 34 benefited from my discussions with John Lakos and from reading his book, *Large-Scale C++ Software Design* (Addison-Wesley, 1996). The envelope/letter terminology in that Item comes from Jim Coplien's *Advanced C++: Programming Styles and Idioms*; John Carolan coined the delightful term, "Cheshire Cat class." The rectangle/square example of Item 35 is taken from Robert Martin's March 1996 *C++ Report* column, "The Liskov Substitution Principle." A long-ago comp.lang.c++ posting by Mark Linton set me straight in my thinking about grasshoppers and crickets in Item 43. My traits examples in Item 49 are taken from Nathan Myers's June 1995 *C++ Report* article, "A New and Useful Template Technique: Traits," and Pete Becker's "C/C++ Q&A" column in the November 1996 *C/C++ User's Journal*; my summary of C++'s internationalization support is based on a pre-publication book draft by Klaus Kreft and Angelika Langer. Of course, "Hello world" comes from *The C Programming Language* by Brian Kernighan and Dennis Ritchie (Prentice-Hall, initially published in 1978).

Many readers of the first edition sent suggestions I was unable to incorporate in that version of the book, but that I've adopted in one form or another for this new edition. Others took advantage of Usenet C++ newsgroups to post insightful remarks about the material in the book. I'm grateful to each of the following individuals, and I've noted where I took advantage of their ideas: Mike Kaelbling and Julio Kuplinsky (Introduction); a person my notes identify only as "a guy at Claris"[†] (Item 5); Joel Regen and Chris Treichel (Item 7); Tom Cargill, Larry Gajdos, Doug Morgan, and Uwe Steinmüller (Item 10); Roger Scott and Steve Burkett (Item 12); David Papurt (Item 13); Alexander Gootman (Item 14); David Bern (Item 16); Tom Cargill, Tom Chappell, Dan Fran-

---

† Note to this guy: I was at Claris the week of November 15, 1993. Contact me and identify yourself as the one who pointed out the importance of specifying which form of delete to use with a typedef, and I'll happily give you proper credit in these acknowledgments. I'll even throw in a little something (*very* little — don't get excited) to help compensate for my pathetic failure to know who you are.

klin, and Jerry Liebelson (Item 17); John "Eljay" Love-Jensen (Item 19); Eric Nagler (Item 22); Roger Eastman, Doug Moore, and Aaron Naiman (Item 23); Dat Thuc Nguyen (Item 25); Tony Hansen, Natraj Kini, and Roger Scott (Item 33); John Harrington, Read Fleming, and Dave Smallberg (Item 34); Johan Bengtsson (Item 36); Rene Rodoni (Item 39); Paul Blankenbaker and Mark Somer (Item 40); Tom Cargill and John Lakos (Item 41); Frieder Knauss and Roger Scott (Item 42); David Braunegg, Steve Clamage, and Dawn Koffman (Item 45); Tom Cargill (Item 46); Wesley Munsil (Item 47); Randy Mangoba (most class definitions); and John "Eljay" Love-Jensen (many places where I use type double).

Partial and/or complete drafts of the manuscript for the first edition were reviewed by Tom Cargill, Glenn Carroll, Tony Davis, Brian Kernighan, Jak Kirman, Doug Lea, Moises Lejter, Eugene Santos, Jr., John Shewchuk, John Stasko, Bjarne Stroustrup, Barbara Tilly, and Nancy L. Urbano. In addition, I received suggestions for improvements that I was able to incorporate in later printings from the following alert readers, whom I've listed in the order in which I received their reports: Nancy L. Urbano, Chris Treichel, David Corbin, Paul Gibson, Steve Vinoski, Tom Cargill, Neil Rhodes, David Bern, Russ Williams, Robert Brazile, Doug Morgan, Uwe Steinmüller, Mark Somer, Doug Moore, Dave Smallberg, Seth Meltzer, Oleg Shteynbuk, David Papurt, Tony Hansen, Peter McCluskey, Stefan Kuhlins, David Braunegg, Paul Chisholm, Adam Zell, Clovis Tondo, Mike Kaelbling, Natraj Kini, Lars Nyman, Greg Lutz, Tim Johnson, John Lakos, Roger Scott, Scott Frohman, Alan Rooks, Robert Poor, Eric Nagler, Antoine Trux, Cade Roux, Chandrika Gokul, Randy Mangoba, and Glenn Teitelbaum. Each of these people was instrumental in improving the book you now hold.

Drafts of the second edition were reviewed by Derek Bosch, Tim Johnson, Brian Kernighan, Junichi Kimura, Scott Lewandowski, Laura Michaels, Dave Smallberg, Clovis Tondo, Chris Van Wyk, and Oleg Zabluda. I am grateful to all these people, but especially to Tim Johnson, whose detailed review influenced the final manuscript in dozens of ways. I am also grateful to Jill Huchital and Steve Reiss for their assistance in finding good reviewers, a task of crucial importance and increasing difficulty. Dawn Koffman and Dave Smallberg suggested improvements to the C++ training materials derived from my books, and many of their ideas have found their way into this revision. Finally, I received comments from the following readers of earlier printings of this book, and I've modified this current printing to take their suggestions into account: Daniel Steinberg, Arunprasad Marathe, Doug Stapp, Robert Hall, Cheryl Ferguson, Gary Bartlett, Michael

Tamm, Kendall Beaman, Eric Nagler, Max Hailperin, Joe Gottman, Richard Weeks, Valentin Bonnard, Jun He, Tim King, Don Maier, Ted Hill, Mark Harrison, Michael Rubenstein, Mark Rodgers, David Goh, Brenton Cooper, Andy Thomas-Cramer, Antoine Trux, John Wait, Brian Sharon, Liam Fitzpatrick, Bernd Mohr, Gary Yee, John O'Hanley, Brady Patterson, Christopher Peterson, Feliks Kluzniak, and Isi Dunietz.

Evi Nemeth (with the cooperation of Addison-Wesley, the USENIX Association, and The Internet Engineering Task Force) has agreed to see to it that leftover copies of the first edition are delivered to computer science laboratories at universities in Eastern Europe; these universities would otherwise find it difficult to acquire such books. Evi voluntarily performs this service for several authors and publishers, and I'm happy to be able to help in some small way. If you'd like more information on this program, contact Evi at evi@cs.colorado.edu.

Sometimes it seems that the players in publishing change nearly as frequently as the trends in programming, so I'm pleased that my editor, John Wait, my marketing director, Kim Dawley, and my production director, Marty Rabinowitz, continue to play the roles they did in those innocent days of 1991 when I first started this whole authoring thing. Sarah Weaver was my project manager for this book, Rosemary Simpson provided advice on indexing, and Lana Langlois acted as my primary contact and all-around *über*coordinator at Addison-Wesley until she left for greener — or at least different — pastures. I thank them and their colleagues for helping with the thousand tasks that separate simple writing from actual publishing.

Kathy Wright had nothing to do with the book, but she'd like to be acknowledged.

For the first edition, I am grateful for the enthusiastic and unflagging encouragement provided by my wife, Nancy L. Urbano, and by my family and hers. Although writing a book was the last thing I was supposed to be doing, and doing so reduced my free time from merely little to effectively none, they made it clear that the effort was worth it if, in the end, the result was an author in the family.

That author has been in the family six years now, yet Nancy continues to tolerate my hours, put up with my technochatter, and encourage my writing. She also has a knack for knowing *just* the right word when I can't think of it. The Nancyless life is not worth living.

Our dog, Persephone, never lets me confuse my priorities. Deadline or no deadline, the time for a walk is always *now*.

Introduction

Learning the fundamentals of a programming language is one thing; learning how to design and implement *effective* programs in that language is something else entirely. This is especially true of C++, a language boasting an uncommon range of power and expressiveness. Built atop a full-featured conventional language (C), it also offers a wide range of object-oriented features, as well as support for templates and exceptions.

Properly used, C++ can be a joy to work with. An enormous variety of designs, both object-oriented and conventional, can be expressed directly and implemented efficiently. You can define new data types that are all but indistinguishable from their built-in counterparts, yet are substantially more flexible. A judiciously chosen and carefully crafted set of classes — one that automatically handles memory management, aliasing, initialization and clean-up, type conversions, and all the other conundrums that are the bane of software developers — can make application programming easy, intuitive, efficient, and nearly error-free. It isn't unduly difficult to write effective C++ programs, *if* you know how to do it.

Used without discipline, C++ can lead to code that is incomprehensible, unmaintainable, inextensible, inefficient, and just plain wrong.

The trick is to discover those aspects of C++ that are likely to trip you up and to learn how to avoid them. That is the purpose of this book. I assume you already know C++ as a *language* and that you have some experience in its use. What I provide here is a guide to using the language *effectively*, so that your software is comprehensible, maintainable, extensible, efficient, and likely to behave as you expect.

The advice I proffer falls into two broad categories: general design strategies, and the nuts and bolts of specific language features.

The design discussions concentrate on how to choose between different approaches to accomplishing something in C++. How do you choose between inheritance and templates? Between templates and generic pointers? Between public and private inheritance? Between private inheritance and layering? Between function overloading and parameter defaulting? Between virtual and nonvirtual functions? Between pass-by-value and pass-by-reference? It is important to get these decisions right at the outset, because an incorrect choice may not become apparent until much later in the development process, at which point its rectification is often difficult, time-consuming, demoralizing, and expensive.

Even when you know exactly what you want to do, getting things just right can be tricky. What's the proper return type for the assignment operator? How should operator new behave when it can't find enough memory? When should a destructor be virtual? How should you write a member initialization list? It's crucial to sweat details like these, because failure to do so almost always leads to unexpected, possibly mystifying, program behavior. More importantly, the aberrant behavior may not be immediately apparent, giving rise to the specter of code that passes through quality control while still harboring a variety of undetected bugs — ticking time-bombs just waiting to go off.

This is not a book that must be read cover to cover to make any sense. You need not even read it front to back. The material is broken down into 50 Items, each of which stands more or less on its own. Frequently, however, one Item will refer to others, so one way to read the book is to start with a particular Item of interest and then follow the references to see where they lead you.

The Items are grouped into general topic areas, so if you are interested in discussions related to a particular issue, such as memory management or object-oriented design, you can start with the relevant section and either read straight through or start jumping around from there. You will find, however, that all of the material in this book is pretty fundamental to effective C++ programming, so almost everything is eventually related to everything else in one way or another.

This is not a reference book for C++, nor is it a way for you to learn the language from scratch. For example, I'm eager to tell you all about the gotchas in writing your own operator new (see Items 7–10), but I assume you can go elsewhere to discover that that function must return a void* and its first argument must be of type size_t. There are a number of introductory books on C++ that contain information such as that.

The purpose of *this* book is to highlight those aspects of C++ programming that are usually treated superficially (if at all). Other books describe the different parts of the language. This book tells you how to combine those parts so you end up with effective programs. Other books tell you how to get your programs to compile. This book tells you how to avoid problems that compilers won't tell you about.

Like most languages, C++ has a rich folklore that is usually passed from programmer to programmer as part of the language's grand oral tradition. This book is my attempt to record some of that accumulated wisdom in a more accessible form.

At the same time, this book limits itself to legitimate, *portable*, C++. Only language features in the ISO/ANSI language standard have been used here. In this book, portability is a key concern, so if you're looking for implementation-dependent hacks and kludges, this is not the place to find them.

Alas, C++ as described by the standard is sometimes different from the C++ supported by your friendly neighborhood compiler vendors. As a result, when I point out places where relatively new language features are useful, I also show you how to produce effective software in their absence. After all, it would be foolish to labor in ignorance of what the future is sure to bring, but by the same token, you can't just put your life on hold until the latest, greatest, be-all-and-end-all C++ compilers appear on your computer. You've got to work with the tools available to you, and this book helps you do just that.

Notice that I refer to *compilers* — plural. Different compilers implement varying approximations to the standard, so I encourage you to develop your code under at least two compilers. Doing so will help you avoid inadvertent dependence on one vendor's proprietary language extension or its misinterpretation of the standard. It will also help keep you away from the bleeding edge of compiler technology, i.e., from new features supported by only one vendor. Such features are often poorly implemented (buggy or slow — frequently both), and upon their introduction, the C++ community lacks experience to advise you in their proper application. Blazing trails can be exciting, but when your goal is producing reliable code, it's often best to let others do the bushwhacking for you.

One thing you will *not* find in this book is the C++ Gospel, the One True Path to perfect C++ software. Each of the 50 Items in this book provides guidance on how to come up with better designs, how to avoid common problems, or how to achieve greater efficiency, but none of the Items is universally applicable. Software design and implementation is a complex task, one invariably colored by the constraints of the hardware, the operating system, and the application, so the best I can do is provide *guidelines* for creating better programs.

If you follow all the guidelines all the time, you are unlikely to fall into the most common traps surrounding C++, but guidelines, by their very nature, have exceptions. That's why each Item has an explanation. The explanations are the most important part of the book. Only by understanding the rationale behind an Item can you reasonably determine whether it applies to the software you are developing and to the unique constraints under which you toil.

The best use of this book, then, is to gain insight into how C++ behaves, why it behaves that way, and how to use its behavior to your advantage. Blind application of the Items in this book is clearly inappropriate, but at the same time, you probably shouldn't violate any of the guidelines without having a good reason for doing so.

There's no point in getting hung up on terminology in a book like this; that form of sport is best left to language lawyers. However, there is a small C++ vocabulary that everybody should understand. The following terms crop up often enough that it is worth making sure we agree on what they mean.

A *declaration* tells compilers about the name and type of an object, function, class, or template, but it omits certain details. These are declarations:

```
extern int x;                    // object declaration

int numDigits(int number);       // function declaration

class Clock;                     // class declaration

template<class T>
class SmartPointer;              // template declaration
```

A *definition*, on the other hand, provides compilers with the details. For an object, the definition is where compilers allocate memory for the object. For a function or a function template, the definition provides the code body. For a class or a class template, the definition lists the members of the class or template:

```
int x;                          // object definition

int numDigits(int number)       // function definition
{                               // (this function returns
  int digitsSoFar = 1;          // the number of digits in
                                // its parameter)
```

```
  if (number < 0) {
    number = -number;
  }

  while (number /= 10) ++digitsSoFar;

  return digitsSoFar;
}
class Clock {                    // class definition
public:
  Clock();
  ~Clock();

  int hour() const;
  int minute() const;
  int second() const;

  ...

};

template<class T>
class SmartPointer {             // template definition
public:
  SmartPointer(T *p = 0);
  ~SmartPointer();

  T * operator->() const;
  T& operator*() const;

  ...

};
```

That brings us to constructors. A *default constructor* is one that can be called without any arguments. Such a constructor either has no parameters or has a default value for every parameter. You generally need a default constructor if you want to define arrays of objects:

```
class A {
public:
  A();                          // default constructor
};

A arrayA[10];                   // 10 constructors called

class B {
public:
  B(int x = 0);                 // default constructor
};

B arrayB[10];                   // 10 constructors called,
                                // each with an arg of 0
```

```
class C {
public:
  C(int x);                      // not a default constructor
};

C arrayC[10];                    // error!
```

You may find that your compilers reject arrays of objects when a class's default constructor has default parameter values. For example, some compilers refuse to accept the definition of arrayB above, even though it receives the blessing of the C++ standard. This is an example of the kind of discrepancy that can exist between the standard's description of C++ and a particular compiler's implementation of the language. Every compiler I know of has a few of these shortcomings. Until compiler vendors catch up to the standard, be prepared to be flexible, and take solace in the certainty that someday in the not-too-distant future, the C++ described in the standard will be the same as the language accepted by C++ compilers.

Incidentally, if you want to create an array of objects for which there is no default constructor, the usual ploy is to define an array of *pointers* instead. Then you can initialize each pointer separately by using new:

```
C *ptrArray[10];                 // no constructors called

ptrArray[0] = new C(22);         // allocate and construct
                                 // 1 C object

ptrArray[1] = new C(4);          // ditto

...
```

Back on the terminology front, a *copy constructor* is used to initialize an object with a different object of the same type:

```
class String {
public:
  String();                     // default constructor
  String(const String& rhs);    // copy constructor

  ...

private:
  char *data;
};

String s1;                       // call default constructor
String s2(s1);                   // call copy constructor
String s3 = s2;                  // call copy constructor
```

Probably the most important use of the copy constructor is to define what it means to pass and return objects by value. As an example, consider the following (inefficient) way of writing a function to concatenate two String objects:

```
const String operator+(String s1, String s2)
{
  String temp;

  delete [] temp.data;

  temp.data =
    new char[strlen(s1.data) + strlen(s2.data) + 1];

  strcpy(temp.data, s1.data);
  strcat(temp.data, s2.data);

  return temp;
}
String a("Hello");
String b(" world");
String c = a + b;                    // c = String("Hello world")
```

This operator+ takes two String objects as parameters and returns one String object as a result. Both the parameters and the result will be passed by value, so there will be one copy constructor called to initialize s1 with a, one to initialize s2 with b, and one to initialize c with temp. In fact, there might even be some additional calls to the copy constructor if a compiler decides to generate intermediate temporary objects, which it is allowed to do. The important point here is that pass-by-value *means* "call the copy constructor."

By the way, you wouldn't really implement operator+ for Strings like this. Returning a const String object is correct (see Items 21 and 23), but you would want to pass the two parameters by reference (see Item 22).

Actually, you wouldn't write operator+ for Strings at all if you could help it, and you should be able to help it almost all the time. That's because the standard C++ library (see Item 49) contains a string type (cunningly named string), as well as an operator+ for string objects that does almost exactly what the operator+ above does. In this book, I use both String and string objects, but I use them in different ways. (Note that the former name is capitalized, the latter name is not.) If I need just a generic string and I don't care how it's implemented, I use the string type that is part of the standard C++ library. That's what you should do, too. Often, however, I want to make a point about how C++ behaves, and in those cases, I need to show some implementation code. That's when I use the (nonstandard) String class. As a programmer, you should use the standard string type whenever you need a string object; the days of developing your own string class as a C++ rite of passage are behind us. However, you still need to understand the issues that go into the development of classes like string. String is convenient for that purpose (and for that purpose only). As for raw char*-based strings, you shouldn't use those antique throw-backs unless you have a *very* good reason. Well-implemented string types can now be superior to char*s in virtually every way — including efficiency (see Item 49).

The next two terms we need to grapple with are *initialization* and *assignment*. An object's initialization occurs when it is given a value for the very first time. For objects of classes or structs with constructors, initialization is *always* accomplished by calling a constructor. This is quite different from object assignment, which occurs when an object that is already initialized is given a new value:

```
string s1;                          // initialization
string s2("Hello");                 // initialization
string s3 = s2;                     // initialization

s1 = s3;                            // assignment
```

From a purely operational point of view, the difference between initialization and assignment is that the former is performed by a constructor while the latter is performed by operator=. In other words, the two processes correspond to different function calls.

The reason for the distinction is that the two kinds of functions must worry about different things. Constructors usually have to check their arguments for validity, whereas most assignment operators can take it for granted that their argument is legitimate (because it has already been constructed). On the other hand, the target of an assignment, unlike an object undergoing construction, may already have resources allocated to it. These resources typically must be released before the new resources can be assigned. Frequently, one of these resources is memory. Before an assignment operator can allocate memory for a new value, it must first deallocate the memory that was allocated for the old value.

Here is how a String constructor and assignment operator could be implemented:

```
// a possible String constructor
String::String(const char *value)
{
  if (value) {                      // if value ptr isn't null
    data = new char[strlen(value) + 1];
    strcpy(data,value);
  }
  else {                            // handle null value ptr†
    data = new char[1];
```

---

† My String's constructor taking a const char* argument handles the case where a null pointer is passed in, but the standard string type is not required to be so tolerant. Attempts to create a string from a null pointer yield undefined results. However, it is safe to create a string object from an empty char*-based string, i.e., from "".

rors. For example, only `const_cast` can be used to cast away the constness of something. If you try to cast away an object's or a pointer's constness using one of the other new casts, your cast expression won't compile.

For more information on the new casts, consult a recent introductory textbook on C++ or see Item 2 of my book, *More Effective C++*. (You'll find an overview of *More Effective C++* on pages 237–238 of this book.)

In the code examples in this book, I have tried to select meaningful names for objects, classes, functions, etc. Many books, when choosing identifiers, embrace the time-honored adage that brevity is the soul of wit, but I'm not as interested in being witty as I am in being clear. I have therefore striven to break the tradition of using cryptic identifiers in books on programming languages. Nonetheless, I have at times succumbed to the temptation to use two of my favorite parameter names, and their meanings may not be immediately apparent, especially if you've never done time on a compiler-writing chain gang.

The names are `lhs` and `rhs`, and they stand for "left-hand side" and "right-hand side," respectively. I use them as parameter names for functions implementing binary operators, especially `operator==` and arithmetic operators like `operator*`. For example, if a and b are objects representing rational numbers, and if rational numbers can be multiplied via a non-member `operator*` function, the expression

```
a * b
```

is equivalent to the function call

```
operator*(a, b)
```

As you will discover in Item 23, I declare `operator*` like this:

```
const Rational operator*(const Rational& lhs,
                         const Rational& rhs);
```

As you can see, the left-hand operand, a, is known as `lhs` inside the function, and the right-hand operand is known as `rhs`.

I've also chosen to abbreviate names for pointers according to this rule: a pointer to an object of type `T` is often called pt, "pointer to T." Here are some examples:

```
string *ps;                     // ps = ptr to string

class Airplane;
Airplane *pa;                   // pa = ptr to Airplane

class BankAccount;
BankAccount *pba;               // pba = ptr to BankAccount
```

I use a similar convention for references. That is, `rs` might be a reference-to-`string` and `ra` a reference-to-`Airplane`.

I occasionally use the name `mf` when I'm talking about member functions.

On the off chance there might be some confusion, any time I mention the C programming language in this book, I mean the ISO/ANSI-sanctified version of C, not the older, less strongly-typed, "classic" C.

Finally, I assume that you recognize common elements of the standard C++ library as such, so I generally omit references to the `std` namespace. Thus, I refer to `cout` instead of `std::cout`, etc. In my opinion, this makes the example code more focused and easier to understand.

Shifting from C to C++

Getting used to C++ takes a little while for everyone, but for grizzled C programmers, the process can be especially unnerving. Because C is effectively a subset of C++, all the old C tricks continue to work, but many of them are no longer appropriate. To C++ programmers, for example, a pointer to a pointer looks a little funny. Why, we wonder, wasn't a *reference* to a pointer used instead?

C is a fairly simple language. All it really offers is macros, pointers, structs, arrays, and functions. No matter what the problem is, the solution will always boil down to macros, pointers, structs, arrays, and functions. Not so in C++. The macros, pointers, structs, arrays and functions are still there, of course, but so are private and protected members, function overloading, default parameters, constructors and destructors, user-defined operators, inline functions, references, friends, templates, exceptions, namespaces, and more. The design space is much richer in C++ than it is in C: there are just a lot more options to consider.

When faced with such a variety of choices, many C programmers hunker down and hold tight to what they're used to. For the most part, that's no great sin, but some C habits run contrary to the spirit of C++. Those are the ones that have simply *got* to go.

Item 1: Prefer const and inline to #define.

This Item might better be called "prefer the compiler to the preprocessor," because #define is often treated as if it's not part of the language *per se*. That's one of its problems. When you do something like this,

```
#define ASPECT_RATIO 1.653
```

the symbolic name ASPECT_RATIO may never be seen by compilers; it may be removed by the preprocessor before the source code ever gets to a compiler. As a result, the name ASPECT_RATIO may not get entered into the symbol table. This can be confusing if you get an error during compilation involving the use of the constant, because the error message may refer to 1.653, not ASPECT_RATIO. If ASPECT_RATIO was defined in a header file you didn't write, you'd then have no idea where that 1.653 came from, and you'd probably waste time tracking it down. This problem can also crop up in a symbolic debugger, because, again, the name you're programming with may not be in the symbol table.

The solution to this sorry scenario is simple and succinct. Instead of using a preprocessor macro, define a constant:

```
const double ASPECT_RATIO = 1.653;
```

This approach works like a charm. There are two special cases worth mentioning, however.

First, things can get a bit tricky when defining constant pointers. Because constant definitions are typically put in header files (where many different source files will include them), it's important that the *pointer* be declared const, usually in addition to what the pointer points to. To define a constant char*-based string in a header file, for example, you have to write const *twice*:

```
const char * const authorName = "Scott Meyers";
```

For a discussion of the meanings and uses of const, especially in conjunction with pointers, see Item 21.

Second, it's often convenient to define class-specific constants, and that calls for a slightly different tack. To limit the scope of a constant to a class, you must make it a member, and to ensure there's at most one copy of the constant, you must make it a *static* member:

```
class GamePlayer {
private:
  static const int NUM_TURNS = 5;   // constant declaration
  int scores[NUM_TURNS];            // use of constant
  ...
};
```

There's a minor wrinkle, however, which is that what you see above is a *declaration* for NUM_TURNS, not a definition. You must still define static class members in an implementation file:

```
const int GamePlayer::NUM_TURNS;  // mandatory definition;
                                  // goes in class impl. file
```

There's no need to lose sleep worrying about this detail. If you forget the definition, your linker should remind you.

Older compilers may not accept this syntax, because it used to be illegal to provide an initial value for a static class member at its point of declaration. Furthermore, in-class initialization is allowed only for integral types (e.g., ints, bools, chars, etc.), and only for constants. In cases where the above syntax can't be used, you put the initial value at the point of definition:

```
class EngineeringConstants {   // this goes in the class
private:                       // header file

  static const double FUDGE_FACTOR;

  ...

};

// this goes in the class implementation file
const double EngineeringConstants::FUDGE_FACTOR = 1.35;
```

This is all you need almost all the time. The only exception is when you need the value of a class constant during compilation of the class, such as in the declaration of the array GamePlayer::scores above (where compilers insist on knowing the size of the array during compilation). Then the accepted way to compensate for compilers that (incorrectly) forbid the in-class specification of initial values for integral class constants is to use what is affectionately known as "the enum hack." This technique takes advantage of the fact that the values of an enumerated type can be used where ints are expected, so GamePlayer could just as well have been defined like this:

```
class GamePlayer {
private:
  enum { NUM_TURNS = 5 };   // "the enum hack" — makes
                            // NUM_TURNS a symbolic name
                            // for 5

  int scores[NUM_TURNS];    // fine

  ...

};
```

Unless you're dealing with compilers of primarily historical interest (i.e., those written before 1995), you shouldn't have to use the enum hack. Still, it's worth knowing what it looks like, because it's not uncommon to encounter it in code dating back to those early, simpler times.

Getting back to the preprocessor, another common (mis)use of the #define directive is using it to implement macros that look like functions but that don't incur the overhead of a function call. The canonical example is computing the maximum of two values:

```
#define max(a,b) ((a) > (b) ? (a) : (b))
```

This little number has so many drawbacks, just thinking about them is painful. You're better off playing in the freeway during rush hour.

Whenever you write a macro like this, you have to remember to parenthesize all the arguments when you write the macro body; otherwise you can run into trouble when somebody calls the macro with an expression. But even if you get that right, look at the weird things that can happen:

```
int a = 5, b = 0;

max(++a, b);                    // a is incremented twice
max(++a, b+10);                 // a is incremented once
```

Here, what happens to a inside max depends on what it is being compared with!

Fortunately, you don't need to put up with this nonsense. You can get all the efficiency of a macro plus all the predictable behavior and type-safety of a regular function by using an inline function (see Item 33):

```
inline int max(int a, int b) { return a > b ? a : b; }
```

Now this isn't quite the same as the macro above, because this version of max can only be called with ints, but a template fixes that problem quite nicely:

```
template<class T>
inline const T& max(const T& a, const T& b)
{ return a > b ? a : b; }
```

This template generates a whole family of functions, each of which takes two objects convertible to the same type and returns a reference to (a constant version of) the greater of the two objects. Because you don't know what the type T will be, you pass and return by reference for efficiency (see Item 22).

By the way, before you consider writing templates for commonly useful functions like max, check the standard library (see Item 49) to see if they already exist. In the case of max, you'll be pleasantly surprised to find that you can rest on others' laurels: max is part of the standard C++ library.

Given the availability of consts and inlines, your need for the pre-processor is reduced, but it's not completely eliminated. The day is far from near when you can abandon #include, and #ifdef/#ifndef continue to play important roles in controlling compilation. It's not yet time to retire the preprocessor, but you should definitely plan to start giving it longer and more frequent vacations.

Item 2:   Prefer `<iostream>` to `<stdio.h>`.

Yes, they're portable. Yes, they're efficient. Yes, you already know how to use them. Yes, yes, yes. But venerated though they are, the fact of the matter is that `scanf` and `printf` and all their ilk could use some improvement. In particular, they're not type-safe and they're not extensible. Because type safety and extensibility are cornerstones of the C++ way of life, you might just as well resign yourself to them right now. Besides, the `printf`/`scanf` family of functions separate the variables to be read or written from the formatting information that controls the reads and writes, just like FORTRAN does. It's time to bid the 1950s a fond farewell.

Not surprisingly, these weaknesses of `printf`/`scanf` are the strengths of `operator>>` and `operator<<`.

```
int i;
Rational r;                       // r is a rational number

...

cin >> i >> r;
cout << i << r;
```

If this code is to compile, there must be functions `operator>>` and `operator<<` that can work with an object of type `Rational`. If these functions are missing, it's an error. (The versions for `int`s are standard.) Furthermore, compilers take care of figuring out which versions of the operators to call for different variables, so you needn't worry about specifying that the first object to be read or written is an `int` and the second is a `Rational`.

In addition, objects to be read are passed using the same syntactic form as are those to be written, so you don't have to remember silly rules like you do for `scanf`, where if you don't already have a pointer, you have to be sure to take an address, but if you've already got a pointer, you have to be sure *not* to take an address. Let C++ compilers take care of those details. They have nothing better to do, and you *do* have better things to do. Finally, note that built-in types like `int` are read and written in the same manner as user-defined types like `Rational`. Try *that* using `scanf` and `printf`!

Here's how you might write an output routine for a class representing rational numbers:

```
class Rational {
public:
  Rational(int numerator = 0, int denominator = 1);

  ...

private:
  int n, d;                    // numerator and denominator

  friend ostream& operator<<(ostream& s, const Rational& r);
};

ostream& operator<<(ostream& s, const Rational& r)
{
  s << r.n << '/' << r.d;
  return s;
}
```

This version of operator<< demonstrates some subtle (but important) points that are discussed elsewhere in this book. For example, operator<< is not a member function (Item 19 explains why), and the Rational object to be output is passed into operator<< as a reference-to-const rather than as an object (see Item 22). The corresponding input function, operator>>, would be declared and implemented in a similar manner.

Reluctant though I am to admit it, there are some situations in which it may make sense to fall back on the tried and true. First, some implementations of iostream operations are less efficient than the corresponding C stream operations, so it's possible (though unlikely) that you have an application in which this makes a significant difference. Bear in mind, though, that this says nothing about iostreams *in general*, only about particular implementations. Second, the iostream library was modified in some rather fundamental ways during the course of its standardization (see Item 49), so applications that must be maximally portable may discover that different vendors support different approximations to the standard. Finally, because the classes of the iostream library have constructors and the functions in <stdio.h> do not, there are rare occasions involving the initialization order of static objects (see Item 47) when the standard C library may be more useful simply because you know that you can always call it with impunity.

The type safety and extensibility offered by the classes and functions in the iostream library are more useful than you might initially imagine, so don't throw them away just because you're used to <stdio.h>. After all, even after the transition, you'll still have your memories.

Incidentally, that's no typo in the Item title; I really mean <iostream> and not <iostream.h>. Technically speaking, there is no such thing as <iostream.h> — the standardization committee eliminated it in favor of <iostream> when they truncated the names of the other non-C standard header names. The reasons for their doing this are explained in Item 49, but what you really need to understand is that if (as is likely) your compilers support both <iostream> and <iostream.h>, the headers are subtly different. In particular, if you #include <iostream>, you get the elements of the iostream library ensconced within the namespace std (see Item 28), but if you #include <iostream.h>, you get those same elements at global scope. Getting them at global scope can lead to name conflicts, precisely the kinds of name conflicts the use of namespaces is designed to prevent.

Item 3:   Prefer new and delete to malloc and free.

The problem with malloc and free (and their variants) is simple: they don't know about constructors and destructors.

Consider the following two ways to get space for an array of 10 string objects, one using malloc, the other using new:

```
string *stringArray1 =
  static_cast<string*>(malloc(10 * sizeof(string)));

string *stringArray2 = new string[10];
```

Here stringArray1 points to enough memory for 10 string objects, but no objects have been constructed in that memory. Furthermore, without jumping through some rather obscure linguistic hoops, you have no way to initialize the objects in the array. In other words, stringArray1 is pretty useless. In contrast, stringArray2 points to an array of 10 fully constructed string objects, each of which can safely be used in any operation taking a string.

Nonetheless, let's suppose you magically managed to initialize the objects in the stringArray1 array. Later on in your program, then, you'd expect to do this:

```
free(stringArray1);

delete [] stringArray2;        // see Item 5 for why the
                               // "[]" is necessary
```

The call to free will release the memory pointed to by stringArray1, but no destructors will be called on the string objects in that memory. If the string objects themselves allocated memory, as string objects are wont to do, all the memory they allocated will be lost. On the other hand, when delete is called on stringArray2, a destructor is called for each object in the array before any memory is released.

Because new and delete interact properly with constructors and destructors, they are clearly the superior choice.

Mixing new and delete with malloc and free is usually a bad idea. When you try to call free on a pointer you got from new or call delete on a pointer you got from malloc, the results are undefined, and we all know what "undefined" means: it means it works during development, it works during testing, and it blows up in your most important customers' faces.

The incompatibility of new/delete and malloc/free can lead to some interesting complications. For example, the strdup function commonly found in <string.h> takes a char*-based string and returns a copy of it:

```
char * strdup(const char *ps);     // return a copy of what
                                    // ps points to
```

At some sites, both C and C++ use the same version of strdup, so the memory allocated inside the function comes from malloc. As a result, unwitting C++ programmers calling strdup might overlook the fact that they must use free on the pointer returned from strdup. But wait! To forestall such complications, some sites might decide to rewrite strdup for C++ and have this rewritten version call new inside the function, thereby mandating that callers later use delete. As you can imagine, this can lead to some pretty nightmarish portability problems as code is shuttled back and forth between sites with different forms of strdup.

Still, C++ programmers are as interested in code reuse as C programmers, and it's a simple fact that there are lots of C libraries based on malloc and free containing code that is very much worth reusing. When taking advantage of such a library, it's likely you'll end up with the responsibility for freeing memory malloced by the library and/or mallocing memory the library itself will free. That's fine. There's nothing wrong with calling malloc and free inside a C++ program as long as you make sure the pointers you get from malloc always meet their maker in free and the pointers you get from new eventually find their way to delete. The problems start when you get sloppy and try to mix new with free or malloc with delete. That's just *asking* for trouble.

Given that `malloc` and `free` are ignorant of constructors and destructors and that mixing `malloc`/`free` with `new`/`delete` can be more volatile than a fraternity rush party, you're best off sticking to an exclusive diet of `new`s and `delete`s whenever you can.

Item 4:   Prefer C++-style comments.

The good old C comment syntax works in C++ too, but the newfangled C++ comment-to-end-of-line syntax has some distinct advantages. For example, consider this situation:

```
if ( a > b ) {
  // int temp = a;              // swap a and b
  // a = b;
  // b = temp;
}
```

Here you have a code block that has been commented out for some reason or other, but in a stunning display of software engineering, the programmer who originally wrote the code actually included a comment to indicate what was going on. When the C++ comment form was used to comment out the block, the embedded comment was of no concern, but there could have been a serious problem had everybody chosen to use C-style comments:

```
if ( a > b ) {
  /* int temp = a;              /* swap a and b */
     a = b;
     b = temp;
  */
}
```

Notice how the embedded comment inadvertently puts a premature end to the comment that is supposed to comment out the code block.

C-style comments still have their place. For example, they're invaluable in header files that are processed by both C and C++ compilers. Still, if you can use C++-style comments, you are often better off doing so.

It's worth pointing out that retrograde preprocessors that were written only for C don't know how to cope with C++-style comments, so things like the following sometimes don't work as expected:

```
#define LIGHT_SPEED 3e8          // m/sec (in a vacuum)
```

Given a preprocessor unfamiliar with C++, the comment at the end of the line becomes *part of the macro!* Of course, as is discussed in Item 1, you shouldn't be using the preprocessor to define constants anyway.

Memory Management

Memory management concerns in C++ fall into two general camps: getting it right and making it perform efficiently. Good programmers understand that these concerns should be addressed in that order, because a program that is dazzlingly fast and astoundingly small is of little use if it doesn't behave the way it's supposed to. For most programmers, getting things right means calling memory allocation and deallocation routines correctly. Making things perform efficiently, on the other hand, often means writing custom versions of the allocation and deallocation routines. Getting things right there is even more important.

On the correctness front, C++ inherits from C one of its biggest headaches, that of potential memory leaks. Even virtual memory, wonderful invention though it is, is finite, and not everybody has virtual memory in the first place.

In C, a memory leak arises whenever memory allocated through `malloc` is never returned through `free`. The names of the players in C++ are `new` and `delete`, but the story is much the same. However, the situation is improved somewhat by the presence of destructors, because they provide a convenient repository for calls to `delete` that all objects must make when they are destroyed. At the same time, there is more to worry about, because `new` implicitly calls constructors and `delete` implicitly calls destructors. Furthermore, there is the complication that you can define your own versions of `operator new` and `operator delete`, both inside and outside of classes. This gives rise to all kinds of opportunities to make mistakes. The following items should help you avoid some of the most common ones.

Item 5: Use the same form in corresponding uses of new and delete.

What's wrong with this picture?

```
string *stringArray = new string[100];

...

delete stringArray;
```

Everything here appears to be in order — the use of new is matched with a use of delete — but something is still quite wrong: your program's behavior is undefined. At the very least, 99 of the 100 string objects pointed to by stringArray are unlikely to be properly destroyed, because their destructors will probably never be called.

When you use new, two things happen. First, memory is allocated (via the function operator new, about which I'll have more to say in Items 7–10). Second, one or more constructors are called for that memory. When you use delete, two other things happen: one or more destructors are called for the memory, then the memory is deallocated (via the function operator delete — see Item 8). The big question for delete is this: *how many* objects reside in the memory being deleted? The answer to that determines how many destructors must be called.

Actually, the question is simpler: does the pointer being deleted point to a single object or to an array of objects? The only way for delete to know is for you to tell it. If you don't use brackets in your use of delete, delete assumes a single object is pointed to. Otherwise, it assumes that an array is pointed to:

```
string *stringPtr1 = new string;
string *stringPtr2 = new string[100];

...

delete stringPtr1;              // delete an object
delete [] stringPtr2;          // delete an array of
                               // objects
```

What would happen if you used the "[]" form on stringPtr1? The result is undefined. What would happen if you didn't use the "[]" form on stringPtr2? Well, that's undefined too. Furthermore, it's undefined even for built-in types like ints, even though such types lack destructors. The rule, then, is simple: if you use [] when you call new, you must use [] when you call delete. If you don't use [] when you call new, don't use [] when you call delete.

This is a particularly important rule to bear in mind when you are writing a class containing a pointer data member and also offering multiple constructors, because then you've got to be careful to use the *same form* of new in all the constructors to initialize the pointer member. If you don't, how will you know what form of delete to use in your destructor? For a further examination of this issue, see Item 11.

This rule is also important for the typedef-inclined, because it means that a typedef's author must document which form of delete should be employed when new is used to conjure up objects of the typedef type. For example, consider this typedef:

```
typedef string AddressLines[4];   // a person's address
                                  // has 4 lines, each of
                                  // which is a string
```

Because AddressLines is an array, this use of new,

```
string *pal = new AddressLines;   // note that "new
                                  // AddressLines" returns
                                  // a string*, just like
                                  // "new string[4]" would
```

must be matched with the *array* form of delete:

```
delete pal;                       // undefined!

delete [] pal;                    // fine
```

To avoid such confusion, you're probably best off abstaining from typedefs for array types. That should be easy, however, because the standard C++ library (see Item 49) includes string and vector templates that reduce the need for built-in arrays to nearly zero. Here, for example, AddressLines could be defined to be a vector of strings. That is, AddressLines could be of type vector<string>.

Item 6:   Use delete on pointer members in destructors.

Most of the time, classes performing dynamic memory allocation will use new in the constructor(s) to allocate the memory and will later use delete in the destructor to free up the memory. This isn't too difficult to get right when you first write the class, provided, of course, that you remember to employ delete on *all* the members that could have been assigned memory in *any* constructor.

However, the situation becomes more difficult as classes are maintained and enhanced, because the programmers making the modifications to the class may not be the ones who wrote the class in the first place. Under those conditions, it's easy to forget that adding a pointer member almost always requires each of the following:

- Initialization of the pointer in each of the constructors. If no memory is to be allocated to the pointer in a particular constructor, the pointer should be initialized to 0 (i.e., the null pointer).

- Deletion of the existing memory and assignment of new memory in the assignment operator. (See also Item 17.)

- Deletion of the pointer in the destructor.

If you forget to initialize a pointer in a constructor, or if you forget to handle it inside the assignment operator, the problem usually becomes apparent fairly quickly, so in practice those issues don't tend to plague you. Failing to delete the pointer in the destructor, however, often exhibits no obvious external symptoms. Instead, it manifests itself as a subtle memory leak, a slowly growing cancer that will eventually devour your address space and drive your program to an early demise. Because this particular problem doesn't usually call attention to itself, it's important that you keep it in mind whenever you add a pointer member to a class.

Note, by the way, that deleting a null pointer is always safe (it does nothing). Thus, if you write your constructors, your assignment operators, and your other member functions such that each pointer member of the class is always either pointing to valid memory or is null, you can merrily `delete` away in the destructor without regard for whether you ever used `new` for the pointer in question.

There's no reason to get fascist about this Item. For example, you certainly don't want to use `delete` on a pointer that wasn't initialized via `new`, and you almost *never* want to delete a pointer that was passed to you in the first place. In other words, your class destructor usually shouldn't be using `delete` unless your class members were the ones who used `new` in the first place.

Item 7:   Be prepared for out-of-memory conditions.

When `operator new` can't allocate the memory you request, it throws an exception. (It used to return 0, and some older compilers still do that. You can make your compilers do it again if you want to, but I'll defer that discussion until the end of this Item.) Deep in your heart of hearts, you know that handling out-of-memory exceptions is the only truly moral course of action. At the same time, you are keenly aware of the fact that doing so is a pain in the neck. As a result, chances are that you omit such handling from time to time. Like always, perhaps.

Still, you must harbor a lurking sense of guilt. I mean, what if new really *does* yield an exception?

You may think that one reasonable way to cope with this matter is to fall back on your days in the gutter, i.e., to use the preprocessor. For example, a common C idiom is to define a type-independent macro to allocate memory and then check to make sure the allocation succeeded. For C++, such a macro might look something like this:

```
#define NEW(PTR, TYPE)                          \
    try { (PTR) = new TYPE; }                   \
    catch (std::bad_alloc&) { assert(0); }
```

("Wait! What's this std::bad_alloc business?", you ask. bad_alloc is the type of exception operator new throws when it can't satisfy a memory allocation request, and std is the name of the namespace (see Item 28) where bad_alloc is defined. "Okay," you continue, "what's this assert business?" Well, if you look in the standard C include file <assert.h> (or its namespace-savvy C++ equivalent, <cassert> — see Item 49), you'll find that assert is a macro. The macro checks to see if the expression it's passed is non-zero, and, if it's not, it issues an error message and calls abort. Okay, it does that only when the standard macro NDEBUG isn't defined, i.e., in debug mode. In production mode, i.e., when NDEBUG *is* defined, assert expands to nothing — to a void statement. You thus check assertions only when debugging.)

This NEW macro suffers from the common error of using an assert to test a condition that might occur in production code (after all, you can run out of memory at any time), but it also has a drawback specific to C++: it fails to take into account the myriad ways in which new can be used. There are three common syntactic forms for getting new objects of type T, and you need to deal with the possibility of exceptions for each of these forms:

```
new T;
```

```
new T(constructor arguments);
```

```
new T[size];
```

This oversimplifies the problem, however, because clients can define their own (overloaded) versions of operator new, so programs may contain an arbitrary number of different syntactic forms for using new.

How, then, to cope? If you're willing to settle for a very simple error-handling strategy, you can set things up so that if a request for memory cannot be satisfied, an error-handling function you specify is called. This strategy relies on the convention that when operator new cannot satisfy a request, it calls a client-specifiable error-handling function — often called a *new-handler* — before it throws an exception. (In truth, what operator new really does is slightly more complicated. Details are provided in Item 8.)

To specify the out-of-memory-handling function, clients call set_new_handler, which is specified in the header <new> more or less like this:

```
typedef void (*new_handler)();
new_handler set_new_handler(new_handler p) throw();
```

As you can see, new_handler is a typedef for a pointer to a function that takes and returns nothing, and set_new_handler is a function that takes and returns a new_handler.

set_new_handler's parameter is a pointer to the function operator new should call if it can't allocate the requested memory. The return value of set_new_handler is a pointer to the function in effect for that purpose before set_new_handler was called.

You use set_new_handler like this:

```
// function to call if operator new can't allocate enough memory
void noMoreMemory()
{
  cerr << "Unable to satisfy request for memory\n";
  abort();
}

int main()
{
  set_new_handler(noMoreMemory);

  int *pBigDataArray = new int[100000000];

  ...

}
```

If, as seems likely, operator new is unable to allocate space for 100,000,000 integers, noMoreMemory will be called, and the program will abort after issuing an error message. This is a marginally better way to terminate the program than a simple core dump. (By the way, consider what happens if memory must be dynamically allocated during the course of writing the error message to cerr...)

When operator new cannot satisfy a request for memory, it calls the new-handler function not once, but *repeatedly* until it *can* find enough memory. The code giving rise to these repeated calls is shown in Item 8, but this high-level description is enough to conclude that a well-designed new-handler function must do one of the following:

■ **Make more memory available**. This may allow operator new's next attempt to allocate the memory to succeed. One way to implement this strategy is to allocate a large block of memory at program start-up, then release it the first time the new-handler is invoked. Such a release is often accompanied by some kind of warning to the user that memory is low and that future requests may fail unless more memory is somehow made available.

- **Install a different new-handler**. If the current new-handler can't make any more memory available, perhaps it knows of a different new-handler that is more resourceful. If so, the current new-handler can install the other new-handler in its place (by calling `set_new_handler`). The next time `operator new` calls the new-handler function, it will get the one most recently installed. (A variation on this theme is for a new-handler to modify its *own* behavior, so the next time it's invoked, it does something different. One way to achieve this is to have the new-handler modify static or global data that affects the new-handler's behavior.)

- **Deinstall the new-handler**, i.e., pass the null pointer to `set_new_handler`. With no new-handler installed, `operator new` will throw an exception of type `std::bad_alloc` when its attempt to allocate memory is unsuccessful.

- **Throw an exception** of type `std::bad_alloc` or some type derived from `std::bad_alloc`. Such exceptions will not be caught by `operator new`, so they will propagate to the site originating the request for memory. (Throwing an exception of a different type will violate `operator new`'s exception specification. The default action when that happens is to call `abort`, so if your new-handler is going to throw an exception, you definitely want to make sure it's from the `std::bad_alloc` hierarchy.)

- **Not return**, typically by calling `abort` or `exit`, both of which are found in the standard C library (and thus in the standard C++ library — see Item 49).

These choices give you considerable flexibility in implementing new-handler functions.

Sometimes you'd like to handle memory allocation failures in different ways, depending on the class of the object being allocated:

```
class X {
public:
  static void outOfMemory();

  ...

};
```

```
class Y {
public:
  static void outOfMemory();

  ...

};
X* p1 = new X;            // if allocation is unsuccessful,
                         // call X::outOfMemory
Y* p2 = new Y;            // if allocation is unsuccessful,
                         // call Y::outOfMemory
```

C++ has no support for class-specific new-handlers, but it doesn't need to. You can implement this behavior yourself. You just have each class provide its own versions of set_new_handler and operator new. The class's set_new_handler allows clients to specify the new-handler for the class (just like the standard set_new_handler allows clients to specify the global new-handler). The class's operator new ensures that the class-specific new-handler is used in place of the global new-handler when memory for class objects is allocated.

Consider a class X for which you want to handle memory allocation failures. You'll have to keep track of the function to call when operator new can't allocate enough memory for an object of type X, so you'll declare a static member of type new_handler to point to the new-handler function for the class. Your class X will look something like this:

```
class X {
public:
  static new_handler set_new_handler(new_handler p);
  static void * operator new(size_t size);

private:
  static new_handler currentHandler;
};
```

Static class members must be defined outside the class definition. Because you'll want to use the default initialization of static objects to 0, you'll define X::currentHandler without initializing it:

```
new_handler X::currentHandler;     // sets currentHandler
                                   // to 0 (i.e., null) by
                                   // default
```

The set_new_handler function in class X will save whatever pointer is passed to it. It will return whatever pointer had been saved prior to the call. This is exactly what the standard version of set_new_handler does:

```
new_handler X::set_new_handler(new_handler p)
{
  new_handler oldHandler = currentHandler;
  currentHandler = p;
  return oldHandler;
}
```

Finally, X's operator new will do the following:

1. Call the standard set_new_handler with X's error-handling function. This will install X's new-handler as the global new-handler. In the code below, notice how you explicitly reference the std scope (where the standard set_new_handler resides) by using the ":: " notation.

2. Call the global operator new to actually allocate the requested memory. If the initial attempt at allocation fails, the global operator new will invoke X's new-handler, because that function was just installed as the global new-handler. If the global operator new is ultimately unable to find a way to allocate the requested memory, it will throw a std::bad_alloc exception, which X's operator new will catch. X's operator new will then restore the global new-handler that was originally in place, and it will return by propagating the exception.

3. Assuming the global operator new was able to successfully allocate enough memory for an object of type X, X's operator new will again call the standard set_new_handler to restore the global error-handling function to what it was originally. It will then return a pointer to the allocated memory.

Here's how you say all that in C++:

```
void * X::operator new(size_t size)
{
  new_handler globalHandler =                 // install X's
    std::set_new_handler(currentHandler);     // handler

  void *memory;

  try {                                       // attempt
    memory = ::operator new(size);            // allocation
  }
  catch (std::bad_alloc&) {                    // restore
    std::set_new_handler(globalHandler);      // handler;
    throw;                                     // propagate
  }                                            // exception
```

```
        std::set_new_handler(globalHandler);      // restore
                                                  // handler
    return memory;
}
```

Clients of class X use its new-handling capabilities like this:

```
void noMoreMemory();                  // decl. of function to
                                      // call if memory allocation
                                      // for X objects fails

X::set_new_handler(noMoreMemory);
                                      // set noMoreMemory as X's
                                      // new-handling function

X *px1 = new X;                       // if memory allocation
                                      // fails, call noMoreMemory

string *ps = new string;              // if memory allocation
                                      // fails, call the global
                                      // new-handling function
                                      // (if there is one)

X::set_new_handler(0);                // set the X-specific
                                      // new-handling function
                                      // to nothing (i.e., null)

X *px2 = new X;                       // if memory allocation
                                      // fails, throw an exception
                                      // immediately. (There is
                                      // no new-handling function
                                      // for class X.)
```

You may note that the code for implementing this scheme is the same regardless of the class, so a reasonable inclination would be to reuse it in other places. As Item 41 explains, both inheritance and templates can be used to create reusable code. However, in this case, it's a combination of the two that gives you what you need.

All you have to do is create a "mixin-style" base class, i.e., a base class that's designed to allow derived classes to inherit a single specific capability — in this case, the ability to set a class-specific new-handler. Then you turn the base class into a template. The base class part of the design lets derived classes inherit the set_new_handler and operator new functions they all need, while the template part of the design ensures that each inheriting class gets a different currentHandler data member. The result may sound a little complicated, but you'll find that the code looks reassuringly familiar. In fact, about the only real difference is that it's now reusable by any class that wants it:

```
template<class T>              // "mixin-style" base class
class NewHandlerSupport {      // for class-specific
public:                        // set_new_handler support
  static new_handler set_new_handler(new_handler p);
  static void * operator new(size_t size);

private:
  static new_handler currentHandler;
};

template<class T>
new_handler NewHandlerSupport<T>::set_new_handler(new_handler p)
{
  new_handler oldHandler = currentHandler;
  currentHandler = p;
  return oldHandler;
}

template<class T>
void * NewHandlerSupport<T>::operator new(size_t size)
{
  new_handler globalHandler =
    std::set_new_handler(currentHandler);

  void *memory;

  try {
    memory = ::operator new(size);
  }
  catch (std::bad_alloc&) {
    std::set_new_handler(globalHandler);
    throw;
  }

  std::set_new_handler(globalHandler);

  return memory;
}

// this sets each currentHandler to 0
template<class T>
new_handler NewHandlerSupport<T>::currentHandler;
```

With this class template, adding set_new_handler support to class X
is easy: X just inherits from newHandlerSupport<X>:

```
class X: public NewHandlerSupport<X> { // note inheritance
                                       // from mixin base
                                       // class template

  ...                  // as before, but no declarations for
};                     // set_new_handler or operator new
```

Clients of X remain oblivious to all the behind-the-scenes action; their old code continues to work. This is good, because one thing you can usually rely on your clients being is oblivious.

Using set_new_handler is a convenient, easy way to cope with the possibility of out-of-memory conditions. Certainly it's a lot more attractive than wrapping every use of new inside a try block. Furthermore, templates like NewHandlerSupport make it simple to add a class-specific new-handler to any class that wants one. Mixin-style inheritance, however, invariably leads to the topic of multiple inheritance, and before starting down that slippery slope, you'll definitely want to read Item 43.

Until 1993, C++ required that operator new return 0 when it was unable to satisfy a memory request. The current behavior is for operator new to throw a std::bad_alloc exception, but a lot of C++ was written before compilers began supporting the revised specification. The C++ standardization committee didn't want to abandon the established test-for-0 code base, so they provided alternative forms of operator new (and operator new[] — see Item 8) that continue to offer the traditional failure-yields-0 behavior. These forms are called "nothrow" forms because, well, they never do a throw, and they employ nothrow objects (defined in the standard header <new>) at the point where new is used:

```
class Widget { ... };

Widget *pw1 = new Widget;        // throws std::bad_alloc if
                                 // allocation fails

if (pw1 == 0) ...                // this test must fail

Widget *pw2 =
  new (nothrow) Widget;          // returns 0 if allocation
                                 // fails

if (pw2 == 0) ...                // this test may succeed
```

Regardless of whether you use "normal" (i.e., exception-throwing) new or "nothrow" new, it's important that you be prepared to handle memory allocation failures. The easiest way to do that is to take advantage of set_new_handler, because it works with both forms.

Item 8: Adhere to convention when writing operator new and operator delete.

When you take it upon yourself to write operator new (Item 10 explains why you might want to), it's important that your function(s) offer behavior that is consistent with the default operator new. In practical terms, this means having the right return value, calling an error-handling function when insufficient memory is available (see Item 7), and being prepared to cope with requests for no memory. You also need to avoid inadvertently hiding the "normal" form of new, but that's a topic for Item 9.

The return value part is easy. If you can supply the requested memory, you just return a pointer to it. If you can't, you follow the rule described in Item 7 and throw an exception of type std::bad_alloc.

It's not quite that simple, however, because operator new actually tries to allocate memory more than once, calling the error-handling function after each failure, the assumption being that the error-handling function might be able to do something to free up some memory. Only when the pointer to the error-handling function is null does operator new throw an exception.

In addition, the C++ standard requires that operator new return a legitimate pointer even when 0 bytes are requested. (Believe it or not, requiring this odd-sounding behavior actually simplifies things elsewhere in the language.)

That being the case, pseudocode for a non-member operator new looks like this:

```
void * operator new(size_t size)    // your operator new might
{                                    // take additional params

  if (size == 0) {                   // handle 0-byte requests
    size = 1;                        // by treating them as
  }                                  // 1-byte requests

  while (true) {
    attempt to allocate size bytes;

    if (the allocation was successful)
      return (a pointer to the memory);

    // allocation was unsuccessful; find out what the
    // current error-handling function is (see Item 7)
    new_handler globalHandler = set_new_handler(0);
    set_new_handler(globalHandler);

    if (globalHandler) (*globalHandler)();
    else throw std::bad_alloc();
  }
}
```

The trick of treating requests for zero bytes as if they were really requests for one byte looks slimy, but it's simple, it's legal, it works, and how often do you expect to be asked for zero bytes, anyway?

You may also look askance at the place in the pseudocode where the error-handling function pointer is set to null, then promptly reset to what it was originally. Unfortunately, there is no way to get at the error-handling function pointer directly, so you have to call set_new_handler to find out what it is. Crude, yes, but also effective.

Item 7 remarks that operator new contains an infinite loop, and the code above shows that loop explicitly — while (true) is about as infinite as it gets. The only way out of the loop is for memory to be successfully allocated or for the new-handling function to do one of the things described in Item 7: make more memory available, install a different new-handler, deinstall the new-handler, throw an exception of or derived from std::bad_alloc, or fail to return. It should now be clear why the new-handler must do one of those things. If it doesn't, the loop inside operator new will never terminate.

One of the things many people don't realize about operator new is that it's inherited by subclasses. That can lead to some interesting complications. In the pseudocode for operator new above, notice that the function tries to allocate size bytes (unless size is 0). That makes perfect sense, because that's the argument that was passed to the function. However, most class-specific versions of operator new (including the one you'll find in Item 10) are designed for a *specific* class, *not* for a class *or* any of its subclasses. That is, given an operator new for a class X, the behavior of that function is almost always carefully tuned for objects of size sizeof(X) — nothing larger and nothing smaller. Because of inheritance, however, it is possible that the operator new in a base class will be called to allocate memory for an object of a derived class:

```
class Base {
public:
  static void * operator new(size_t size);
  ...
};

class Derived: public Base      // Derived doesn't declare
{ ... };                         // operator new

Derived *p = new Derived;        // calls Base::operator new!
```

If Base's class-specific operator new wasn't designed to cope with this — and chances are slim that it was — the best way for it to handle the situation is to slough off calls requesting the "wrong" amount of memory to the standard operator new, like this:

```
void * Base::operator new(size_t size)
{
  if (size != sizeof(Base))          // if size is "wrong,"
    return ::operator new(size);     // have standard operator
                                     // new handle the request

    ...                              // otherwise handle
                                     // the request here
}
```

"Hold on!" I hear you cry, "You forgot to check for the pathological-but-nevertheless-possible case where size is zero!" Actually, I didn't, and please stop using hyphens when you cry out. The test is still there, it's just been incorporated into the test of size against sizeof(Base). The C++ standard works in mysterious ways, and one of those ways is to decree that all freestanding classes have nonzero size. By definition, sizeof(Base) can never be zero (even if it has no members), so if size is zero, the request will be forwarded to ::operator new, and it will become that function's responsibility to treat the request in a reasonable fashion.

If you'd like to control memory allocation for arrays on a per-class basis, you need to implement operator new's array-specific cousin, operator new[]. (This function is usually called "array new," because it's hard to figure out how to pronounce "operator new[]".) If you decide to write operator new[], remember that all you're doing is allocating raw memory — you can't do anything to the as-yet-nonexistent objects in the array. In fact, you can't even figure out how many objects will be in the array, because you don't know how big each object is. After all, a base class's operator new[] might, through inheritance, be called to allocate memory for an array of derived class objects, and derived class objects are usually bigger than base class objects. Hence, you can't assume inside Base::operator new[] that the size of each object going into the array is sizeof(Base), and that means you can't assume that the number of objects in the array is (*bytes requested*)/sizeof(Base).

So much for the conventions you need to follow when writing operator new (and operator new[]). For operator delete (and its array counterpart, operator delete[]), things are simpler. About all you need to remember is that C++ guarantees it's always safe to delete the null pointer, so you need to honor that guarantee. Here's pseudocode for a non-member operator delete:

```
void operator delete(void *rawMemory)
{
  if (rawMemory == 0) return;   // do nothing if the null
                                // pointer is being deleted

  deallocate the memory pointed to by rawMemory;

  return;
}
```

The member version of this function is simple, too, except you've got to
be sure to check the size of what's being deleted. Assuming your class-
specific operator new forwards requests of the "wrong" size to ::op-
erator new, you've got to forward "wrongly sized" deletion requests to
::operator delete:

```
class Base {                    // same as before, but now
public:                         // op. delete is declared
  static void * operator new(size_t size);
  static void operator delete(void *rawMemory, size_t size);
  ...
};

void Base::operator delete(void *rawMemory, size_t size)
{
  if (rawMemory == 0) return;       // check for null pointer

  if (size != sizeof(Base)) {       // if size is "wrong,"
    ::operator delete(rawMemory);   // have standard operator
    return;                         // delete handle the request
  }

  deallocate the memory pointed to by rawMemory;

  return;
}
```

The conventions, then, for operator new and operator delete (and
their array counterparts) are not particularly onerous, but it is important that you obey them. If your allocation routines support new-handler functions and correctly deal with zero-sized requests, you're all
but finished, and if your deallocation routines cope with null pointers,
there's little more to do. Add support for inheritance in member versions of the functions, and *presto!* — you're done.

Item 9: Avoid hiding the "normal" form of new.

A declaration of a name in an inner scope hides the same name in
outer scopes, so for a function f at both global and class scope, the
member function will hide the global function:

```
void f();                       // global function

class X {
public:
  void f();                     // member function
};

X x;

f();                            // calls global f

x.f();                          // calls X::f
```

This is unsurprising and normally causes no confusion, because global and member functions are usually invoked using different syntactic forms. However, if you add to this class an operator new taking additional parameters, the result is likely to be an eye-opener:

```
class X {
public:
  void f();

  // operator new allowing specification of a
  // new-handling function
  static void * operator new(size_t size, new_handler p);
};

void specialErrorHandler();     // definition is elsewhere

X *px1 =
  new (specialErrorHandler) X;  // calls X::operator new

X *px2 = new X;                 // error!
```

By declaring a function called "operator new" inside the class, you inadvertently block access to the "normal" form of new. Why this is so is discussed in Item 50. Here we're more interested in figuring out how to avoid the problem.

One solution is to write a class-specific operator new that supports the "normal" invocation form. If it does the same thing as the global version, that can be efficiently and elegantly encapsulated as an inline function:

```
class X {
public:
  void f();

  static void * operator new(size_t size, new_handler p);

  static void * operator new(size_t size)
  { return ::operator new(size); }
};
```

```
X *px1 =
  new (specialErrorHandler) X;  // calls X::operator
                                // new(size_t, new_handler)

X* px2 = new X;                 // calls X::operator
                                // new(size_t)
```

An alternative is to provide a default parameter value (see Item 24) for each additional parameter you add to operator new:

```
class X {
public:
  void f();

  static
    void * operator new(size_t size,          // note default
                        new_handler p = 0);   // value for p
};

X *px1 = new (specialErrorHandler) X;         // fine

X* px2 = new X;                               // also fine
```

Either way, if you later decide to customize the behavior of the "normal" form of new, all you need to do is rewrite the function; callers will get the customized behavior automatically when they relink.

Item 10: **Write operator delete if you write operator new.**

Let's step back for a moment and return to fundamentals. Why would anybody want to write their own version of operator new or operator delete in the first place?

More often than not, the answer is efficiency. The default versions of operator new and operator delete are perfectly adequate for general-purpose use, but their flexibility inevitably leaves room for improvements in their performance in a more circumscribed context. This is especially true for applications that dynamically allocate a large number of small objects.

As an example, consider a class for representing airplanes, where the Airplane class contains only a pointer to the actual representation for airplane objects (a technique discussed in Item 34):

```
class AirplaneRep { ... };       // representation for an
                                 // Airplane object
class Airplane {
public:
  ...
private:
  AirplaneRep *rep;              // pointer to representation
};
```

An `Airplane` object is not very big; it contains but a single pointer. (As explained in Item 14, it may implicitly contain a second pointer if the `Airplane` class declares virtual functions.) When you allocate an `Airplane` object by calling `operator new`, however, you probably get back more memory than is needed to store this pointer (or pair of pointers). The reason for this seemingly wayward behavior has to do with the need for `operator new` and `operator delete` to communicate with one another.

Because the default version of `operator new` is a general-purpose allocator, it must be prepared to allocate blocks of any size. Similarly, the default version of `operator delete` must be prepared to deallocate blocks of whatever size `operator new` allocated. For `operator delete` to know how much memory to deallocate, it must have some way of knowing how much memory `operator new` allocated in the first place. A common way for `operator new` to tell `operator delete` how much memory it allocated is by prepending to the memory it returns some additional data that specifies the size of the allocated block. That is, when you say this,

```
Airplane *pa = new Airplane;
```

you don't necessarily get back a block of memory that looks like this:

Instead, you often get back a block of memory that looks more like this:

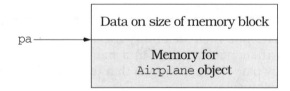

For small objects like those of class `Airplane`, this additional book-keeping data can more than double the amount of memory needed for each dynamically allocated object (especially if the class contains no virtual functions).

If you're developing software for an environment in which memory is precious, you may not be able to afford this kind of spendthrift allocation. By writing your own `operator new` for the `Airplane` class, you can take advantage of the fact that all `Airplane` objects are the same size, so there isn't any need for bookkeeping information to be kept with each allocated block.

One way to implement your class-specific operator new is to ask the default operator new for big blocks of raw memory, each block of sufficient size to hold a large number of Airplane objects. The memory chunks for Airplane objects themselves will be taken from these big blocks. Currently unused chunks will be organized into a linked list — the *free list* — of chunks that are available for future Airplane use. This may make it sound like you'll have to pay for the overhead of a next field in every object (to support the list), but you won't: the space for the rep field (which is necessary only for memory chunks in use as Airplane objects) will also serve as the place to store the next pointer (because that pointer is needed only for chunks of memory *not* in use as Airplane objects). You'll arrange for this job-sharing in the usual fashion: you'll use a union.

To turn this design into reality, you have to modify the definition of Airplane to support custom memory management. You do it as follows:

```
class Airplane {           // modified class — now supports
public:                    // custom memory management

  static void * operator new(size_t size);

  ...

private:
  union {
    AirplaneRep *rep;        // for objects in use
    Airplane *next;          // for objects on free list
  };

  // this class-specific constant (see Item 1) specifies how
  // many Airplane objects fit into a big memory block;
  // it's initialized below
  static const int BLOCK_SIZE;

  static Airplane *headOfFreeList;

};
```

Here you've added the declarations for operator new, the union that allows the rep and next fields to occupy the same memory, a class-specific constant for specifying how big each allocated block should be, and a static pointer to keep track of the head of the free list. It's important to use a static member for this last task, because there's one free list for the entire *class*, not one free list for each Airplane *object*.

The next thing to do is to write the new operator new:

```
void * Airplane::operator new(size_t size)
{
  // send requests of the "wrong" size to ::operator new();
  // for details, see Item 8
  if (size != sizeof(Airplane))
    return ::operator new(size);

  Airplane *p =                 // p is now a pointer to the
    headOfFreeList;             // head of the free list

  // if p is valid, just move the list head to the
  // next element in the free list
  if (p)
    headOfFreeList = p->next;

  else {
    // The free list is empty. Allocate a block of memory
    // big enough to hold BLOCK_SIZE Airplane objects
    Airplane *newBlock =
      static_cast<Airplane*>(::operator new(BLOCK_SIZE *
                                          sizeof(Airplane)));

    // form a new free list by linking the memory chunks
    // together; skip the zeroth element, because you'll
    // return that to the caller of operator new
    for (int i = 1; i < BLOCK_SIZE-1; ++i)
      newBlock[i].next = &newBlock[i+1];

    // terminate the linked list with a null pointer
    newBlock[BLOCK_SIZE-1].next = 0;

    // set p to front of list, headOfFreeList to
    // chunk immediately following
    p = newBlock;
    headOfFreeList = &newBlock[1];
  }

  return p;
}
```

If you've read Item 8, you know that when operator new can't satisfy a request for memory, it's supposed to perform a series of ritualistic steps involving new-handler functions and exceptions. There is no sign of such steps above. That's because this operator new gets all the memory it manages from ::operator new. That means this operator new can fail only if ::operator new does. But if ::operator new fails, *it* must engage in the new-handling ritual (possibly culminating in the throwing of an exception), so there is no need for Airplane's operator new to do it, too. In other words, the new-handler behavior is there, you just don't see it, because it's hidden inside ::operator new.

Given this operator new, the only thing left to do is provide the obligatory definitions of Airplane's static data members:

```
Airplane *Airplane::headOfFreeList;       // these definitions
                                          // go in an implemen-
const int Airplane::BLOCK_SIZE = 512;     // tation file, not
                                          // a header file
```

There's no need to explicitly set headOfFreeList to the null pointer, because static members are initialized to 0 by default. The value for BLOCK_SIZE, of course, determines the size of each memory block we get from ::operator new.

This version of operator new will work just fine. Not only will it use a lot less memory for Airplane objects than the default operator new, it's also likely to be faster, possibly as much as *two orders of magnitude* faster. That shouldn't be surprising. After all, the general version of operator new has to cope with memory requests of different sizes, has to worry about internal and external fragmentation, etc., whereas your version of operator new just manipulates a couple of pointers in a linked list. It's easy to be fast when you don't have to be flexible.

At long last we are in a position to discuss operator delete. Remember operator delete? This Item is *about* operator delete. As currently written, your Airplane class declares operator new, but it does not declare operator delete. Now consider what happens when a client writes the following, which is nothing if not eminently reasonable:

```
Airplane *pa = new Airplane;      // calls
                                  // Airplane::operator new
...

delete pa;                        // calls ::operator delete
```

If you listen closely when you read this code, you can hear the sound of an airplane crashing and burning, with much weeping and wailing by the programmers who knew it. The problem is that operator new (the one defined in Airplane) returns a pointer to memory *without any header information*, but operator delete (the default, global one) assumes that the memory it's passed *does* contain header information! Surely this is a recipe for disaster.

This example illustrates the general rule: operator new and operator delete must be written in concert so that they share the same assumptions. If you're going to roll your own memory allocation routine, be sure to roll one for deallocation, too.

Here's how you solve the problem with the Airplane class:

```
class Airplane {        // same as before, except there's
public:                 // now a decl. for operator delete
  ...

  static void operator delete(void *deadObject,
                              size_t size);

};

// operator delete is passed a memory chunk, which,
// if it's the right size, is just added to the
// front of the list of free chunks
void Airplane::operator delete(void *deadObject,
                               size_t size)
{
  if (deadObject == 0) return;        // see Item 8

  if (size != sizeof(Airplane)) {     // see Item 8
    ::operator delete(deadObject);
    return;
  }

  Airplane *carcass =
    static_cast<Airplane*>(deadObject);

  carcass->next = headOfFreeList;
  headOfFreeList = carcass;
}
```

Because you were careful in operator new to ensure that calls of the "wrong" size were forwarded to the global operator new (see Item 8), you must demonstrate equal care in ensuring that such "improperly sized" objects are handled by the global version of operator delete. If you did not, you'd run into precisely the problem you have been laboring so arduously to avoid — a semantic mismatch between new and delete.

Interestingly, the size_t value C++ passes to operator delete may be *incorrect* if the object being deleted was derived from a base class lacking a virtual destructor. This is reason enough for making sure your base classes have virtual destructors, but Item 14 describes a second, arguably better reason. For now, simply note that if you omit virtual destructors in base classes, operator delete functions may not work correctly.

All of which is well and good, but I can tell by the furrow in your brow that what you're really concerned about is the memory leak. With all the software development experience you bring to the table, there's no way you'd fail to notice that Airplane's operator new calls ::operator new to get big blocks of memory, but Airplane's operator delete fails to release those blocks.† *Memory leak! Memory leak!* I can almost hear the alarm bells going off in your head.

Listen to me carefully: *there is no memory leak.*

A memory leak arises when memory is allocated, then all pointers to that memory are lost. Absent garbage collection or some other extralinguistic mechanism, such memory cannot be reclaimed. But this design has no memory leak, because it's never the case that all pointers to memory are lost. Each big block of memory is first broken down into `Airplane`-sized chunks, and these chunks are then placed on the free list. When clients call `Airplane::operator new`, chunks are removed from the free list, and clients receive pointers to them. When clients call `operator delete`, the chunks are put back on the free list. With this design, all memory chunks are either in use as `Airplane` objects (in which case it's the clients' responsibility to avoid leaking their memory) or are on the free list (in which case there's a pointer to the memory). There is no memory leak.

Nevertheless, the blocks of memory returned by `::operator new` are never released by `Airplane::operator delete`, and there has to be *some* name for that. There is. You've created a memory *pool.* Call it semantic gymnastics if you must, but there is an important difference between a memory leak and a memory pool. A memory leak may grow indefinitely, even if clients are well-behaved, but a memory pool never grows larger than the maximum amount of memory requested by its clients at any given time.

It would not be difficult to modify `Airplane`'s memory management routines so that the blocks of memory returned by `::operator new` were automatically released when they were no longer in use, but there are two reasons why you might not want to do it.

The first concerns your likely motivation for tackling custom memory management. There are many reasons why you might do it, but the most common one is that you've determined that the default `operator new` and `operator delete` use too much memory or are too slow (or both). That being the case, every additional byte and every additional statement you devote to tracking and releasing those big memory blocks comes straight off the bottom line: your software runs slower and uses more memory than it would if you adopted the pool strategy. For libraries and applications in which performance is at a premium

---

† I write this with certainty, because I failed to address this issue in the first edition of this book, and *many* readers upbraided me for the omission. There's nothing quite like a few thousand proofreaders to demonstrate one's fallibility, sigh.

and you can expect pool sizes to be reasonably bounded, the pool approach may well be best.

The second reason has to do with pathological behavior. Suppose Airplane's memory management routines are modified so Airplane's operator delete releases any big block of memory that has no active objects in it. Now consider this program:

```
int main()
{
  Airplane *pa = new Airplane;    // first allocation: get big
                                  // block, make free list, etc.

  delete pa;                      // block is now empty;
                                  // release it

  pa = new Airplane;              // uh oh, get block again,
                                  // make free list, etc.

  delete pa;                      // okay, block is empty
                                  // again; release it

  ...                             // you get the idea...

  return 0;
}
```

This nasty little program will run slower and use more memory than with even the *default* operator new and operator delete, much less the pool-based versions of those functions!

Of course, there are ways to deal with this pathology, but the more you code for uncommon special cases, the closer you get to reimplementing the default memory management functions, and then what have you gained? A memory pool is not the answer to all memory management questions, but it's a reasonable answer to many of them.

In fact, it's a reasonable answer often enough that you may be bothered by the need to reimplement it for different classes. "Surely," you think to yourself, "there should be a way to package the notion of a fixed-sized memory allocator so it's easily reused." There is, though this Item has droned on long enough that I'll leave the details in the form of the dreaded exercise for the reader.

Instead, I'll simply show a minimal interface (see Item 18) to a *Pool* class, where each object of type Pool is an allocator for objects of the size specified in the Pool's constructor:

```
class Pool {
public:
  Pool(size_t n);                 // Create an allocator for
                                  // objects of size n
```

```
void * alloc(size_t n);          // Allocate enough memory
                                 // for one object; follow
                                 // operator new conventions
                                 // from Item 8

void free(void *p, size_t n);    // Return to the pool the
                                 // memory pointed to by p;
                                 // follow operator delete
                                 // conventions from Item 8

~Pool();                         // Deallocate all memory in
                                 // the pool
};
```

This class allows Pool objects to be created, to perform allocation and deallocation operations, and to be destroyed. When a Pool object is destroyed, it releases all the memory it allocated. This means there is now a way to avoid the memory leak-like behavior that Airplane's functions exhibited. However, this also means that if a Pool's destructor is called too soon (before all the objects using its memory have been destroyed), some objects will find their memory yanked out from under them before they're done using it. To say that the resulting behavior is undefined is being generous.

Given this Pool class, even a Java programmer can add custom memory management capabilities to Airplane without breaking a sweat:

```
class Airplane {
public:

   ...                          // usual Airplane functions

   static void * operator new(size_t size);
   static void operator delete(void *p, size_t size);
private:
   AirplaneRep *rep;            // pointer to representation

   static Pool memPool;         // memory pool for Airplanes; see
};                              // below for a remark on this

inline void * Airplane::operator new(size_t size)
{ return memPool.alloc(size); }

inline void Airplane::operator delete(void *p,
                                      size_t size)
{ memPool.free(p, size); }

// create a new pool for Airplane objects; this goes in
// the class implementation file
Pool Airplane::memPool(sizeof(Airplane));
```

This is a much cleaner design than the one we saw earlier, because the Airplane class is no longer cluttered with non-airplane details. Gone are the union, the head of the free list, the constant defining how big each raw memory block should be, etc. That's all hidden inside Pool, which is really where it should be. Let Pool's author worry about memory management minutiae. Your job is to make the Airplane class work properly.

As an aside, Airplane::memPool is what the C++ standard charmingly refers to as a "non-local static object." Care must be taken to guarantee that it's not possible to use such objects before they've been initialized. For all the whats, whys, and hows, turn to Item 47.

Now, it's interesting to see how custom memory management routines can improve program performance, and it's worthwhile to see how such routines can be encapsulated inside a class like Pool, but let us not lose sight of the main point. That point is that operator new and operator delete need to work together, so if you write operator new, be sure to write operator delete, as well.

Constructors, Destructors, and Assignment Operators

Almost every class you write will have one or more constructors, a destructor, and an assignment operator. Little wonder. These are your bread-and-butter functions, the ones that control the fundamental operations of bringing a new object into existence and making sure it's initialized; getting rid of an object and making sure it's been properly cleaned up; and giving an object a new value. Making mistakes in these functions will lead to far-reaching and distinctly unpleasant repercussions throughout your classes, so it's vital that you get them right. In this section, I offer guidance on putting together the functions that comprise the backbone of well-formed classes.

Item 11: Declare a copy constructor and an assignment operator for classes with dynamically allocated memory.

Consider a class for representing String objects:

```
// a poorly designed String class
class String {
public:
  String(const char *value);
  ~String();

  ...                                // no copy ctor or operator=

private:
  char *data;
};
```

```
String::String(const char *value)
{
  if (value) {
    data = new char[strlen(value) + 1];
    strcpy(data, value);
  }
  else {
    data = new char[1];
    *data = '\0';
  }
}

inline String::~String() { delete [] data; }
```

Note that there is no assignment operator or copy constructor declared in this class. As you'll see, this has some unfortunate consequences.

If you make these object definitions,

```
String a("Hello");
String b("World");
```

the situation is as shown below:

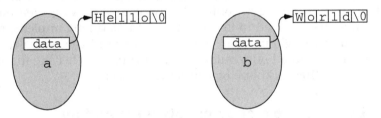

Inside object a is a pointer to memory containing the character string "Hello". Separate from that is an object b containing a pointer to the character string "World". If you now perform an assignment,

```
b = a;
```

there is no client-defined operator= to call, so C++ generates and calls the default assignment operator instead (see Item 45). This default assignment operator performs memberwise assignment from the members of a to the members of b, which for pointers (a.data and b.data) is just a bitwise copy. The result of this assignment is shown below.

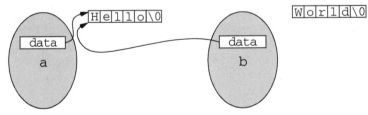

There are at least two problems with this state of affairs. First, the memory that b used to point to was never deleted; it is lost forever. This is a classic example of how a memory leak can arise. Second, both a and b now contain pointers to the same character string. When one of them goes out of scope, its destructor will delete the memory still pointed to by the other. For example:

```
String a("Hello");              // define and construct a

{                               // open new scope
  String b("World");            // define and construct b

  ...

  b = a;                        // execute default op=,
                                // lose b's memory

}                               // close scope, call b's
                                // destructor

String c = a;                   // c.data is undefined!
                                // a.data is already deleted
```

The last statement in this example is a call to the copy constructor, which also isn't defined in the class, hence will be generated by C++ in the same manner as the assignment operator (again, see Item 45) and with the same behavior: bitwise copy of the underlying pointers. That leads to the same kind of problem, but without the worry of a memory leak, because the object being initialized can't yet point to any allocated memory. In the case of the code above, for example, there is no memory leak when c.data is initialized with the value of a.data, because c.data doesn't yet point anywhere. However, after c is initialized with a, both c.data and a.data point to the same place, so that place will be deleted twice: once when c is destroyed, once again when a is destroyed.

The case of the copy constructor differs a little from that of the assignment operator, however, because of the way it can bite you: pass-by-value. Of course, Item 22 demonstrates that you should only rarely pass objects by value, but consider this anyway:

```
void doNothing(String localString) {}

String s = "The Truth Is Out There";

doNothing(s);
```

Everything looks innocuous enough, but because localString is passed by value, it must be initialized from s via the (default) copy constructor. Hence, localString has a copy of the *pointer* that is inside s. When doNothing finishes executing, localString goes out of scope, and its destructor is called. The end result is by now familiar: s contains a pointer to memory that localString has already deleted.

By the way, the result of using delete on a pointer that has already been deleted is undefined, so even if s is never used again, there could well be a problem when it goes out of scope.

The solution to these kinds of pointer aliasing problems is to write your own versions of the copy constructor and the assignment operator if you have any pointers in your class. Inside those functions, you can either copy the pointed-to data structures so that every object has its own copy, or you can implement some kind of reference-counting scheme to keep track of how many objects are currently pointing to a particular data structure. The reference-counting approach is more complicated, and it calls for extra work inside the constructors and destructors, too, but in some (though by no means all) applications, it can result in significant memory savings and substantial increases in speed.

For some classes, it's more trouble than it's worth to implement copy constructors and assignment operators, especially when you have reason to believe that your clients won't make copies or perform assignments. The examples above demonstrate that omitting the corresponding member functions reflects poor design, but what do you do if writing them isn't practical, either? Simple: you follow this Item's advice. You *declare* the functions (private, as it turns out), but you don't define (i.e., implement) them at all. That prevents clients from calling them, and it prevents compilers from generating them, too. For details on this nifty trick, see Item 27.

One more thing about the String class I used in this Item. In the constructor body, I was careful to use [] with new both times I called it, even though in one of the places I wanted only a single object. As described in Item 5, it's essential to employ the same form in corresponding applications of new and delete, so I was careful to be consistent in my uses of new. This is something you do not want to forget. *Always* make sure that you use [] with delete if and only if you used [] with the corresponding use of new.

Item 12: Prefer initialization to assignment in constructors.

Consider a template for generating classes that allow a name to be associated with a pointer to an object of some type T:

```
template<class T>
class NamedPtr {
public:
  NamedPtr(const string& initName, T *initPtr);
  ...

private:
  string name;
  T *ptr;
};
```

(In light of the aliasing that can arise during the assignment and copy construction of objects with pointer members (see Item 11), you might wish to consider whether NamedPtr should implement these functions. Hint: it should (see Item 27).)

When you write the NamedPtr constructor, you have to transfer the values of the parameters to the corresponding data members. There are two ways to do this. The first is to use the member initialization list:

```
template<class T>
NamedPtr<T>::NamedPtr(const string& initName, T *initPtr)
: name(initName), ptr(initPtr)
{}
```

The second is to make assignments in the constructor body:

```
template<class T>
NamedPtr<T>::NamedPtr(const string& initName, T *initPtr)
{
  name = initName;
  ptr = initPtr;
}
```

There are important differences between these two approaches.

From a purely pragmatic point of view, there are times when the initialization list *must* be used. In particular, const and reference members may *only* be initialized, never assigned. So, if you decided that a NamedPtr<T> object could never change its name or its pointer, you might follow the advice of Item 21 and declare the members const:

```
template<class T>
class NamedPtr {
public:
  NamedPtr(const string& initName, T *initPtr);
  ...

private:
  const string name;
  T * const ptr;
};
```

This class definition *requires* that you use a member initialization list, because const members may only be initialized, never assigned.

You'd obtain very different behavior if you decided that a NamedPtr<T> object should contain a *reference* to an existing name. Even so, you'd still have to initialize the reference on your constructors' member initialization lists. Of course, you could also combine the two, yielding NamedPtr<T> objects with read-only access to names that might be modified outside the class:

```
template<class T>
class NamedPtr {
public:
  NamedPtr(const string& initName, T *initPtr);
  ...

private:
  const string& name;        // must be initialized via
                             // initializer list

  T * const ptr;             // must be initialized via
                             // initializer list
};
```

The original class template, however, contains no const or reference members. Even so, using a member initialization list is still preferable to performing assignments inside the constructor. This time the reason is efficiency. When a member initialization list is used, only a single string member function is called. When assignment inside the constructor is used, two are called. To understand why, consider what happens when you declare a NamedPtr<T> object.

Construction of objects proceeds in two phases:

1. Initialization of data members. (See also Item 13.)

2. Execution of the body of the constructor that was called.

(For objects with base classes, base class member initialization and constructor body execution occurs prior to that for derived classes.)

For the NamedPtr classes, this means that a constructor for the string object name will *always* be called before you ever get inside the body of a NamedPtr constructor. The only question, then, is this: which string constructor will be called?

That depends on the member initialization list in the NamedPtr classes. If you fail to specify an initialization argument for name, the default string constructor will be called. When you later perform an assignment to name inside the NamedPtr constructors, you will call operator= on name. That will total two calls to string member functions: one for the default constructor and one more for the assignment.

On the other hand, if you use a member initialization list to specify that name should be initialized with initName, name will be initialized through the copy constructor at a cost of only a single function call.

Even in the case of the lowly string type, the cost of an unnecessary function call may be significant, and as classes become larger and more complex, so do their constructors, and so does the cost of constructing objects. If you establish the habit of using a member initialization list whenever you can, not only do you satisfy a requirement for const and reference members, you also minimize the chances of initializing data members in an inefficient manner.

In other words, initialization via a member initialization list is *always* legal, is *never* less efficient than assignment inside the body of the constructor, and is often *more* efficient. Furthermore, it simplifies maintenance of the class, because if a data member's type is later modified to something that *requires* use of a member initialization list, nothing has to change.

There is one time, however, when it may make sense to use assignment instead of initialization for the data members in a class. That is when you have a large number of data members of *built-in types*, and you want them all initialized the same way in each constructor. For example, here's a class that might qualify for this kind of treatment:

```cpp
class ManyDataMbrs {
public:
  // default constructor
  ManyDataMbrs();

  // copy constructor
  ManyDataMbrs(const ManyDataMbrs& x);

private:
  int a, b, c, d, e, f, g, h;
  double i, j, k, l, m;
};
```

Suppose you want to initialize all the ints to 1 and all the doubles to 0, even if the copy constructor is used. Using member initialization lists, you'd have to write this:

```
ManyDataMbrs::ManyDataMbrs()
: a(1), b(1), c(1), d(1), e(1), f(1), g(1), h(1), i(0),
  j(0), k(0), l(0), m(0)
{ ... }

ManyDataMbrs::ManyDataMbrs(const ManyDataMbrs& x)
: a(1), b(1), c(1), d(1), e(1), f(1), g(1), h(1), i(0),
  j(0), k(0), l(0), m(0)
{ ... }
```

This is more than just unpleasant drudge work. It is error-prone in the short term and difficult to maintain in the long term.

However, you can take advantage of the fact that there is no operational difference between initialization and assignment for (non-const, non-reference) objects of built-in types, so you can safely replace the memberwise initialization lists with a function call to a common initialization routine:

```
class ManyDataMbrs {
public:
  // default constructor
  ManyDataMbrs();

  // copy constructor
  ManyDataMbrs(const ManyDataMbrs& x);

private:
  int a, b, c, d, e, f, g, h;
  double i, j, k, l, m;

  void init();                      // used to initialize data
                                    // members
};

void ManyDataMbrs::init()
{
  a = b = c = d = e = f = g = h = 1;
  i = j = k = l = m = 0;
}

ManyDataMbrs::ManyDataMbrs()
{
  init();

  ...

}

ManyDataMbrs::ManyDataMbrs(const ManyDataMbrs& x)
{
  init();

  ...

}
```

Because the initialization routine is an implementation detail of the class, you are, of course, careful to make it `private`, right?

Note that `static` class members should *never* be initialized in a class's constructor. Static members are initialized only once per program run, so it makes no sense to try to "initialize" them each time an object of the class's type is created. At the very least, doing so would be inefficient: why pay to "initialize" an object multiple times? Besides, initialization of static class members is different enough from initialization of their nonstatic counterparts that an entire Item — Item 47 — is devoted to the topic.

Item 13: List members in an initialization list in the order in which they are declared.

Unrepentant Pascal and Ada programmers often yearn for the ability to define arrays with arbitrary bounds, i.e., from 10 to 20 instead of from 0 to 10. Long-time C programmers will insist that everybody who's anybody will always start counting from 0, but it's easy enough to placate the `begin`/`end` crowd. All you have to do is define your own Array class template:

```
template<class T>
class Array {
public:
  Array(int lowBound, int highBound);
  ...

private:
  vector<T> data;            // the array data is stored
                             // in a vector object; see
                             // Item 49 for info about
                             // the vector template

  size_t size;               // # of elements in array

  int lBound, hBound;        // lower bound, higher bound
};

template<class T>
Array<T>::Array(int lowBound, int highBound)
: size(highBound - lowBound + 1),
  lBound(lowBound), hBound(highBound),
  data(size)
{}
```

An industrial-strength constructor would perform sanity checking on its parameters to ensure that `highBound` was at least as great as `low-Bound`, but there is a much nastier error here: even with perfectly good values for the array's bounds, you have absolutely no idea how many elements data holds.

"How can that be?" I hear you cry. "I carefully initialized size before passing it to the vector constructor!" Unfortunately, you didn't — you just tried to. The rules of the game are that class members are initialized *in the order of their declaration in the class*; the order in which they are listed in a member initialization list makes not a whit of difference. In the classes generated by your Array template, data will always be initialized first, followed by size, lBound, and hBound. Always.

Perverse though this may seem, there is a reason for it. Consider this scenario:

```
class Wacko {
public:
  Wacko(const char *s): s1(s), s2(0) {}
  Wacko(const Wacko& rhs): s2(rhs.s1), s1(0) {}

private:
  string s1, s2;
};

Wacko w1 = "Hello world!";
Wacko w2 = w1;
```

If members were initialized in the order of their appearance in an initialization list, the data members of w1 and w2 would be constructed in different orders. Recall that the destructors for the members of an object are always called in the inverse order of their constructors. Thus, if the above were allowed, compilers would have to keep track of the order in which the members were initialized for *each object*, just to ensure that the destructors would be called in the right order. That would be an expensive proposition. To avoid that overhead, the order of construction and destruction is the same for all objects of a given type, and the order of members in an initialization list is ignored.

Actually, if you really want to get picky about it, only nonstatic data members are initialized according to the rule. Static data members act like global and namespace objects, so they are initialized only once; see Item 47 for details. Furthermore, base class data members are initialized before derived class data members, so if you're using inheritance, you should list base class initializers at the very beginning of your member initialization lists. (If you're using *multiple* inheritance, your base classes will be initialized in the order in which you *inherit* from them; the order in which they're listed in your member initialization lists will again be ignored. However, if you're using multiple inheritance, you've probably got more important things to worry about. If you don't, Item 43 would be happy to make suggestions regarding aspects of multiple inheritance that are worrisome.)

The bottom line is this: if you hope to understand what is really going on when your objects are initialized, be sure to list the members in an initialization list in the order in which those members are declared in the class.

Item 14: **Make sure base classes have virtual destructors.**

Sometimes it's convenient for a class to keep track of how many objects of its type exist. The straightforward way to do this is to create a static class member for counting the objects. The member is initialized to 0, is incremented in the class constructors, and is decremented in the class destructor.

You might envision a military application, in which a class representing enemy targets might look something like this:

```
class EnemyTarget {
public:
  EnemyTarget() { ++numTargets; }
  EnemyTarget(const EnemyTarget&) { ++numTargets; }
  ~EnemyTarget() { --numTargets; }

  static size_t numberOfTargets()
  { return numTargets; }

  virtual bool destroy();                  // returns success of
                                           // attempt to destroy
                                           // EnemyTarget object

private:
  static size_t numTargets;                // object counter
};
// class statics must be defined outside the class;
// initialization is to 0 by default
size_t EnemyTarget::numTargets;
```

This class is unlikely to win you a government defense contract, but it will suffice for our purposes here, which are substantially less demanding than are those of the Department of Defense. Or so we may hope.

Let us suppose that a particular kind of enemy target is an enemy tank, which you model, naturally enough (see Item 35), as a publicly derived class of EnemyTarget. Because you are interested in the total number of enemy tanks as well as the total number of enemy targets, you'll pull the same trick with the derived class that you did with the base class:

```
class EnemyTank: public EnemyTarget {
public:
  EnemyTank() { ++numTanks; }

  EnemyTank(const EnemyTank& rhs)
   : EnemyTarget(rhs)
   { ++numTanks; }

  ~EnemyTank() { --numTanks; }

  static size_t numberOfTanks()
  { return numTanks; }

  virtual bool destroy();

private:
  static size_t numTanks;        // object counter for tanks
};

size_t EnemyTank::numTanks;      // initialization of counter
```

Finally, let's assume that somewhere in your application, you dynamically create an EnemyTank object using new, which you later get rid of via delete:

```
EnemyTarget *targetPtr = new EnemyTank;

...

delete targetPtr;
```

Everything you've done so far seems completely kosher. Both classes undo in the destructor what they did in the constructor, and there's certainly nothing wrong with your application, in which you were careful to use delete after you were done with the object you conjured up with new. Nevertheless, there is something very troubling here. Your program's behavior is *undefined* — you have no way of knowing *what* will happen.

The C++ language standard is unusually clear on this topic. When you try to delete a derived class object through a base class pointer and the base class has a *nonvirtual* destructor (as EnemyTarget does), the results are undefined. That means compilers may generate code to do whatever they like: reformat your disk, send suggestive mail to your boss, fax source code to your competitors, whatever. (What often happens at runtime is that the derived class's destructor is never called. In this example, that would mean your count of EnemyTanks would not be adjusted when targetPtr was deleted. Your count of enemy tanks would thus be wrong, a rather disturbing prospect to combatants dependent on accurate battlefield information.)

To avoid this problem, you have only to make the EnemyTarget destructor *virtual*. Declaring the destructor virtual ensures well-defined behavior that does precisely what you want: both EnemyTank's and EnemyTarget's destructors will be called before the memory holding the object is deallocated.

Now, the EnemyTarget class contains a virtual function, which is generally the case with base classes. After all, the purpose of virtual functions is to allow customization of behavior in derived classes (see Item 36), so almost all base classes contain virtual functions.

If a class does *not* contain any virtual functions, that is often an indication that it is not meant to be used as a base class. When a class is not intended to be used as a base class, making the destructor virtual is usually a bad idea. Consider this example, based on a discussion in the ARM (see Item 50):

```
// class for representing 2D points
class Point {
public:
  Point(short int xCoord, short int yCoord);
  ~Point();

private:
  short int x, y;
};
```

If a short int occupies 16 bits, a Point object can fit into a 32-bit register. Furthermore, a Point object can be passed as a 32-bit quantity to functions written in other languages such as C or FORTRAN. If Point's destructor is made virtual, however, the situation changes.

The implementation of virtual functions requires that objects carry around with them some additional information that can be used at runtime to determine which virtual functions should be invoked on the object. In most compilers, this extra information takes the form of a pointer called a vptr ("virtual table pointer"). The vptr points to an array of function pointers called a vtbl ("virtual table"); each class with virtual functions has an associated vtbl. When a virtual function is invoked on an object, the actual function called is determined by following the object's vptr to a vtbl and then looking up the appropriate function pointer in the vtbl.

The details of how virtual functions are implemented are unimportant. What *is* important is that if the Point class contains a virtual function, objects of that type will implicitly *double* in size, from two 16-bit shorts to two 16-bit shorts plus a 32-bit vptr! No longer will Point objects fit in a 32-bit register. Furthermore, Point objects in C++ no longer look like the same structure declared in another language such as C, because their foreign language counterparts will lack the vptr. As a result, it is no longer possible to pass Points to and from functions written in other languages unless you explicitly compensate for the vptr, which is itself an implementation detail and hence unportable.

The bottom line is that gratuitously declaring all destructors virtual is just as wrong as never declaring them virtual. In fact, many people summarize the situation this way: declare a virtual destructor in a class if and only if that class contains at least one virtual function.

This is a good rule, one that works most of the time, but unfortunately, it is possible to get bitten by the nonvirtual destructor problem even in the absence of virtual functions. For example, Item 13 considers a class template for implementing arrays with client-defined bounds. Suppose you decide to write a template for derived classes representing named arrays, i.e., classes where every array has a name:

```cpp
template<class T>                    // base class template
class Array {                        // (from Item 13)
public:
  Array(int lowBound, int highBound);
  ~Array();

private:
  vector<T> data;
  size_t size;
  int lBound, hBound;
};

template<class T>
class NamedArray: public Array<T> {
public:
  NamedArray(int lowBound, int highBound, const string& name);
  ...

private:
  string arrayName;
};
```

If anywhere in an application you somehow convert a pointer-to-Named-Array into a pointer-to-Array and you then use delete on the Array pointer, you are instantly transported to the realm of undefined behavior:

```cpp
NamedArray<int> *pna =
  new NamedArray<int>(10, 20, "Impending Doom");

Array<int> *pa;

...
```

```
pa = pna;                    // NamedArray<int>* -> Array<int>*

...

delete pa;                   // undefined! (Insert theme to
                             // Twilight Zone here); in practice,
                             // pa->arrayName will often be leaked,
                             // because the NamedArray part of
                             // *pa will never be destroyed
```

This situation can arise more frequently than you might imagine, because it's not uncommon to want to take an existing class that does something, `Array` in this case, and derive from it a class that does all the same things, plus more. `NamedArray` doesn't redefine any of the behavior of `Array` — it inherits all its functions without change — it just adds some additional capabilities. Yet the nonvirtual destructor problem persists.

Finally, it's worth mentioning that it can be convenient to declare pure virtual destructors in some classes. Recall that pure virtual functions result in *abstract* classes — classes that can't be instantiated (i.e., you can't create objects of that type). Sometimes, however, you have a class that you'd like to be abstract, but you don't happen to have any functions that are pure virtual. What to do? Well, because an abstract class is intended to be used as a base class, and because a base class should have a virtual destructor, and because a pure virtual function yields an abstract class, the solution is simple: declare a pure virtual destructor in the class you want to be abstract.

Here's an example:

```
class AWOV {                 // AWOV = "Abstract w/o
                             // Virtuals"
public:
  virtual ~AWOV() = 0;       // declare pure virtual
                             // destructor
};
```

This class has a pure virtual function, so it's abstract, and it has a virtual destructor, so you can rest assured that you won't have to worry about the destructor problem. There is one twist, however: you must provide a *definition* for the pure virtual destructor:

```
AWOV::~AWOV() {}             // definition of pure
                             // virtual destructor
```

You need this definition, because the way virtual destructors work is that the most derived class's destructor is called first, then the destructor of each base class is called. That means that compilers will generate a call to ~AWOV even though the class is abstract, so you have to be sure to provide a body for the function. If you don't, the linker will complain about a missing symbol, and you'll have to go back and add one.

You can do anything you like in that function, but, as in the example above, it's not uncommon to have nothing to do. If that is the case, you'll probably be tempted to avoid paying the overhead cost of a call to an empty function by declaring your destructor inline. That's a perfectly sensible strategy, but there's a twist you should know about.

Because your destructor is virtual, its address must be entered into the class's vtbl. But inline functions aren't supposed to exist as freestanding functions (that's what inline means, right?), so special measures must be taken to get addresses for them. Item 33 tells the full story, but the bottom line is this: if you declare a virtual destructor inline, you're likely to avoid function call overhead when it's invoked, but your compiler will still have to generate an out-of-line copy of the function somewhere, too.

Item 15: Have operator= return a reference to *this.

Bjarne Stroustrup, the designer of C++, went to a lot of trouble to ensure that user-defined types would mimic the built-in types as closely as possible. That's why you can overload operators, write type conversion functions, take control of assignment and copy construction, etc. After so much effort on his part, the least you can do is keep the ball rolling.

Which brings us to assignment. With the built-in types, you can chain assignments together, like so:

```
int w, x, y, z;

w = x = y = z = 0;
```

As a result, you should be able to chain together assignments for user-defined types, too:

```
string w, x, y, z;          // string is "user-defined"
                            // by the standard C++
                            // library (see Item 49)

w = x = y = z = "Hello";
```

As fate would have it, the assignment operator is right-associative, so the assignment chain is parsed like this:

```
w = (x = (y = (z = "Hello")));
```

It's worthwhile to write this in its completely equivalent functional form. Unless you're a closet LISP programmer, this example should make you grateful for the ability to define infix operators:

```
w.operator=(x.operator=(y.operator=(z.operator=("Hello"))));
```

This form is illustrative because it emphasizes that the argument to w.operator=, x.operator=, and y.operator= is the return value of a previous call to operator=. As a result, the return type of operator= must be acceptable as an input to the function itself. For the default version of operator= in a class C, the signature of the function is as follows (see Item 45):

```
C& C::operator=(const C&);
```

You'll almost always want to follow this convention of having operator= both take and return a reference to a class object, although at times you may overload operator= so that it takes different argument types. For example, the standard string type provides two different versions of the assignment operator:

```
string&                       // assign a string
operator=(const string& rhs); // to a string

string&                       // assign a char*
operator=(const char *rhs);   // to a string
```

Notice, however, that even in the presence of overloading, the return type is a reference to an object of the class.

A common error amongst new C++ programmers is to have operator= return void, a decision that seems reasonable until you realize it prevents chains of assignment. So don't do it.

Another common error is to have operator= return a reference to a const object, like this:

```
class Widget {
public:
  ...                                            // note
  const Widget& operator=(const Widget& rhs);    // const
  ...                                            // return
};                                               // type
```

The usual motivation is to prevent clients from doing silly things like this:

```
Widget w1, w2, w3;

...

(w1 = w2) = w3;              // assign w2 to w1, then w3 to
                             // the result! (Giving Widget's
                             // operator= a const return value
                             // prevents this from compiling.)
```

Silly this may be, but not so silly that it's prohibited for the built-in types:

```
int i1, i2, i3;

...

(i1 = i2) = i3;              // legal! assigns i2 to
                             // i1, then i3 to i1!
```

I know of no practical use for this kind of thing, but if it's good enough for the ints, it's good enough for me and my classes. It should be good enough for you and yours, too. Why introduce gratuitous incompatibilities with the conventions followed by the built-in types?

Within an assignment operator bearing the default signature, there are two obvious candidates for the object to be returned: the object on the left hand side of the assignment (the one pointed to by this) and the object on the right-hand side (the one named in the parameter list). Which is correct?

Here are the possibilities for a String class (a class for which you'd definitely want to write an assignment operator, as explained in Item 11):

```
String& String::operator=(const String& rhs)
{

  ...

  return *this;              // return reference
                             // to left-hand object
}
String& String::operator=(const String& rhs)
{

  ...

  return rhs;                // return reference to
                             // right-hand object
}
```

This might strike you as a case of six of one versus a half a dozen of the other, but there are important differences.

First, the version returning rhs won't compile. That's because rhs is a reference-to-*const*-String, but operator= returns a reference-to-String. Compilers will give you no end of grief for trying to return a reference-to-non-const when the object itself is const. That seems easy enough to get around, however — just redeclare operator= like this:

```
String& String::operator=(String& rhs) { ... }
```

Alas, now the client code won't compile! Look again at the last part of the original chain of assignments:

```
z = "Hello";                      // same as z.op=("Hello");
```

Because the right-hand argument of the assignment is not of the correct type — it's a char array, not a String — compilers would have to create a temporary String object (via the String constructor) to make the call succeed. That is, they'd have to generate code roughly equivalent to this:

```
const String temp("Hello");    // create temporary

z = temp;                      // pass temporary to op=
```

Compilers are willing to create such a temporary (unless the needed constructor is explicit — see Item 19), but note that the temporary object is const. This is important, because it prevents you from accidentally passing a temporary into a function that modifies its parameter. If that were allowed, programmers would be surprised to find that only the compiler-generated temporary was modified, *not* the argument they actually provided at the call site. (We know this for a fact, because early versions of C++ allowed these kinds of temporaries to be generated, passed, and modified, and the result was a lot of surprised programmers.)

Now we can see why the client code above won't compile if String's operator= is declared to take a reference-to-non-const String: it's never legal to pass a const object to a function that fails to declare the corresponding parameter const. That's just simple const-correctness.

You thus find yourself in the happy circumstance of having no choice whatsoever: you'll always want to define your assignment operators in such a way that they return a reference to their left-hand argument, *this. If you do anything else, you prevent chains of assignments, you prevent implicit type conversions at call sites, or both.

Item 16: Assign to all data members in operator=.

Item 45 explains that C++ will write an assignment operator for you if you don't declare one yourself, and Item 11 describes why you often won't much care for the one it writes for you, so perhaps you're wondering if you can somehow have the best of both worlds, whereby you let C++ generate a default assignment operator and you selectively override those parts you don't like. No such luck. If you want to take control of any part of the assignment process, you must do the entire thing yourself.

In practice, this means that you need to assign to *every* data member of your object when you write your assignment operator(s):

```
template<class T>        // template for classes associating
class NamedPtr {         // names with pointers (from Item 12)
public:
  NamedPtr(const string& initName, T *initPtr);
  NamedPtr& operator=(const NamedPtr& rhs);

private:
  string name;
  T *ptr;
};

template<class T>
NamedPtr<T>& NamedPtr<T>::operator=(const NamedPtr<T>& rhs)
{
  if (this == &rhs)
    return *this;                 // see Item 17

  // assign to all data members
  name = rhs.name;                // assign to name

  *ptr = *rhs.ptr;                // for ptr, assign what's
                                  // pointed to, not the
                                  // pointer itself

  return *this;                   // see Item 15
}
```

This is easy enough to remember when the class is originally written, but it's equally important that the assignment operator(s) be updated if new data members are added to the class. For example, if you decide to upgrade the NamedPtr template to carry a timestamp marking when the name was last changed, you'll have to add a new data member, and this will require updating the constructor(s) as well as the assignment operator(s). In the hustle and bustle of upgrading a class and adding new member functions, etc., it's easy to let this kind of thing slip your mind.

The real fun begins when inheritance joins the party, because a derived class's assignment operator(s) must also handle assignment of its base class members! Consider this:

```
class Base {
public:
  Base(int initialValue = 0): x(initialValue) {}

private:
  int x;
};

class Derived: public Base {
public:
  Derived(int initialValue)
  : Base(initialValue), y(initialValue) {}

  Derived& operator=(const Derived& rhs);

private:
  int y;
};
```

The logical way to write Derived's assignment operator is like this:

```
// erroneous assignment operator
Derived& Derived::operator=(const Derived& rhs)
{
  if (this == &rhs) return *this;    // see Item 17

  y = rhs.y;                         // assign to Derived's
                                     // lone data member

  return *this;                      // see Item 15
}
```

Unfortunately, this is incorrect, because the data member x in the Base part of a Derived object is unaffected by this assignment operator. For example, consider this code fragment:

```
void assignmentTester()
{
  Derived d1(0);                // d1.x = 0, d1.y = 0
  Derived d2(1);                // d2.x = 1, d2.y = 1

  d1 = d2;                      // d1.x = 0, d1.y = 1!
}
```

Notice how the Base part of d1 is unchanged by the assignment.

The straightforward way to fix this problem would be to make an assignment to x in Derived::operator=. Unfortunately, that's not legal, because x is a private member of Base. Instead, you have to make an explicit assignment to the Base *part* of Derived from inside Derived's assignment operator.

This is how you do it:

```
// correct assignment operator
Derived& Derived::operator=(const Derived& rhs)
{
  if (this == &rhs) return *this;

  Base::operator=(rhs);          // call this->Base::operator=
  y = rhs.y;

  return *this;
}
```

Here you just make an explicit call to Base::operator=. That call, like all calls to member functions from within other member functions, will use *this as its implicit left-hand object. The result will be that Base::operator= will do whatever work it does on the Base part of *this — precisely the effect you want.

Alas, some compilers (incorrectly) reject this kind of call to a base class's assignment operator if that assignment operator was generated by the compiler (see Item 45). To pacify these renegade translators, you need to implement Derived::operator= this way:

```
Derived& Derived::operator=(const Derived& rhs)
{
  if (this == &rhs) return *this;

  static_cast<Base&>(*this) = rhs;    // call operator= on
                                      // Base part of *this
  y = rhs.y;

  return *this;
}
```

This monstrosity casts *this to be a reference to a Base, then makes an assignment to the result of the cast. That makes an assignment to only the Base part of the Derived object. Careful now! It is important that the cast be to a *reference* to a Base object, not to a Base object itself. If you cast *this to be a Base object, you'll end up calling the copy constructor for Base, and the new object you construct will be the target of the assignment; *this will remain unchanged. Hardly what you want.

Regardless of which of these approaches you employ, once you've assigned the Base part of the Derived object, you then continue with Derived's assignment operator, making assignments to all the data members of Derived.

A similar inheritance-related problem often arises when implementing derived class copy constructors. Take a look at the following, which is the copy constructor analogue of the code we just examined:

```
class Base {
public:
  Base(int initialValue = 0): x(initialValue) {}
  Base(const Base& rhs): x(rhs.x) {}

private:
  int x;
};

class Derived: public Base {
public:
  Derived(int initialValue)
  : Base(initialValue), y(initialValue) {}

  Derived(const Derived& rhs)      // erroneous copy
  : y(rhs.y) {}                    // constructor

private:
  int y;
};
```

Class Derived demonstrates one of the nastiest bugs in all C++-dom: it fails to copy the base class part when a Derived object is copy constructed. Of course, the Base part of such a Derived object *is* constructed, but it's constructed using Base's *default* constructor. Its member x is initialized to 0 (the default constructor's default parameter value), regardless of the value of x in the object being copied!

To avoid this problem, Derived's copy constructor must make sure that Base's copy constructor is invoked instead of Base's default constructor. That's easily done. Just be sure to specify an initializer value for Base in the member initialization list of Derived's copy constructor:

```
class Derived: public Base {
public:
  Derived(const Derived& rhs): Base(rhs), y(rhs.y) {}

  ...

};
```

Now when a client creates a Derived by copying an existing object of that type, its Base part will be copied, too.

Item 17: Check for assignment to self in operator=.

An assignment to self occurs when you do something like this:

```
class X { ... };

X a;

a = a;                          // a is assigned to itself
```

This looks like a silly thing to do, but it's perfectly legal, so don't doubt for a moment that programmers do it. More importantly, assignment to self can appear in this more benign-looking form:

```
a = b;
```

If b is another name for a (for example, a reference that has been initialized to a), then this is also an assignment to self, though it doesn't outwardly look like it. This is an example of *aliasing*: having two or more names for the same underlying object. As you'll see at the end of this Item, aliasing can crop up in any number of nefarious disguises, so you need to take it into account any time you write a function.

Two good reasons exist for taking special care to cope with possible aliasing in assignment operator(s). The lesser of them is efficiency. If you can detect an assignment to self at the top of your assignment operator(s), you can return right away, possibly saving a lot of work that you'd otherwise have to go through to implement assignment. For example, Item 16 points out that a proper assignment operator in a derived class must call an assignment operator for each of its base classes, and those classes might themselves be derived classes, so skipping the body of an assignment operator in a derived class might save a large number of other function calls.

A more important reason for checking for assignment to self is to ensure correctness. Remember that an assignment operator must typically free the resources allocated to an object (i.e., get rid of its old value) before it can allocate the new resources corresponding to its new value. When assigning to self, this freeing of resources can be disastrous, because the old resources might be needed during the process of allocating the new ones.

Consider assignment of String objects, where the assignment operator fails to check for assignment to self:

```
class String {
public:
  String(const char *value);       // see Item 11 for
                                   // function definition

  ~String();                       // see Item 11 for
                                   // function definition

  ...

  String& operator=(const String& rhs);
```

```
private:
  char *data;
};

// an assignment operator that omits a check
// for assignment to self
String& String::operator=(const String& rhs)
{
  delete [] data;                      // delete old memory

  // allocate new memory and copy rhs's value into it
  data = new char[strlen(rhs.data) + 1];
  strcpy(data, rhs.data);

  return *this;                        // see Item 15
}
```

Consider now what happens in this case:

```
String a = "Hello";

a = a;                               // same as a.operator=(a)
```

Inside the assignment operator, *this and rhs seem to be different objects, but in this case they happen to be different names for the same object. You can envision it like this:

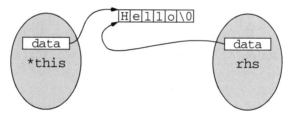

The first thing the assignment operator does is use delete on data, and the result is the following state of affairs:

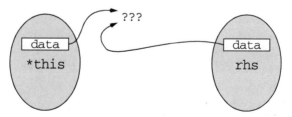

Now when the assignment operator tries to do a strlen on rhs.data, the results are undefined. This is because rhs.data was deleted when data was deleted, which happened because data, this->data, and rhs.data are all the same pointer! From this point on, things can only get worse.

By now you know that the solution to the dilemma is to check for an assignment to self and to return immediately if such an assignment is detected. Unfortunately, it's easier to talk about such a check than it is to write it, because you are immediately forced to figure out what it means for two objects to be "the same."

The topic you confront is technically known as that of *object identity*, and it's a well-known topic in object-oriented circles. This book is no place for a discourse on object identity, but it is worthwhile to mention the two basic approaches to the problem.

One approach is to say that two objects are the same (have the same identity) if they have the same value. For example, two String objects would be the same if they represented the same sequence of characters:

```
String a = "Hello";
String b = "World";
String c = "Hello";
```

Here a and c have the same value, so they are considered identical; b is different from both of them. If you wanted to use this definition of identity in your String class, your assignment operator might look like this:

```
String& String::operator=(const String& rhs)
{
  if (strcmp(data, rhs.data) == 0) return *this;

  . . .

}
```

Value equality is usually determined by operator==, so the general form for an assignment operator for a class C that uses value equality for object identity is this:

```
C& C::operator=(const C& rhs)
{
  // check for assignment to self
  if (*this == rhs)                // assumes op== exists
    return *this;

  . . .

}
```

Note that this function is comparing *objects* (via operator==), not pointers. Using value equality to determine identity, it doesn't matter whether two objects occupy the same memory; all that matters is the values they represent.

The other possibility is to equate an object's identity with its address in memory. Using this definition of object equality, two objects are the same if and only if they have the same address. This definition is more common in C++ programs, probably because it's easy to implement and the computation is fast, neither of which is always true when object identity is based on values. Using address equality, a general assignment operator looks like this:

```
C& C::operator=(const C& rhs)
{
  // check for assignment to self
  if (this == &rhs) return *this;

  ...

}
```

This suffices for a great many programs.

If you need a more sophisticated mechanism for determining whether two objects are the same, you'll have to implement it yourself. The most common approach is based on a member function that returns some kind of object identifier:

```
class C {
public:
  ObjectID identity() const;              // see also Item 36

  ...

};
```

Given object pointers a and b, then, the objects they point to are identical if and only if a->identity() == b->identity(). Of course, you are responsible for writing operator== for ObjectIDs.

The problems of aliasing and object identity are hardly confined to operator=. That's just a function in which you are particularly likely to run into them. In the presence of references and pointers, any two names for objects of compatible types may in fact refer to the same object. Here are some other situations in which aliasing can show its Medusa-like visage:

```
class Base {
  void mf1(Base& rb);            // rb and *this could be
                                 // the same
  ...

};

void f1(Base& rb1,Base& rb2);    // rb1 and rb2 could be
                                 // the same
```

```
class Derived: public Base {
  void mf2(Base& rb);              // rb and *this could be
                                   // the same

  ...

};
int f2(Derived& rd, Base& rb);  // rd and rb could be
                                // the same
```

These examples happen to use references, but pointers would serve just as well.

As you can see, aliasing can crop up in a variety of guises, so you can't just forget about it and hope you'll never run into it. Well, maybe *you* can, but most of us can't. At the expense of mixing my metaphors, this is a clear case in which an ounce of prevention is worth its weight in gold. Anytime you write a function in which aliasing could conceivably be present, you *must* take that possibility into account when you write the code.

Classes and Functions:
Design and Declaration

Declaring a new class in a program creates a new type: class design is *type* design. You probably don't have much experience with type design, because most languages don't offer you the opportunity to get any practice. In C++, it is of fundamental importance, not just because you can do it if you want to, but because you *are* doing it every time you declare a class, whether you mean to or not.

Designing good classes is challenging because designing good types is challenging. Good types have a natural syntax, an intuitive semantics, and one or more efficient implementations. In C++, a poorly thought out class definition can make it impossible to achieve any of these goals. Even the performance characteristics of a class's member functions are determined as much by the declarations of those member functions as they are by their definitions.

How, then, do you go about designing effective classes? First, you must understand the issues you face. Virtually every class requires that you confront the following questions, the answers to which often lead to constraints on your design:

- *How should objects be created and destroyed?* How this is done strongly influences the design of your constructors and destructor, as well as your versions of operator new, operator new[], operator delete, and operator delete[], if you write them.

- *How does object initialization differ from object assignment?* The answer to this question determines the behavior of and the differences between your constructors and your assignment operators.

- *What does it mean to pass objects of the new type by value?* Remember, the copy constructor defines what it means to pass an object by value.

- *What are the constraints on legal values for the new type?* These constraints determine the kind of error checking you'll have to do inside your member functions, especially your constructors and assignment operators. It may also affect the exceptions your functions throw and, if you use them, your functions' exception specifications.

- *Does the new type fit into an inheritance graph?* If you inherit from existing classes, you are constrained by the design of those classes, particularly by whether the functions you inherit are virtual or nonvirtual. If you wish to allow other classes to inherit from your class, that will affect whether the functions you declare are virtual.

- *What kind of type conversions are allowed?* If you wish to allow objects of type A to be *implicitly* converted into objects of type B, you will want to write either a type conversion function in class A or a non-explicit constructor in class B that can be called with a single argument. If you wish to allow *explicit* conversions only, you'll want to write functions to perform the conversions, but you'll want to avoid making them type conversion operators or non-explicit single-argument constructors.

- *What operators and functions make sense for the new type?* The answer to this question determines which functions you'll declare in your class interface.

- *What standard operators and functions should be explicitly disallowed?* Those are the ones you'll need to declare private.

- *Who should have access to the members of the new type?* This question helps you determine which members are public, which are protected, and which are private. It also helps you determine which classes and/or functions should be friends, as well as whether it makes sense to nest one class inside another.

- *How general is the new type?* Perhaps you're not really defining a new type. Perhaps you're defining a whole *family* of types. If so, you don't want to define a new class, you want to define a new class *template*.

These are difficult questions to answer, so defining effective classes in C++ is far from simple. Done properly, however, user-defined classes in C++ yield types that are all but indistinguishable from built-in types, and that makes all the effort worthwhile.

A discussion of the details of each of the above issues would comprise a book in its own right, so the guidelines that follow are anything but comprehensive. However, they highlight some of the most important design considerations, warn about some of the most frequent errors, and provide solutions to some of the most common problems encountered by class designers. Much of the advice is as applicable to non-member functions as it is to member functions, so in this section I consider the design and declaration of global and namespace-resident functions, too.

Item 18: Strive for class interfaces that are complete and minimal.

The client interface for a class is the interface that is accessible to the programmers who use the class. Typically, only functions exist in this interface, because having data members in the client interface has a number of drawbacks (see Item 20).

Trying to figure out what functions should be in a class interface can drive you crazy. You're pulled in two completely different directions. On the one hand, you'd like to build a class that is easy to understand, straightforward to use, and easy to implement. That usually implies a fairly small number of member functions, each of which performs a distinct task. On the other hand, you'd like your class to be powerful and convenient to use, which often means adding functions to provide support for commonly performed tasks. How do you decide which functions go into the class and which ones don't?

Try this: aim for a class interface that is *complete* and *minimal*.

A *complete* interface is one that allows clients to do anything they might reasonably want to do. That is, for any reasonable task that clients might want to accomplish, there is a reasonable way to accomplish it, although it may not be as convenient as clients might like. A *minimal* interface, on the other hand, is one with as few functions in it as possible, one in which no two member functions have overlapping functionality. If you offer a complete, minimal interface, clients can do whatever they want to do, but the class interface is no more complicated than absolutely necessary.

The desirability of a complete interface seems obvious enough, but why a minimal interface? Why not just give clients everything they ask for, adding functionality until everyone is happy?

Aside from the moral issue — is it really *right* to mollycoddle your clients? — there are definite technical disadvantages to a class interface that is crowded with functions. First, the more functions in an interface, the harder it is for potential clients to understand. The harder it is for them to understand, the more reluctant they will be to learn how to use it. A class with 10 functions looks tractable to most people, but a class with 100 functions is enough to make many programmers run and hide. By expanding the functionality of your class to make it as attractive as possible, you may actually end up discouraging people from learning how to use it.

A large interface can also lead to confusion. Suppose you create a class that supports cognition for an artificial intelligence application. One of your member functions is called think, but you later discover that some people want the function to be called ponder, and others prefer the name ruminate. In an effort to be accommodating, you offer all three functions, even though they do the same thing. Consider then the plight of a potential client of your class who is trying to figure things out. The client is faced with three different functions, all of which are supposed to do the same thing. Can that really be true? Isn't there some subtle difference between the three, possibly in efficiency or generality or reliability? If not, why are there three different functions? Rather than appreciating your flexibility, such a potential client is likely to wonder what on earth you were thinking (or pondering, or ruminating over).

A second disadvantage to a large class interface is that of maintenance. It's simply more difficult to maintain and enhance a class with many functions than it is a class with few. It is more difficult to avoid duplicated code (with the attendant duplicated bugs), and it is more difficult to maintain consistency across the interface. It's also more difficult to document.

Finally, long class definitions result in long header files. Because header files typically have to be read every time a program is compiled (see Item 34), class definitions that are longer than necessary can incur a substantial penalty in total compile-time over the life of a project.

The long and short of it is that the gratuitous addition of functions to an interface is not without costs, so you need to think carefully about whether the convenience of a new function (a new function can *only* be added for convenience if the interface is already complete) justifies the additional costs in complexity, comprehensibility, maintainability, and compilation speed.

Yet there's no sense in being unduly miserly. It is often justifiable to offer more than a minimal set of functions. If a commonly performed task can be implemented much more efficiently as a member function, that may well justify its addition to the interface. If the addition of a member function makes the class substantially easier to use, that may be enough to warrant its inclusion in the class. And if adding a member function is likely to prevent client errors, that, too, is a powerful argument for its being part of the interface.

Consider a concrete example: a template for classes that implement arrays with client-defined upper and lower bounds and that offer optional bounds-checking. The beginning of such an array template is shown below:

```
template<class T>
class Array {
public:
  enum BoundsCheckingStatus {NO_CHECK_BOUNDS = 0,
                             CHECK_BOUNDS = 1};

  Array(int lowBound, int highBound,
        BoundsCheckingStatus check = NO_CHECK_BOUNDS);

  Array(const Array& rhs);

  ~Array();

  Array& operator=(const Array& rhs);
private:
  int lBound, hBound;           // low bound, high bound

  vector<T> data;               // contents of array; see
                                // Item 49 for vector info

  BoundsCheckingStatus checkingBounds;
};
```

The member functions declared so far are the ones that require basically no thinking (or pondering or ruminating). You have a constructor to allow clients to specify each array's bounds, a copy constructor, an assignment operator, and a destructor. In this case, you've declared the destructor nonvirtual, which implies that this class is not to be used as a base class (see Item 14).

The declaration of the assignment operator is actually less clear-cut than it might at first appear. After all, built-in arrays in C++ don't allow assignment, so you might want to disallow it for your Array objects, too (see Item 27). On the other hand, the array-like vector template (in the standard library — see Item 49) permits assignments between vector objects. In this example, you'll follow vector's lead, and that decision, as you'll see below, will affect other portions of the Array classes's interface.

Old-time C hacks would cringe to see this interface. Where is the support for declaring an array of a particular size? It would be easy enough to add another constructor,

```
Array(int size,
      BoundsCheckingStatus check = NO_CHECK_BOUNDS);
```

but this is not part of a minimal interface, because the constructor taking an upper and lower bound can be used to accomplish the same thing. Nonetheless, it might be a wise political move to humor the old geezers, possibly under the rubric of consistency with the base language.

What other functions do you need? Certainly it is part of a complete interface to index into an array:

```
// return element for read/write
T& operator[](int index);

// return element for read-only
const T& operator[](int index) const;
```

By declaring the same function twice, once `const` and once non-`const`, you provide support for both `const` and non-const `Array` objects. The difference in return types is significant, as is explained in Item 21.

As it now stands, the `Array` template supports construction, destruction, pass-by-value, assignment, and indexing, which may strike you as a complete interface. But look closer. Suppose a client wants to loop through an array of integers, printing out each of its elements, like so:

```
Array<int> a(10, 20);          // bounds on a are 10 to 20

...

for (int i = lower bound of a; i <= upper bound of a; ++i)
    cout << "a[" << i << "] = " << a[i] << '\n';
```

How is the client to get the bounds of a? The answer depends on what happens during assignment of `Array` objects, i.e., on what happens inside `Array::operator=`. In particular, if assignment can change the bounds of an `Array` object, you must provide member functions to return the current bounds, because the client has no way of knowing *a priori* what the bounds are at any given point in the program. In the example above, if a was the target of an assignment between the time it was defined and the time it was used in the loop, the client would have no way to determine the current bounds of a.

On the other hand, if the bounds of an `Array` object cannot be changed during assignment, then the bounds are fixed at the point of definition, and it would be possible (though cumbersome) for a client to keep track of these bounds. In that case, though it would be convenient to offer functions to return the current bounds, such functions would not be part of a truly minimal interface.

Proceeding on the assumption that assignment can modify the bounds of an object, the bounds functions could be declared thus:

```
int lowBound() const;
int highBound() const;
```

Because these functions don't modify the object on which they are invoked, and because you prefer to use const whenever you can (see Item 21), these are both declared const member functions. Given these functions, the loop above would be written as follows:

```
for (int i = a.lowBound(); i <= a.highBound(); ++i)
  cout << "a[" << i << "] = " << a[i] << '\n';
```

Needless to say, for such a loop to work for an array of objects of type T, an operator<< function must be defined for objects of type T. (That's not quite true. What must exist is an operator<< for T or for some other type to which T may be implicitly converted. But you get the idea.)

Some designers would argue that the Array class should also offer a function to return the number of elements in an Array object. The number of elements is simply highBound()-lowBound()+1, so such a function is not really necessary, but in view of the frequency of off-by-one errors, it might not be a bad idea to add such a function.

Other functions that might prove worthwhile for this class include those for input and output, as well as the various relational operators (e.g., <, >, ==, etc.). None of those functions is part of a minimal interface, however, because they can all be implemented in terms of loops containing calls to operator[].

Speaking of functions like operator<<, operator>>, and the relational operators, Item 19 discusses why they are frequently implemented as non-member friend functions instead of as member functions. That being the case, don't forget that friend functions are, for all practical purposes, part of a class's interface. That means that friend functions count toward a class interface's completeness and minimalness.

Item 19: Differentiate among member functions, non-member functions, and friend functions.

The biggest difference between member functions and non-member functions is that member functions can be virtual and non-member functions can't. As a result, if you have a function that has to be dynamically bound (see Item 38), you've got to use a virtual function, and that virtual function must be a member of some class. It's as simple as that. If your function doesn't need to be virtual, however, the water begins to muddy a bit.

Consider a class for representing rational numbers:

```
class Rational {
public:
  Rational(int numerator = 0, int denominator = 1);
  int numerator() const;
  int denominator() const;

private:
  ...
};
```

As it stands now, this is a pretty useless class. (Using the terms of Item 18, the interface is certainly minimal, but it's *far* from complete.) You know you'd like to support arithmetic operations like addition, subtraction, multiplication, etc., but you're unsure whether you should implement them via a member function, a non-member function, or possibly a non-member function that's a friend.

When in doubt, be object-oriented. You know that, say, multiplication of rational numbers is related to the Rational class, so try bundling the operation with the class by making it a member function:

```
class Rational {
public:

  ...

  const Rational operator*(const Rational& rhs) const;
};
```

(If you're unsure why this function is declared the way it is — returning a const by-value result, but taking a reference-to-const as its argument — consult Items 21–23.)

Now you can multiply rational numbers with the greatest of ease:

```
Rational oneEighth(1, 8);
Rational oneHalf(1, 2);

Rational result = oneHalf * oneEighth;   // fine

result = result * oneEighth;             // fine
```

But you're not satisfied. You'd also like to support mixed-mode operations, where Rationals can be multiplied with, for example, ints. When you try to do this, however, you find that it works only half the time:

```
result = oneHalf * 2;                    // fine
result = 2 * oneHalf;                    // error!
```

This is a bad omen. Multiplication is supposed to be commutative, remember?

The source of the problem becomes apparent when you rewrite the last two examples in their equivalent functional form:

```
result = oneHalf.operator*(2);           // fine
result = 2.operator*(oneHalf);           // error!
```

The object oneHalf is an instance of a class that contains an operator*, so your compilers call that function. However, the integer 2 has no associated class, hence no operator* member function. Your compilers will also look for a non-member operator* (i.e., one that's in a visible namespace or is global) that can be called like this,

```
result = operator*(2, oneHalf);          // error!
```

but there is no non-member operator* taking an int and a Rational, so the search fails.

Look again at the call that succeeds. You'll see that its second parameter is the integer 2, yet Rational::operator* takes a Rational object as its argument. What's going on here? Why does 2 work in one position and not in the other?

What's going on is implicit type conversion. Your compilers know you're passing an int and the function requires a Rational, but they also know that they can conjure up a suitable Rational by calling the Rational constructor with the int you provided, so that's what they do. In other words, they treat the call as if it had been written more or less like this:

```
const Rational temp(2);        // create a temporary
                               // Rational object from 2
result = oneHalf * temp;       // same as
                               // oneHalf.operator*(temp);
```

Of course, they do this only when non-explicit constructors are involved, because explicit constructors can't be used for implicit conversions; that's what explicit means. If Rational were defined like this,

```
class Rational {
public:
  explicit Rational(int numerator = 0,    // this ctor is
                    int denominator = 1);  // now explicit

  ...

  const Rational operator*(const Rational& rhs) const;

  ...

};
```

neither of these statements would compile:

```
result = oneHalf * 2;                // error!
result = 2 * oneHalf;                // error!
```

That would hardly qualify as support for mixed-mode arithmetic, but at least the behavior of the two statements would be consistent.

The Rational class we've been examining, however, is designed to allow implicit conversions from built-in types to Rationals — that's why Rational's constructor isn't declared explicit. That being the case, compilers *will* perform the implicit conversion necessary to allow result's first assignment to compile. In fact, your handy-dandy compilers will perform this kind of implicit type conversion, if it's needed, on *every* parameter of *every* function call. But they will do it only for parameters *listed in the parameter list, never* for the object on which a member function is invoked, i.e., the object corresponding to *this inside a member function. That's why this call works,

```
result = oneHalf.operator*(2); // converts int -> Rational
```

and this one does not:

```
result = 2.operator*(oneHalf); // doesn't convert
                               // int -> Rational
```

The first case involves a parameter listed in the function declaration, but the second one does not.

Nonetheless, you'd still like to support mixed-mode arithmetic, and the way to do it is by now perhaps clear: make operator* a non-member function, thus allowing compilers to perform implicit type conversions on *all* arguments:

```
class Rational {

  ...                            // contains no operator*

};
```

```
// declare this globally or within a namespace
const Rational operator*(const Rational& lhs,
                         const Rational& rhs)
{
  return Rational(lhs.numerator() * rhs.numerator(),
                  lhs.denominator() * rhs.denominator());
}

Rational oneFourth(1, 4);
Rational result;

result = oneFourth * 2;        // fine
result = 2 * oneFourth;        // hooray, it works!
```

This is certainly a happy ending to the tale, but there is a nagging worry. Should operator* be made a friend of the Rational class?

In this case, the answer is no, because operator* can be implemented entirely in terms of the class's public interface. The code above shows one way to do it. Whenever you can avoid friend functions, you should, because, much as in real life, friends are often more trouble than they're worth.

However, it's not uncommon for functions that are not members, yet are still conceptually part of a class interface, to need access to the non-public members of the class.

As an example, let's fall back on a workhorse of this book, the String class. If you try to overload operator>> and operator<< for reading and writing String objects, you'll quickly discover that they shouldn't be member functions. If they were, you'd have to put the String object on the left when you called the functions:

```
// a class that incorrectly declares operator>> and
// operator<< as member functions
class String {
public:
  String(const char *value);

  ...

  istream& operator>>(istream& input);
  ostream& operator<<(ostream& output);

private:
  char *data;
};
```

```
String s;

s >> cin;                        // legal, but contrary
                                 // to convention

s << cout;                       // ditto
```

That would confuse everyone. As a result, these functions shouldn't be member functions. Notice that this is a different case from the one we discussed above. Here the goal is a natural calling syntax; earlier we were concerned about implicit type conversions.

If you were designing these functions, you'd come up with something like this:

```
istream& operator>>(istream& input, String& string)
{
  delete [] string.data;

  read from input into some memory, and make string.data
  point to it

  return input;
}
ostream& operator<<(ostream& output,
                    const String& string)
{
  return output << string.data;
}
```

Notice that both functions need access to the data field of the String class, a field that's private. However, you already know that you have to make these functions non-members. You're boxed into a corner and have no choice: non-member functions with a need for access to non-public members of a class must be made friends of that class.

The lessons of this Item are summarized below, in which it is assumed that f is the function you're trying to declare properly and C is the class to which it is conceptually related:

- **Virtual functions must be members**. If f needs to be virtual, make it a member function of C.

- **operator>> and operator<< are never members**. If f is operator>> or operator<<, make f a non-member function. If, in addition, f needs access to non-public members of C, make f a friend of C.

- **Only non-member functions get type conversions on their left-most argument**. If f needs type conversions on its left-most argument, make f a non-member function. If, in addition, f needs access to non-public members of C, make f a friend of C.

- **Everything else should be a member function**. If none of the other cases apply, make f a member function of C.

Item 20: Avoid data members in the public interface.

First, let's look at this issue from the point of view of consistency. If everything in the public interface is a function, clients of your class won't have to scratch their heads trying to remember whether to use parentheses when they want to access a member of your class. They'll just *do* it, because everything is a function. Over the course of a lifetime, that can save a lot of head scratching.

You don't buy the consistency argument? How about the fact that using functions gives you much more precise control over the accessibility of data members? If you make a data member public, everybody has read/write access to it, but if you use functions to get and set its value, you can implement no access, read-only access, and read-write access. Heck, you can even implement write-only access if you want to:

```
class AccessLevels {
public:
  int getReadOnly() const{ return readOnly; }

  void setReadWrite(int value) { readWrite = value; }
  int getReadWrite() const { return readWrite; }

  void setWriteOnly(int value) { writeOnly = value; }
private:
  int noAccess;              // no access to this int

  int readOnly;              // read-only access to
                             // this int

  int readWrite;             // read-write access to
                             // this int

  int writeOnly;             // write-only access to
                             // this int
};
```

Still not convinced? Then it's time to bring out the big gun: functional abstraction. If you implement access to a data member through a function, you can later replace the data member with a computation, and nobody using your class will be any the wiser.

For example, suppose you are writing an application in which some automated equipment is monitoring the speed of passing cars. As each car passes, its speed is computed, and the value is added to a collection of all the speed data collected so far:

```
class SpeedDataCollection {
public:
  void addValue(int speed);     // add a new data value

  double averageSoFar() const; // return average speed
};
```

Now consider the implementation of the member function averageSo-Far. One way to implement it is to have a data member in the class that is a running average of all the speed data so far collected. Whenever averageSoFar is called, it just returns the value of that data member. A different approach is to have averageSoFar compute its value anew each time it's called, something it could do by examining each data value in the collection.

The first approach — keeping a running average — makes each SpeedDataCollection object bigger, because you have to allocate space for the data member holding the running average. However, averageSoFar can be implemented very efficiently; it's just an inline function (see Item 33) that returns the value of the data member. Conversely, computing the average whenever it's requested will make averageSoFar run slower, but each SpeedDataCollection object will be smaller.

Who's to say which is best? On a machine where memory is tight, and in an application where averages are needed only infrequently, computing the average each time is a better solution. In an application where averages are needed frequently, speed is of the essence, and memory is not an issue, keeping a running average is preferable. The important point is that by accessing the average through a member function, you can use *either* implementation, a valuable source of flexibility that you wouldn't have if you made a decision to include the running average data member in the public interface.

The upshot of all this is that you're just asking for trouble by putting data members in the public interface, so play it safe by hiding all your data members behind a wall of functional abstraction. If you do it *now*, we'll throw in consistency and fine-grained access control at no extra cost!

Item 21: Use const whenever possible.

The wonderful thing about const is that it allows you to specify a certain semantic constraint — a particular object should *not* be modified — and compilers will enforce that constraint. It allows you to communicate to both compilers and other programmers that a value should remain invariant. Whenever that is true, you should be sure to say so explicitly, because that way you enlist your compilers' aid in making sure the constraint isn't violated.

The const keyword is remarkably versatile. Outside of classes, you can use it for global or namespace constants (see Items 1 and 47) and for static objects (local to a file or a block). Inside classes, you can use it for both static and nonstatic data members (see also Item 12).

For pointers, you can specify whether the pointer itself is const, the data it points to is const, both, or neither:

```
char *p               = "Hello";      // non-const pointer,
                                      // non-const data†

const char *p         = "Hello";      // non-const pointer,
                                      // const data

char * const p        = "Hello";      // const pointer,
                                      // non-const data

const char * const p  = "Hello";      // const pointer,
                                      // const data
```

This syntax isn't quite as capricious as it looks. Basically, you mentally draw a vertical line through the asterisk of a pointer declaration, and if the word const appears to the left of the line, what's *pointed to* is constant; if the word const appears to the right of the line, the *pointer itself* is constant; if const appears on both sides of the line, both are constant.

When what's pointed to is constant, some programmers list const before the type name. Others list it after the type name but before the asterisk. As a result, the following functions take the same parameter type:

```
class Widget { ... };

void f1(const Widget *pw);     // f1 takes a pointer to a
                              // constant Widget object

void f2(Widget const *pw);     // so does f2
```

Because both forms exist in real code, you should accustom yourself to both of them.

---

† According to the C++ standard, the type of "Hello" is const char[], a type that's almost always treated as const char*. We'd therefore expect it to be a violation of const correctness to initialize a char* variable with a string literal like "Hello". The practice is so common in C, however, that the standard grants a special dispensation for initializations like this. Nevertheless, you should try to avoid them, because they're deprecated.

Some of the most powerful uses of const stem from its application to function declarations. Within a function declaration, const can refer to the function's return value, to individual parameters, and, for member functions, to the function as a whole.

Having a function return a constant value often makes it possible to reduce the incidence of client errors without giving up safety or efficiency. In fact, as Item 29 demonstrates, using const with a return value can make it possible to *improve* the safety and efficiency of a function that would otherwise be problematic.

For example, consider the declaration of the operator* function for rational numbers that is introduced in Item 19:

```
const Rational operator*(const Rational& lhs,
                         const Rational& rhs);
```

Many programmers squint when they first see this. Why should the result of operator* be a const object? Because if it weren't, clients would be able to commit atrocities like this:

```
Rational a, b, c;

...

(a * b) = c;                    // assign to the product
                                // of a*b!
```

I don't know why any programmer would want to make an assignment to the product of two numbers, but I do know this: it would be flat-out illegal if a, b, and c were of a built-in type. One of the hallmarks of good user-defined types is that they avoid gratuitous behavioral incompatibilities with the built-ins, and allowing assignments to the product of two numbers seems pretty gratuitous to me. Declaring operator*'s return value const prevents it, and that's why It's The Right Thing To Do.

There's nothing particularly new about const parameters — they act just like local const objects. Member functions that are const, however, are a different story.

The purpose of const member functions, of course, is to specify which member functions may be invoked on const objects. Many people overlook the fact that member functions differing *only* in their constness can be overloaded, however, and this is an important feature of C++. Consider the String class once again:

```
class String {
public:

  ...

  // operator[] for non-const objects
  char& operator[](int position)
  { return data[position]; }

  // operator[] for const objects
  const char& operator[](int position) const
  { return data[position]; }
private:
  char *data;
};
String s1 = "Hello";
cout << s1[0];                       // calls non-const
                                     // String::operator[]
const String s2 = "World";
cout << s2[0];                       // calls const
                                     // String::operator[]
```

By overloading `operator[]` and giving the different versions different return values, you are able to have `const` and non-`const` `String`s handled differently:

```
String s = "Hello";           // non-const String object

cout << s[0];                 // fine — reading a
                              // non-const String

s[0] = 'x';                   // fine — writing a
                              // non-const String

const String cs = "World";    // const String object

cout << cs[0];                // fine — reading a
                              // const String

cs[0] = 'x';                  // error! — writing a
                              // const String
```

By the way, note that the error here has only to do with the *return value* of the `operator[]` that is called; the calls to `operator[]` themselves are all fine. The error arises out of an attempt to make an assignment to a `const char&`, because that's the return value from the `const` version of `operator[]`.

Also note that the return type of the non-`const` `operator[]` must be a *reference* to a `char` — a `char` itself will not do. If `operator[]` did return a simple `char`, statements like this wouldn't compile:

```
s[0] = 'x';
```

That's because it's never legal to modify the return value of a function that returns a built-in type. Even if it were legal, the fact that C++ returns objects by value (see Item 22) would mean that a *copy* of s.data[0] would be modified, not s.data[0] itself, and that's not the behavior you want, anyway.

Let's take a brief time-out for philosophy. What exactly does it mean for a member function to be const? There are two prevailing notions: bitwise constness and conceptual constness.

The bitwise const camp believes that a member function is const if and only if it doesn't modify any of the object's data members (excluding those that are static), i.e., if it doesn't modify any of the bits inside the object. The nice thing about bitwise constness is that it's easy to detect violations: compilers just look for assignments to data members. In fact, bitwise constness is C++'s definition of constness, and a const member function isn't allowed to modify any of the data members of the object on which it is invoked.

Unfortunately, many member functions that don't act very const pass the bitwise test. In particular, a member function that modifies what a pointer *points to* frequently doesn't act const. But if only the *pointer* is in the object, the function is bitwise const, and compilers won't complain. That can lead to counterintuitive behavior:

```
class String {
public:
  // the constructor makes data point to a copy
  // of what value points to
  String(const char *value);

  ...

  operator char *() const { return data;}
private:
  char *data;
};

const String s = "Hello";      // declare constant object

char *nasty = s;               // calls op char*() const

*nasty = 'M';                  // modifies s.data[0]

cout << s;                     // writes "Mello"
```

Surely there is something wrong when you create a constant object with a particular value and you invoke only const member functions on it, yet you are still able to change its value! (For a more detailed discussion of this example, see Item 29.)

This leads to the notion of conceptual constness. Adherents to this philosophy argue that a const member function might modify some of the bits in the object on which it's invoked, but only in ways that are undetectable by clients. For example, your String class might want to cache the length of the object whenever it's requested:

```
class String {
public:
  // the constructor makes data point to a copy
  // of what value points to
  String(const char *value): lengthIsValid(false) { ... }

  ...

  size_t length() const;

private:
  char *data;

  size_t dataLength;          // last calculated length
                              // of string

  bool lengthIsValid;         // whether length is
                              // currently valid
};
size_t String::length() const
{
  if (!lengthIsValid) {
    dataLength = strlen(data);  // error!
    lengthIsValid = true;       // error!
  }

  return dataLength;
}
```

This implementation of length is certainly not bitwise const — both dataLength and lengthIsValid may be modified — yet it seems as though it should be valid for const String objects. Compilers, you will find, respectfully disagree; they insist on bitwise constness. What to do?

The solution is simple: take advantage of the const-related wiggle room the C++ standardization committee thoughtfully provided for just these types of situations. That wiggle room takes the form of the keyword mutable. When applied to nonstatic data members, mutable frees those members from the constraints of bitwise constness:

```
class String {
public:

  ...                              // same as above

private:
  char *data;

  mutable size_t dataLength;       // these data members are
                                   // now mutable; they may be
  mutable bool lengthIsValid;      // modified anywhere, even
                                   // inside const member
};                                 // functions

size_t String::length() const
{
  if (!lengthIsValid) {
    dataLength = strlen(data);     // now fine
    lengthIsValid = true;          // also fine
  }

  return dataLength;
}
```

mutable is a wonderful solution to the bitwise-constness-is-not-quite-what-I-had-in-mind problem, but it was added to C++ relatively late in the standardization process, so your compilers may not support it yet. If that's the case, you must descend into the dark recesses of C++, where life is cheap and constness may be cast away.

Inside a member function of class C, the this pointer behaves as if it had been declared as follows:

```
C * const this;                  // for non-const member
                                 // functions

const C * const this;            // for const member
                                 // functions
```

That being the case, all you have to do to make the problematic version of String::length (i.e., the one you could fix with mutable if your compilers supported it) valid for both const and non-const objects is to change the type of this from const C * const to C * const. You can't do that directly, but you can fake it by initializing a local pointer to point to the same object as this does. Then you can access the members you want to modify through the local pointer:

```
size_t String::length() const
{
  // make a local version of this that's
  // not a pointer-to-const
  String * const localThis =
    const_cast<String * const>(this);
```

```
  if (!lengthIsValid) {
    localThis->dataLength = strlen(data);
    localThis->lengthIsValid = true;
  }

  return dataLength;
}
```

Pretty this ain't, but sometimes a programmer's just gotta do what a programmer's gotta do.

Unless, of course, it's not guaranteed to work, and sometimes the old cast-away-constness trick isn't. In particular, if the object this points to is truly const, i.e., was declared const at its point of definition, the results of casting away its constness are undefined. If you want to cast away constness in one of your member functions, you'd best be sure that the object you're doing the casting on wasn't originally defined to be const.

There is one other time when casting away constness may be both useful and safe. That's when you have a const object you want to pass to a function taking a non-const parameter, and *you know the parameter won't be modified inside the function*. The second condition is important, because it is always safe to cast away the constness of an object that will only be read — not written — even if that object was originally defined to be const.

For example, some libraries have been known to incorrectly declare the strlen function as follows:

```
size_t strlen(char *s);
```

Certainly strlen isn't going to modify what s points to — at least not the strlen I grew up with. Because of this declaration, however, it would be invalid to call it on pointers of type const char *. To get around the problem, you can safely cast away the constness of such pointers when you pass them to strlen:

```
const char *klingonGreeting = "nuqneH";    // "nuqneH" is
                                           // "Hello" in
                                           // Klingon
size_t length =
  strlen(const_cast<char*>(klingonGreeting));
```

Don't get cavalier about this, though. It is guaranteed to work only if the function being called, strlen in this case, doesn't try to modify what its parameter points to.

Item 22: Prefer pass-by-reference to pass-by-value.

In C, everything is passed by value, and C++ honors this heritage by adopting the pass-by-value convention as its default. Unless you specify otherwise, function parameters are initialized with *copies* of the actual arguments, and function callers get back a *copy* of the value returned by the function.

As I pointed out in the Introduction to this book, the meaning of passing an object by value is defined by the copy constructor of that object's class. This can make pass-by-value an extremely expensive operation. For example, consider the following (rather contrived) class hierarchy:

```
class Person {
public:
  Person();                    // parameters omitted for
                               // simplicity
  ~Person();

  . . .

private:
  string name, address;
};
class Student: public Person {
public:
  Student();                   // parameters omitted for
                               // simplicity
  ~Student();

  . . .

private:
  string schoolName, schoolAddress;
};
```

Now consider a simple function returnStudent that takes a Student argument (by value) and immediately returns it (also by value), plus a call to that function:

```
Student returnStudent(Student s) { return s; }

Student plato;                   // Plato studied under
                                 // Socrates

returnStudent(plato);            // call returnStudent
```

What happens during the course of this innocuous-looking function call?

The simple explanation is this: the Student copy constructor is called to initialize s with plato. Then the Student copy constructor is called again to initialize the object returned by the function with s. Next, the destructor is called for s. Finally, the destructor is called for the object returned by returnStudent. So the cost of this do-nothing function is two calls to the Student copy constructor and two calls to the Student destructor.

But wait, there's more! A Student object has two string objects within it, so every time you construct a Student object you must also construct two string objects. A Student object also inherits from a Person object, so every time you construct a Student object you must also construct a Person object. A Person object has two additional string objects inside it, so each Person construction also entails two more string constructions. The end result is that passing a Student object by value leads to one call to the Student copy constructor, one call to the Person copy constructor, and four calls to the string copy constructor. When the copy of the Student object is destroyed, each constructor call is matched by a destructor call, so the overall cost of passing a Student by value is six constructors and six destructors. Because the function returnStudent uses pass-by-value twice (once for the parameter, once for the return value), the complete cost of a call to that function is *twelve* constructors and *twelve* destructors!

In fairness to the C++ compiler-writers of the world, this is a worst-case scenario. Compilers are allowed to eliminate some of these calls to copy constructors (the C++ standard — see Item 50 — describes the precise conditions under which they are allowed to perform this kind of magic). Some compilers take advantage of this license to optimize. Until such optimizations become ubiquitous, however, you've got to be wary of the cost of passing objects by value.

To avoid this potentially exorbitant cost, you need to pass things not by value, but by reference:

```
const Student& returnStudent(const Student& s)
{ return s; }
```

This is much more efficient: no constructors or destructors are called, because no new objects are being created.

Passing parameters by reference has another advantage: it avoids what is sometimes called the "slicing problem." When a derived class object is passed as a base class object, all the specialized features that make it behave like a derived class object are "sliced" off, and you're left with a simple base class object. This is almost never what you want. For example, suppose you're working on a set of classes for implementing a graphical window system:

```
class Window {
public:
  string name() const;        // return name of window
  virtual void display() const;   // draw window and contents
};

class WindowWithScrollBars: public Window {
public:
  virtual void display() const;
};
```

All `Window` objects have a name, which you can get at through the name function, and all windows can be displayed, which you can bring about by invoking the `display` function. The fact that `display` is virtual tells you that the way in which simple base class `Window` objects are displayed is apt to differ from the way in which the fancy, high-priced `WindowWithScrollBars` objects are displayed (see Items 36 and 37).

Now suppose you'd like to write a function to print out a window's name and then display the window. Here's the *wrong* way to write such a function:

```
// a function that suffers from the slicing problem
void printNameAndDisplay(Window w)
{
  cout << w.name();
  w.display();
}
```

Consider what happens when you call this function with a Window-WithScrollBars object:

```
WindowWithScrollBars wwsb;
```

```
printNameAndDisplay(wwsb);
```

The parameter w will be constructed — it's passed by value, remember? — as a *Window* object, and all the specialized information that made wwsb act like a `WindowWithScrollBars` object will be sliced off. Inside `printNameAndDisplay`, w will always act like an object of class `Window` (because it *is* an object of class `Window`), regardless of the type of object that is passed to the function. In particular, the call to display inside printNameAndDisplay will *always* call `Window::display`, never `WindowWithScrollBars::display`.

The way around the slicing problem is to pass w by reference:

```
// a function that doesn't suffer from the slicing problem
void printNameAndDisplay(const Window& w)
{
  cout << w.name();
  w.display();
}
```

Now w will act like whatever kind of window is actually passed in. To emphasize that w isn't modified by this function even though it's passed by reference, you've followed the advice of Item 21 and carefully declared it to be const; how good of you.

Passing by reference is a wonderful thing, but it leads to certain complications of its own, the most notorious of which is aliasing, a topic that is discussed in Item 17. In addition, it's important to recognize that you sometimes *can't* pass things by reference; see Item 23. Finally, the brutal fact of the matter is that references are almost always *implemented* as pointers, so passing something by reference usually means really passing a pointer. As a result, if you have a small object — an int, for example — it may actually be more efficient to pass it by value than to pass it by reference.

Item 23: Don't try to return a reference when you must return an object.

It is said that Albert Einstein once offered this advice: make things as simple as possible, but no simpler. The C++ analogue might well be to make things as efficient as possible, but no more efficient.

Once programmers grasp the efficiency implications of pass-by-value for objects (see Item 22), they become crusaders, determined to root out the evil of pass-by-value wherever it may hide. Unrelenting in their pursuit of pass-by-reference purity, they invariably make a fatal mistake: they start to pass references to objects that don't exist. This is not a good thing.

Consider a class for representing rational numbers, including a friend function (see Item 19) for multiplying two rationals together:

```
class Rational {
public:
  Rational(int numerator = 0, int denominator = 1);

  ...

private:
  int n, d;                     // numerator and denominator
```

```
friend
  const Rational                    // see Item 21 for why
    operator*(const Rational& lhs,  // the return value is
              const Rational& rhs); // const
};

inline const Rational operator*(const Rational& lhs,
                                const Rational& rhs)
{
  return Rational(lhs.n * rhs.n, lhs.d * rhs.d);
}
```

Clearly, this version of operator* is returning its result object by value, and you'd be shirking your professional duties if you failed to worry about the cost of that object's construction and destruction. Another thing that's clear is that you're cheap and you don't want to pay for such a temporary object if you don't have to. So the question is this: do you have to pay?

Well, you don't have to if you can return a reference instead. But remember that a reference is just a *name*, a name for some *existing* object. Whenever you see the declaration for a reference, you should immediately ask yourself what it is another name for, because it must be another name for *something*. In the case of operator*, if the function is to return a reference, it must return a reference to some other Rational object that already exists and that contains the product of the two objects that are to be multiplied together.

There is certainly no reason to expect that such an object exists prior to the call to operator*. That is, if you have

```
Rational a(1, 2);           // a = 1/2
Rational b(3, 5);           // b = 3/5
Rational c = a * b;         // c should be 3/10
```

it seems unreasonable to expect that there already exists a rational number with the value three-tenths. No, if operator* is to return a reference to such a number, it must create that number object itself.

A function can create a new object in only two ways: on the stack or on the heap. Creation on the stack is accomplished by defining a local variable. Using that strategy, you might try to write your operator* as follows:

```
// the first wrong way to write this function
inline const Rational& operator*(const Rational& lhs,
                                 const Rational& rhs)
{
  Rational result(lhs.n * rhs.n, lhs.d * rhs.d);
  return result;
}
```

You can reject this approach out of hand, because your goal was to avoid a constructor call, and `result` will have to be constructed just like any other object. In addition, this function has a more serious problem in that it returns a reference to a local object, an error that is discussed in depth in Item 31.

That leaves you with the possibility of constructing an object on the heap and then returning a reference to it. Heap-based objects come into being through the use of new. This is how you might write operator* in that case:

```
// the second wrong way to write this function
inline const Rational& operator*(const Rational& lhs,
                                 const Rational& rhs)
{
  Rational *result =
    new Rational(lhs.n * rhs.n, lhs.d * rhs.d);
  return *result;
}
```

Well, you *still* have to pay for a constructor call, because the memory allocated by new is initialized by calling an appropriate constructor (see Item 5), but now you have a different problem: who will apply delete to the object that was conjured up by your use of new?

In fact, this is a guaranteed memory leak. Even if callers of operator* could be persuaded to take the address of the function's result and use delete on it (astronomically unlikely — Item 31 shows what the code would have to look like), complicated expressions would yield unnamed temporaries that programmers would never be able to get at. For example, in

```
Rational w, x, y, z;

w = x * y * z;
```

both calls to operator* yield unnamed temporaries that the programmer never sees, hence can never delete. (Again, see Item 31.)

But perhaps you think you're smarter than the average bear — or the average programmer. Perhaps you notice that both the on-the-stack and the on-the-heap approaches suffer from having to call a constructor for each result returned from operator*. Perhaps you recall that our initial goal was to avoid such constructor invocations. Perhaps you think you know of a way to avoid all but one constructor call. Perhaps the following implementation occurs to you, an implementation based on operator* returning a reference to a *static* Rational object, one defined *inside* the function:

```
// the third wrong way to write this function
inline const Rational& operator*(const Rational& lhs,
                                 const Rational& rhs)
{
  static Rational result;        // static object to which a
                                 // reference will be returned

  somehow multiply lhs and rhs and put the
  resulting value inside result;

  return result;
}
```

This looks promising, though when you try to compose real C++ for the italicized pseudocode above, you'll find that it's all but impossible to give result the correct value without invoking a Rational constructor, and avoiding such a call is the whole reason for this game. Let us posit that you manage to find a way, however, because no amount of cleverness can ultimately save this star-crossed design.

To see why, consider this perfectly reasonable client code:

```
bool operator==(const Rational& lhs,       // an operator==
                const Rational& rhs);      // for Rationals

Rational a, b, c, d;

...

if ((a * b) == (c * d))  {

  do whatever's appropriate when the products are equal;

} else {

  do whatever's appropriate when they're not;

}
```

Now ponder this: the expression ((a*b) == (c*d)) will *always* evaluate to true, regardless of the values of a, b, c, and d!

It's easiest to understand this vexing behavior by rewriting the test for equality in its equivalent functional form:

```
if (operator==(operator*(a, b), operator*(c, d)))
```

Notice that when operator== is called, there will already be *two* active calls to operator*, each of which will return a reference to the static Rational object inside operator*. Thus, operator== will be asked to compare the value of the static Rational object inside operator* with the value of the static Rational object inside operator*. It would be surprising indeed if they did not compare equal. Always.

With luck, this is enough to convince you that returning a reference from a function like operator* is a waste of time, but I'm not so naive as to believe that luck is always sufficient. Some of you — and you know who you are — are at this very moment thinking, "Well, if *one* static isn't enough, maybe a static *array* will do the trick..."

Stop. Please. Haven't we suffered enough already?

I can't bring myself to dignify this design with example code, but I can sketch why even *entertaining* the notion should cause you to blush in shame. First, you must choose *n*, the size of the array. If *n* is too small, you may run out of places to store function return values, in which case you'll have gained nothing over the single-static design we just discredited. But if *n* is too big, you'll decrease the performance of your program, because *every* object in the array will be constructed the first time the function is called. That will cost you *n* constructors and *n* destructors, even if the function in question is called only once. If "optimization" is the process of improving software performance, this kind of thing should be called "pessimization." Finally, think about how you'd put the values you need into the array's objects and what it would cost you to do it. The most direct way to move a value between objects is via assignment, but what is the cost of an assignment? In general, it's about the same as a call to a destructor (to destroy the old value) plus a call to a constructor (to copy over the new value). But your goal is to avoid the costs of construction and destruction! Face it: this approach just isn't going to pan out.

No, the right way to write a function that must return a new object is to have that function return a new object. For Rational's operator*, that means either the following code (which we first saw back on page 102) or something essentially equivalent:

```
inline const Rational operator*(const Rational& lhs,
                                const Rational& rhs)
{
  return Rational(lhs.n * rhs.n, lhs.d * rhs.d);
}
```

Sure, you may incur the cost of constructing and destructing operator*'s return value, but in the long run, that's a small price to pay for correct behavior. Besides, the bill that so terrifies you may never arrive. Like all programming languages, C++ allows compiler implementers to apply certain optimizations to improve the performance of the generated code, and it turns out that in some cases, operator*'s return value can be safely eliminated. When compilers take advantage of that fact (and current compilers often do), your program continues to behave the way it's supposed to, it just does it faster than you expected.

It all boils down to this: when deciding between returning a reference and returning an object, your job is to make the choice that does the right thing. Let your compiler vendors wrestle with figuring out how to make that choice as inexpensive as possible.

Item 24: Choose carefully between function overloading and parameter defaulting.

The confusion over function overloading and parameter defaulting stems from the fact that they both allow a single function name to be called in more than one way:

```
void f();                    // f is overloaded
void f(int x);

f();                         // calls f()
f(10);                       // calls f(int)

void g(int x = 0);           // g has a default
                             // parameter value

g();                         // calls g(0)
g(10);                       // calls g(10)
```

So which should be used when?

The answer depends on two other questions. First, is there a value you can use for a default? Second, how many algorithms do you want to use? In general, if you can choose a reasonable default value and you want to employ only a single algorithm, you'll use default parameters (see also Item 38). Otherwise you'll use function overloading.

Here's a function to compute the maximum of up to five ints. This function uses — take a deep breath and steel yourself — std::numeric_limits<int>::min() as a default parameter value. I'll have more to say about that in a moment, but first, here's the code:

```
int max(int a,
        int b = std::numeric_limits<int>::min(),
        int c = std::numeric_limits<int>::min(),
        int d = std::numeric_limits<int>::min(),
        int e = std::numeric_limits<int>::min())
{
  int temp = a > b ? a : b;
  temp = temp > c ? temp : c;
  temp = temp > d ? temp : d;
  return temp > e ? temp : e;
}
```

Now, calm yourself. `std::numeric_limits<int>::min()` is just the fancy new-fangled way the standard C++ library says what C says via the `INT_MIN` macro in `<limits.h>`: it's the minimum possible value for an `int` in whatever compiler happens to be processing your C++ source code. True, it's a deviation from the terseness for which C is renowned, but there's a method behind all those colons and other syntactic strychnine.

Suppose you'd like to write a function template taking any built-in numeric type as its parameter, and you'd like the functions generated from the template to print the minimum value representable by their instantiation type. Your template would look something like this:

```
template<class T>
void printMinimumValue()
{
  cout << the minimum value representable by T;
}
```

This is a difficult function to write if all you have to work with is `<limits.h>` and `<float.h>`. You don't know what `T` is, so you don't know whether to print out `INT_MIN` or `DBL_MIN` or what.

To sidestep these difficulties, the standard C++ library (see Item 49) defines in the header `<limits>` a class template, `numeric_limits`, which itself defines several static member functions. Each function returns information about the type instantiating the template. That is, the functions in `numeric_limits<int>` return information about type `int`, the functions in `numeric_limits<double>` return information about type `double`, etc. Among the functions in `numeric_limits` is `min`. `min` returns the minimum representable value for the instantiating type, so `numeric_limits<int>::min()` returns the minimum representable integer value.

Given `numeric_limits` (which, like nearly everything in the standard library, is in namespace `std` — see Item 28; `numeric_limits` itself is in the header `<limits>`), writing `printMinimumValue` is as easy as can be:

```
template<class T>
void printMinimumValue()
{
  cout << std::numeric_limits<T>::min();
}
```

This `numeric_limits`-based approach to specifying type-dependent constants may look expensive, but it's not. That's because the long-windedness of the source code fails to be reflected in the resultant object code. In fact, calls to functions in numeric_limits generate no instructions at all. To see how that can be, consider the following, which is an obvious way to implement numeric_limits<int>::min:

```
#include <limits.h>

namespace std {

  inline int numeric_limits<int>::min() throw ()
  { return INT_MIN; }

}
```

Because this function is declared inline, calls to it should be replaced by its body (see Item 33). That's just INT_MIN, which is itself a simple #define for some implementation-defined constant. So even though the max function at the beginning of this Item looks like it's making a function call for each default parameter value, it's just using a clever way of referring to a type-dependent constant, in this case the value of INT_MIN. Such efficient cleverness abounds in C++'s standard library. You really should read Item 49.

Getting back to the max function, the crucial observation is that max uses the same (rather inefficient) algorithm to compute its result, regardless of the number of arguments provided by the caller. Nowhere in the function do you attempt to figure out which parameters are "real" and which are defaults. Instead, you have chosen a default value that cannot possibly affect the validity of the computation for the algorithm you're using. That's what makes the use of default parameter values a viable solution.

For many functions, there is no reasonable default value. For example, suppose you want to write a function to compute the average of up to five ints. You can't use default parameter values here, because the result of the function is dependent on the number of parameters passed in: if 3 values are passed in, you'll divide their sum by 3; if 5 values are passed in, you'll divide their sum by 5. Furthermore, there is no "magic number" you can use as a default to indicate that a parameter wasn't actually provided by the client, because all possible ints are valid values for the parameters. In this case, you have no choice: you *must* use overloaded functions:

```
double avg(int a);
double avg(int a, int b);
double avg(int a, int b, int c);
double avg(int a, int b, int c, int d);
double avg(int a, int b, int c, int d, int e);
```

The other case in which you need to use overloaded functions occurs when you want to accomplish a particular task, but the algorithm that you use depends on the inputs that are given. This is commonly the case with constructors: a default constructor will construct an object from scratch, whereas a copy constructor will construct one from an existing object:

```cpp
// A class for representing natural numbers
class Natural {
public:
  Natural(int initValue);
  Natural(const Natural& rhs);

private:
  unsigned int value;

  void init(int initValue);
  void error(const string& msg);
};

inline
void Natural::init(int initValue) { value = initValue; }

Natural::Natural(int initValue)
{
  if (initValue > 0) init(initValue);
  else error("Illegal initial value");
}

inline Natural::Natural(const Natural& x)
{ init(x.value); }
```

The constructor taking an `int` has to perform error checking, but the copy constructor doesn't, so two different functions are needed. That means overloading. However, note that both functions must assign an initial value for the new object. This could lead to code duplication in the two constructors, so you maneuver around that problem by writing a private member function `init` that contains the code common to the two constructors. This tactic — using overloaded functions that call a common underlying function for some of their work — is worth remembering, because it's frequently useful (see, e.g., Item 12).

Item 25: Avoid overloading on a pointer and a numerical type.

Trivia question for the day: what is zero?

More specifically, what will happen here?

```cpp
void f(int x);
void f(string *ps);

f(0);                              // calls f(int) or f(string*)?
```

The answer is that 0 is an int — a literal integer constant, to be precise — so f(int) will always be called. Therein lies the problem, because that's not what people always want. This is a situation unique in the world of C++: a place where people think a call should be ambiguous, but compilers do not.

It would be nice if you could somehow tiptoe around this problem by use of a symbolic name, say, NULL for null pointers, but that turns out to be a lot tougher than you might imagine.

Your first inclination might be to declare a constant called NULL, but constants have types, and what type should NULL have? It needs to be compatible with all pointer types, but the only type satisfying that requirement is void*, and you can't pass void* pointers to typed pointers without an explicit cast. Not only is that ugly, at first glance it's not a whole lot better than the original situation:

```
void * const NULL = 0;             // potential NULL definition

f(0);                              // still calls f(int)
f(static_cast<string*>(NULL));     // calls f(string*)
f(static_cast<string*>(0));        // calls f(string*)
```

On second thought, however, the use of NULL as a void* constant is a shade better than what you started with, because you avoid ambiguity if you use only NULL to indicate null pointers:

```
f(0);                              // calls f(int)
f(NULL);                           // error! — type mis-match
f(static_cast<string*>(NULL));     // okay, calls f(string*)
```

At least now you've traded a runtime error (the call to the "wrong" f for 0) for a compile-time error (the attempt to pass a void* into a string* parameter). This improves matters somewhat (see Item 46), but the cast is still unsatisfying.

If you shamefacedly crawl back to the preprocessor, you find that it doesn't really offer a way out, either, because the obvious choices seem to be

```
#define NULL 0
```

and

```
#define NULL ((void*) 0)
```

and the first possibility is just the literal 0, which is fundamentally an integer constant (your original problem, as you'll recall), while the second possibility gets you back into the trouble with passing void* pointers to typed pointers.

If you've boned up on the rules governing type conversions, you may know that C++ views a conversion from a long int to an int as neither better nor worse than a conversion from the long int 0 to the null pointer. You can take advantage of that to introduce the ambiguity into the int/pointer question you probably believe should be there in the first place:

```
#define NULL 0L                    // NULL is now a long int

void f(int x);
void f(string *p);

f(NULL);                          // error! — ambiguous
```

However, this fails to help if you overload on a long int and a pointer:

```
#define NULL 0L

void f(long int x);               // this f now takes a long
void f(string *p);

f(NULL);                          // fine, calls f(long int)
```

In practice, this is probably safer than defining NULL to be an int, but it's more a way of moving the problem around than of eliminating it.

The problem can be exterminated, but it requires the use of a late-breaking addition to the language: *member function templates* (often simply called *member templates*). Member function templates are exactly what they sound like: templates within classes that generate member functions for those classes. In the case of NULL, you want an object that acts like the expression static_cast<T*>(0) for every type T. That suggests that NULL should be an object of a class containing an implicit conversion operator for every possible pointer type. That's a lot of conversion operators, but a member template lets you force C++ into generating them for you:

```
// a first cut at a class yielding NULL pointer objects
class NullClass {
public:
  template<class T>                   // generates
    operator T*() const { return 0; } // operator T* for
};                                    // all types T; each
                                      // function returns
                                      // the null pointer

const NullClass NULL;      // NULL is an object of
                           // type NullClass

void f(int x);             // same as we originally had

void f(string *p);         // ditto

f(NULL);                   // fine, converts NULL to
                           // string*, then calls f(string*)
```

This is a good initial draft, but it can be refined in several ways. First, we don't really need more than one `NullClass` object, so there's no reason to give the class a name; we can just use an unnamed class and make `NULL` of that type. Second, as long as we're making it possible to convert `NULL` to any type of pointer, we should handle pointers to members, too. That calls for a second member template, one to convert 0 to type `T C::*` ("pointer to member of type `T` in class `C`") for all classes `C` and all types `T`. (If that makes no sense to you, or if you've never heard of — much less used — pointers to members, relax. Pointers to members are uncommon beasts, rarely seen in the wild, and you'll probably never have to deal with them. The terminally curious may wish to consult Item 30, which discusses pointers to members in a bit more detail.) Finally, we should prevent clients from taking the address of `NULL`, because `NULL` isn't supposed to act like a *pointer*, it's supposed to act like a pointer *value*, and pointer values (e.g., 0x453AB002) don't have addresses.

The jazzed-up `NULL` definition looks like this:

```
const                            // this is a const object...
class {
public:
  template<class T>              // convertible to any type
    operator T*() const          // of null non-member
    { return 0; }                // pointer...

  template<class C, class T>     // or any type of null
    operator T C::*() const      // member pointer...
    { return 0; }

private:
  void operator&() const;        // whose address can't be
                                 // taken (see Item 27)...

} NULL;                          // and whose name is NULL
```

This is truly a sight to behold, though you may wish to make a minor concession to practicality by giving the class a name after all. If you don't, compiler messages referring to `NULL`'s type are likely to be pretty unintelligible.

An important point about all these attempts to come up with a workable `NULL` is that they help only if you're the *caller*. If you're the *author* of the functions being called, having a foolproof `NULL` won't help you at all, because you can't compel your callers to use it. For example, even if you offer your clients the space-age `NULL` we just developed, you still can't keep them from doing this,

```
f(0);                            // still calls f(int),
                                 // because 0 is still an int
```

and that's just as problematic now as it was at the beginning of this Item.

As a designer of overloaded functions, then, the bottom line is that you're best off avoiding overloading on a numerical and a pointer type if you can possibly avoid it.

Item 26: Guard against potential ambiguity.

Everybody has to have a philosophy. Some people believe in *laissez faire* economics, others believe in reincarnation. Some people even believe that COBOL is a real programming language. C++ has a philosophy, too: it believes that potential ambiguity is not an error.

Here's an example of potential ambiguity:

```
class B;                            // forward declaration for
                                    // class B
class A {
public:
  A(const B&);                      // an A can be
                                    // constructed from a B
};
class B {
public:
  operator A() const;               // a B can be
                                    // converted to an A
};
```

There's nothing wrong with these class declarations — they can coexist in the same program without the slightest trouble. However, look what happens when you combine these classes with a function that takes an A object, but is actually passed a B object:

```
void f(const A&);

B b;

f(b);                               // error! — ambiguous
```

Seeing the call to f, compilers know they must somehow come up with an object of type A, even though what they have in hand is an object of type B. There are two equally good ways to do this. On one hand, the class A constructor could be called; this would construct a new A object using b as an argument. On the other hand, b could be converted into an A object by calling the client-defined conversion operator in class B. Because these two approaches are considered equally good, compilers refuse to choose between them.

Of course, you could use this program for some time without ever running across the ambiguity. That's the insidious peril of potential ambiguity. It can lie dormant in a program for long periods of time, undetected and inactive, until the day when some unsuspecting programmer does something that actually *is* ambiguous, at which point pandemonium breaks out. This gives rise to the disconcerting possibility that you might release a library that can be called ambiguously without even being aware that you're doing it.

A similar form of ambiguity arises from standard conversions in the language — you don't even need any classes:

```
void f(int);
void f(char);

double d = 6.02;

f(d);                           // error! — ambiguous
```

Should d be converted into an int or a char? The conversions are equally good, so compilers won't judge. Fortunately, you can get around this problem by using an explicit cast:

```
f(static_cast<int>(d));        // fine, calls f(int)
f(static_cast<char>(d));       // fine, calls f(char)
```

Multiple inheritance (see Item 43) is rife with possibilities for potential ambiguity. The most straightforward case occurs when a derived class inherits the same member name from more than one base class:

```
class Base1 {
public:
  int doIt();
};

class Base2 {
public:
  void doIt();
};

class Derived: public Base1,     // Derived doesn't declare
               public Base2 {    // a function called doIt

  ...

};

Derived d;

d.doIt();                        // error! — ambiguous
```

When class Derived inherits two functions with the same name, C++ utters not a whimper; at this point the ambiguity is only potential. However, the call to doIt forces compilers to face the issue, and unless you explicitly disambiguate the call by specifying which base class function you want, the call is an error:

```
d.Base1::doIt();                    // fine, calls Base1::doIt

d.Base2::doIt();                    // fine, calls Base2::doIt
```

That doesn't upset too many people, but the fact that accessibility restrictions don't enter into the picture has caused more than one otherwise pacifistic soul to contemplate distinctly unpacifistic actions:

```
class Base1 { ... };                // same as above

class Base2 {
private:
  void doIt();                      // this function is now
};                                  // private

class Derived: public Base1, public Base2
{ ... };                            // same as above

Derived d;

int i = d.doIt();                   // error! — still ambiguous!
```

The call to doIt continues to be ambiguous, even though only the function in Base1 is accessible! The fact that only Base1::doIt returns a value that can be used to initialize an int is also irrelevant — the call remains ambiguous. If you want to make this call, you simply *must* specify which class's doIt is the one you want.

As is the case for most initially unintuitive rules in C++, there is a good reason why access restrictions are not taken into account when disambiguating references to multiply inherited members. It boils down to this: changing the accessibility of a class member should never change the meaning of a program.

For example, assume that in the previous example, access restrictions were taken into account. Then the expression d.doIt() would resolve to a call to Base1::doIt, because Base2's version was inaccessible. Now assume that Base1 was changed so that its version of doIt was protected instead of public, and Base2 was changed so that its version was public instead of private.

Suddenly the same expression, d.doIt(), would result in a *completely different function call*, even though neither the calling code nor the functions had been modified! Now *that's* unintuitive, and there would be no way for compilers to issue even a warning. Considering your choices, you may decide that having to explicitly disambiguate references to multiply inherited members isn't quite as unreasonable as you originally thought.

Given that there are all these different ways to write programs and libraries harboring potential ambiguity, what's a good software developer to do? Primarily, you need to keep an eye out for it. It's next to impossible to root out all the sources of potential ambiguity, particularly when programmers combine libraries that were developed independently (see also Item 28), but by understanding the situations that often lead to potential ambiguity, you're in a better position to minimize its presence in the software you design and develop.

Item 27: Explicitly disallow use of implicitly generated member functions you don't want.

Suppose you want to write a class template, `Array`, whose generated classes behave like built-in C++ arrays in every way, except they perform bounds checking. One of the design problems you would face is how to prohibit assignment between `Array` objects, because assignment isn't legal for C++ arrays:

```
double values1[10];
double values2[10];

values1 = values2;              // error!
```

For most functions, this wouldn't be a problem. If you didn't want to allow a function, you simply wouldn't put it in the class. However, the assignment operator is one of those distinguished member functions that C++, always the helpful servant, writes for you if you neglect to write it yourself (see Item 45). What then to do?

The solution is to declare the function, `operator=` in this case, *private*. By declaring a member function explicitly, you prevent compilers from generating their own version, and by making the function private, you keep people from calling it.

However, the scheme isn't foolproof; member and friend functions can still call your private function. *Unless*, that is, you are clever enough not to *define* the function. Then if you inadvertently call the function, you'll get an error at link-time (see Item 46).

For `Array`, your template definition would start out like this:

```
template<class T>
class Array {
private:
  // Don't define this function!
  Array& operator=(const Array& rhs);

  ...
};
```

Now if a client tries to perform assignments on Array objects, compilers will thwart the attempt, and if you inadvertently try it in a member or a friend function, the linker will yelp.

Don't assume from this example that this Item applies only to assignment operators. It doesn't. It applies to each of the compiler-generated functions described in Item 45. In practice, you'll find that the behavioral similarities between assignment and copy construction (see Items 11 and 16) almost always mean that anytime you want to disallow use of one, you'll want to disallow use of the other, too.

Item 28: Partition the global namespace.

The biggest problem with the global scope is that there's only one of them. In a large software project, there is usually a bevy of people putting names in this singular scope, and invariably this leads to name conflicts. For example, library1.h might define a number of constants, including the following:

```
const double LIB_VERSION = 1.204;
```

Ditto for library2.h:

```
const int LIB_VERSION = 3;
```

It doesn't take great insight to see that there is going to be a problem if a program tries to include both library1.h and library2.h. Unfortunately, outside of cursing under your breath, sending hate mail to the library authors, and editing the header files until the name conflicts are eliminated, there is little you can do about this kind of problem.

You can, however, take pity on the poor souls who'll have *your* libraries foisted on them. You probably already prepend some hopefully-unique prefix to each of your global symbols, but surely you must admit that the resulting identifiers are less than pleasing to gaze upon.

A better solution is to use a C++ namespace. Boiled down to its essence, a namespace is just a fancy way of letting you use the prefixes you know and love without making people look at them all the time. So instead of this,

```
const double sdmBOOK_VERSION = 2.0;   // in this library,
                                      // each symbol begins
class sdmHandle { ... };              // with "sdm"

sdmHandle& sdmGetHandle();            // see Item 47 for why you
                                      // might want to declare
                                      // a function like this
```

you write this:

```
namespace sdm {
  const double BOOK_VERSION = 2.0;
  class Handle { ... };
  Handle& getHandle();
}
```

Clients then access symbols in your namespace in any of the usual three ways: by importing all the symbols in a namespace into a scope, by importing individual symbols into a scope, or by explicitly qualifying a symbol for one-time use. Here are some examples:

```
void f1()
{
  using namespace sdm;          // make all symbols in sdm
                                // available w/o qualification
                                // in this scope

  cout << BOOK_VERSION;         // okay, resolves to
                                // sdm::BOOK_VERSION
  ...

  Handle h = getHandle();       // okay, Handle resolves to
                                // sdm::Handle, getHandle
  ...                           // resolves to sdm::getHandle

}

void f2()
{
  using sdm::BOOK_VERSION;      // make only BOOK_VERSION
                                // available w/o qualification
                                // in this scope

  cout << BOOK_VERSION;         // okay, resolves to
                                // sdm::BOOK_VERSION
  ...

  Handle h = getHandle();       // error! neither Handle
                                // nor getHandle were
  ...                           // imported into this scope

}

void f3()
{
  cout << sdm::BOOK_VERSION;    // okay, makes BOOK_VERSION
                                // available for this one use
  ...                           // only

  double d = BOOK_VERSION;      // error! BOOK_VERSION is
                                // not in scope

  Handle h = getHandle();       // error! neither Handle
                                // nor getHandle were
  ...                           // imported into this scope

}
```

One of the nicest things about namespaces is that potential ambiguity is not an error (see Item 26). As a result, you can import the same symbol from more than one namespace, yet still live a carefree life (provided you never actually use the symbol). For instance, if, in addition to namespace sdm, you had need to make use of this namespace,

```
namespace AcmeWindowSystem {

  ...

  typedef int Handle;

  ...

}
```

you could use both sdm and AcmeWindowSystem without conflict, provided you never referenced the symbol Handle. If you did refer to it, you'd have to explicitly say which namespace's Handle you wanted:

```
void f()
{
  using namespace sdm;                 // import sdm symbols
  using namespace AcmeWindowSystem;    // import Acme symbols

  ...                                  // freely refer to sdm
                                       // and Acme symbols
                                       // other than Handle

  Handle h;                            // error! which Handle?

  sdm::Handle h1;                      // fine, no ambiguity

  AcmeWindowSystem::Handle h2;         // also no ambiguity

  ...

}
```

Contrast this with the conventional header-file-based approach, where the mere inclusion of both sdm.h and acme.h would cause compilers to complain about multiple definitions of the symbol Handle.

Namespaces were added to C++ relatively late in the standardization game, so perhaps you think they're not that important and you can live without them. You can't. You can't, because almost everything in the standard library (see Item 49) lives inside the namespace std. That may strike you as a minor detail, but it affects you in a very direct manner: it's why C++ now sports funny-looking extensionless header names like <iostream>, <string>, etc. For details, turn to Item 49.

Because namespaces were introduced comparatively recently, your compilers might not yet support them. If that's the case, there's still no reason to pollute the global namespace, because you can approximate namespaces with `structs`. You do it by creating a struct to hold your global names, then putting your global names inside this struct as static members:

```
// definition of a struct emulating a namespace
struct sdm {
  static const double BOOK_VERSION;
  class Handle { ... };
  static Handle& getHandle();
};
const double sdm::BOOK_VERSION = 2.0;   // obligatory defn
                                        // of static data
                                        // member
```

Now when people want to access your global names, they simply prefix them with the struct name:

```
void f()
{
  cout << sdm::BOOK_VERSION;

  ...

  sdm::Handle h = sdm::getHandle();

  ...
}
```

If there are no name conflicts at the global level, clients of your library may find it cumbersome to use the fully qualified names. Fortunately, there is a way you can let them have their scopes and ignore them, too.

For your type names, provide typedefs that remove the need for explicit scoping. That is, for a type name `T` in your namespace-like struct `S`, provide a (global) typedef such that `T` is a synonym for `S::T`:

```
typedef sdm::Handle Handle;
```

For each (static) object `X` in your struct, provide a (global) reference `X` that is initialized with `S::X`:

```
const double& BOOK_VERSION = sdm::BOOK_VERSION;
```

Frankly, after you've read Item 47, the thought of defining a non-local static object like BOOK_VERSION will probably make you queasy. (You'll want to replace such objects with the functions described in Item 47.)

Functions are treated much like objects, but even though it's legal to define references to functions, future maintainers of your code will dislike you a lot less if you employ pointers to functions instead:

```
sdm::Handle& (* const getHandle)() =      // getHandle is a
  sdm::getHandle;                         // const pointer (see
                                          // Item 21) to
                                          // sdm::getHandle
```

Note that getHandle is a *const* pointer. You don't really want to let clients make it point to something other than sdm::getHandle, do you?

(If you're dying to know how to define a reference to a function, this should revitalize you:

```
sdm::Handle& (&getHandle)() =    // getHandle is a reference
  sdm::getHandle;                // to sdm::getHandle
```

Personally, I think this is kind of cool, but there's a reason you've probably never seen this before. Except for how they're initialized, references to functions and const pointers to functions behave identically, and pointers to functions are much more readily understood.)

Given these typedefs and references, clients not suffering from global name conflicts can just use the unqualified type and object names, while clients who do have conflicts can ignore the typedef and reference definitions and use fully qualified names. It's unlikely that all your clients will want to use the shorthand names, so you should be sure to put the typedefs and references in a different header file from the one containing your namespace-emulating struct.

structs are a nice approximation to namespaces, but they're a long trek from the real thing. They fall short in a variety of ways, one of the most obvious of which is their treatment of operators. Simply put, operators defined as static member functions of structs can be invoked only through a function call, never via the natural infix syntax that operators are designed to support:

```
// define a namespace-emulating struct containing
// types and functions for Widgets. Widget objects
// support addition via operator+
struct widgets {
  class Widget { ... };

  // see Item 21 for why the return value is const
  static const Widget operator+(const Widget& lhs,
                                const Widget& rhs);

  ...

};

// attempt to set up global (unqualified) names for
// Widget and operator+ as described above

typedef widgets::Widget Widget;
```

```
      const Widget (* const operator+)(const Widget&,    // error!
                                       const Widget&);    // operator+
                                                          // can't be a
                                                          // pointer name

Widget w1, w2, sum;

sum = w1 + w2;                               // error! no operator+
                                             // taking Widgets is
                                             // declared at this
                                             // scope

sum = widgets::operator+(w1, w2);            // legal, but hardly
                                             // "natural" syntax
```

Such limitations should spur you to adopt real namespaces as soon as your compilers make it practical.

Classes and Functions: Implementation

Because C++ is strongly typed, coming up with appropriate definitions for your classes and templates and appropriate declarations for your functions is the lion's share of the battle. Once you've got those right, it's hard to go wrong with the template, class, and function implementations. Yet, somehow, people manage to do it.

Some problems arise from inadvertently violating abstraction: accidentally allowing implementation details to peek out from behind the class and function boundaries that are supposed to contain them. Others originate in confusion over the length of an object's lifetime. Still others stem from premature optimization, typically traceable to the seductive nature of the `inline` keyword. Finally, some implementation strategies, while fine on a local scale, result in levels of coupling between source files that can make it unacceptably costly to rebuild large systems.

Each of these problems, as well as others like them, can be avoided if you know what to watch out for. The items that follow identify some situations in which you need to be especially vigilant.

Item 29: Avoid returning "handles" to internal data.

A scene from an object-oriented romance:

> Object A: Darling, don't ever change!

> Object B: Don't worry, dear, I'm `const`.

Yet just as in real life, A wonders, "Can B be trusted?" And just as in real life, the answer often hinges on B's nature: the constitution of its member functions.

Suppose B is a constant String object:

```
class String {
public:
  String(const char *value);        // see Item 11 for pos-
  ~String();                        // sible implementations

  operator char *() const;          // convert String -> char*

  ...

private:
  char *data;
};

const String B("Hello World");      // B is a const object
```

Because B is const, it had better be the case that the value of B now and evermore is "Hello World". Of course, this supposes that programmers working with B are playing the game in a civilized fashion. In particular, it depends on the fact that nobody is "casting away the constness" of B through nefarious ploys such as this (see Item 21):

```
String& alsoB =                     // make alsoB another name
  const_cast<String&>(B);           // for B, but without the
                                    // constness
```

Given that no one is doing such evil deeds, however, it seems a safe bet that B will never change. Or does it? Consider this sequence of events:

```
char *str = B;                      // calls B.operator char*()

strcpy(str, "Hi Mom");              // modifies what str
                                    // points to
```

Does B still have the value "Hello World", or has it suddenly mutated into something you might say to your mother? The answer depends entirely on the implementation of String::operator char*.

Here's a careless implementation, one that does the wrong thing. However, it does it very efficiently, which is why so many programmers fall into this trap:

```
// a fast, but incorrect implementation
inline String::operator char*() const
{ return data; }
```

The flaw in this function is that it's returning a "handle" — in this case, a pointer — to information that should be hidden inside the String object on which the function is invoked. That handle gives callers unrestricted access to what the private field data points to. In other words, after the statement

```
char *str = B;
```

the situation looks like this:

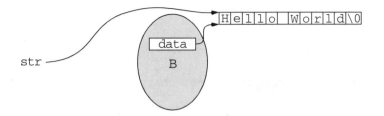

Clearly, any modification to the memory pointed to by str will also change the effective value of B. Thus, even though B is declared const, and even though only const member functions are invoked on B, B might still acquire different values as the program runs. In particular, if str modifies what it points to, B will also change.

There's nothing inherently wrong with the way String::operator char* is written. What's troublesome is that it can be applied to constant objects. If the function weren't declared const, there would be no problem, because it couldn't be applied to objects like B.

Yet it seems perfectly reasonable to turn a String object, even a constant one, into its equivalent char*, so you'd like to keep this function const. If you want to do that, you must rewrite your implementation to avoid returning a handle to the object's internal data:

```
// a slower, but safer implementation
inline String::operator char*() const
{
  char *copy = new char[strlen(data) + 1];
  strcpy(copy, data);

  return copy;

}
```

This implementation is safe, because it returns a pointer to memory that contains a *copy* of the data to which the String object points; there is no way to change the value of the String object through the pointer returned by this function. As usual, such safety commands a price: this version of String::operator char* is slower than the simple version above, and callers of this function must remember to use delete on the pointer that's returned.

If you think this version of operator char* is too slow, or if the potential memory leak makes you nervous (as well it should), a slightly different tack is to return a pointer to *constant* chars:

```
class String {
public:
    operator const char *() const;

    ...

};

inline String::operator const char*() const
{ return data; }
```

This function is fast and safe, and, though it's not the same as the function you originally specified, it suffices for most applications. It's also the moral equivalent of the C++ standardization committee's solution to the string/char* conundrum: the standard string type contains a member function c_str that returns a const char* version of the string in question. For more information on the standard string type, turn to Item 49.

A pointer isn't the only way to return a handle to internal data. References are just as easy to abuse. Here's a common way to do it, again using the String class:

```
class String {
public:

    ...

  char& operator[](int index) const
  { return data[index]; }

private:
  char *data;
};

String s = "I'm not constant";

s[0] = 'x';                      // fine, s isn't const

const String cs = "I'm constant";

cs[0] = 'x';                     // this modifies the const
                                 // string, but compilers
                                 // won't notice
```

Notice how String::operator[] returns its result by reference. That means that the caller of this function gets back *another name* for the internal element data[index], and that other name can be used to modify the internal data of the supposedly constant object. This is the same problem you saw before, but this time the culprit is a reference as a return value, not a pointer.

The general solutions to this kind of problem are the same as they were for pointers: either make the function non-const, or rewrite it so that no handle is returned. For a solution to this *particular* problem — how to write String::operator[] so that it works for both const and non-const objects — see Item 21.

const member functions aren't the only ones that need to worry about returning handles. Even non-const member functions must reconcile themselves to the fact that the validity of a handle expires at the same time as the object to which it corresponds. This may be sooner than a client expects, especially when the object in question is a compiler-generated temporary object.

For example, take a look at this function, which returns a String object:

```
String someFamousAuthor()          // randomly chooses and
{                                  // returns an author's name

  switch (rand() % 3) {            // rand() is in <stdlib.h>
                                   // (and <cstdlib> — see
                                   // Item 49)
  case 0:
    return "Margaret Mitchell";    // Wrote "Gone with the
                                   // Wind," a true classic
  case 1:
    return "Stephen King";         // His stories have kept
                                   // millions from sleeping
                                   // at night
  case 2:
    return "Scott Meyers";         // Ahem, one of these
  }                                // things is not like the
                                   // others...

  return "";                       // we can't get here, but
                                   // all paths in a value-
                                   // returning function must
}                                  // return a value, sigh
```

Kindly set aside your concerns about how "random" the values returned from rand are, and please humor my delusions of grandeur in associating myself with real writers. Instead, focus on the fact that the return value of someFamousAuthor is a String object, a *temporary* String object. Such objects are transient — their lifetimes generally extend only until the end of the expression containing the call to the function creating them. In this case, that would be until the end of the expression containing the call to someFamousAuthor.

Now consider this use of someFamousAuthor, in which we assume that String declares an operator const char* member function as described above:

```
const char *pc = someFamousAuthor();

cout << pc;                    // uh oh...
```

Believe it or not, you can't predict what this code will do, at least not with any certainty. That's because by the time you try to print out the sequence of characters pointed to by pc, that sequence is undefined. The difficulty arises from the events that transpire during the initialization of pc:

1. A temporary String object is created to hold someFamousAuthor's return value.

2. That String is converted to a const char* via String's operator const char* member function, and pc is initialized with the resulting pointer.

3. The temporary String object is destroyed, which means its destructor is called. Within the destructor, its data pointer is deleted (the code is shown in Item 11). However, data points to the same memory as pc does, so pc now points to deleted memory — memory with undefined contents.

Because pc was initialized with a handle into a temporary object and temporary objects are destroyed shortly after they're created, the handle became invalid before pc could do anything with it. For all intents and purposes, pc was dead on arrival. Such is the danger of handles into temporary objects.

For const member functions, then, returning handles is ill-advised, because it violates abstraction. Even for non-const member functions, however, returning handles can lead to trouble, especially when temporary objects get involved. Handles can dangle, just like pointers, and just as you labor to avoid dangling pointers, you should strive to avoid dangling handles, too.

Still, there's no reason to get fascist about it. It's not possible to stomp out all possible dangling pointers in nontrivial programs, and it's rarely possible to eliminate all possible dangling handles, either. Nevertheless, if you avoid returning handles when there's no compelling need, your programs will benefit, and so will your reputation.

Item 30: Avoid member functions that return non-const pointers or references to members less accessible than themselves.

The reason for making a member private or protected is to limit access to it, right? Your overworked, underpaid C++ compilers go to lots of trouble to make sure that your access restrictions aren't circumvented, right? So it doesn't make a lot of sense for you to write functions that give random clients the ability to freely access restricted members, now, does it? If you think it *does* make sense, please reread this paragraph over and over until you agree that it doesn't.

It's easy to violate this simple rule. Here's an example:

```
class Address { ... };          // where someone lives

class Person {
public:
  Address& personAddress() { return address; }
  ...

private:
  Address address;
  ...
};
```

The member function personAddress provides the caller with the Address object contained in the Person object, but, probably due to efficiency considerations, the result is returned by reference instead of by value (see Item 22). Unfortunately, the presence of this member function defeats the purpose of making Person::address private:

```
Person scott(...);              // parameters omitted for
                                // simplicity

Address& addr =                 // assume that addr is
  scott.personAddress();        // global
```

Now the global object addr is *another name* for scott.address, and it can be used to read and write scott.address at will. For all practical purposes, scott.address is no longer private; it is public, and the source of this promotion in accessibility is the member function personAddress. Of course, there is nothing special about the access level private in this example; if address were protected, exactly the same reasoning would apply.

References aren't the only cause for concern. Pointers can play this game, too. Here's the same example, but using pointers this time:

```
class Person {
public:
  Address * personAddress() { return &address; }
  ...

private:
  Address address;
  ...
};

Address *addrPtr =
  scott.personAddress();          // same problem as above
```

With pointers, however, you have to worry not only about data members, but also about member *functions*. That's because it's possible to return a pointer to a member function:

```
class Person;                     // forward declaration

// PPMF = "pointer to Person member function"
typedef void (Person::*PPMF)();

class Person {
public:
  static PPMF verificationFunction()
  { return &Person::verifyAddress; }

  ...

private:
  Address address;

  void verifyAddress();

};
```

If you're not used to socializing with pointers to member functions and typedefs thereof, the declaration for Person::verificationFunction may seem daunting. Don't be intimidated. All it says is

- verificationFunction is a member function that takes no parameters;

- its return value is a pointer to a member function of the Person class;

- the pointed-to function (i.e., verificationFunction's return value) takes no parameters and returns nothing, i.e., void.

As for the word static, that means what it always means in a member declaration: there is only one copy of the member for the entire class, and the member can be accessed without an object. For the complete story, consult your favorite introductory C++ textbook. (If your favorite introductory C++ textbook doesn't discuss static members, carefully tear out all its pages and recycle them. Dispose of the book's cover in an environmentally sound manner, then borrow or buy a better textbook.)

In this last example, `verifyAddress` is a private member function, indicating that it's really an implementation detail of the class; only class members should know about it (and friends, too, of course). However, the public member function `verificationFunction` returns a pointer to `verifyAddress`, so clients can again pull this kind of thing:

```
PPMF pmf = scott.verificationFunction();

(scott.*pmf)();                    // same as calling
                                   // scott.verifyAddress
```

Here, `pmf` has become a synonym for `Person::verifyAddress`, with the crucial difference that there are no restrictions on its use.

In spite of the foregoing discussion, you may someday be faced with a situation in which, pressed to achieve performance constraints, you honestly need to write a member function that returns a reference or a pointer to a less-accessible member. At the same time, however, you won't want to sacrifice the access restrictions that `private` and `protected` afford you. In those cases, you can almost always achieve both goals by returning a pointer or a reference to a `const` object. For details, take a look at Item 21.

Item 31: Never return a reference to a local object or to a dereferenced pointer initialized by new within the function.

This Item may sound complicated, but it's not. It's simple common sense. Really. Honest. *Trust me.*

Consider first the matter of returning a reference to a local object. The problem here is that local objects are just that, *local*. That means they're constructed when they're defined, and they're destructed when they go out of scope. Their scope, however, is that of the function body in which they're located. When the function returns, control leaves its scope, so the objects local to that function are automatically destructed. As a result, if you return a reference to a local object, that local object has been destructed before the caller of the function ever gets its computational hands on it.

This problem usually raises its ugly head when you try to improve the efficiency of a function by returning its result by reference instead of by value. The following example is the same as the one in Item 23, which pursues in detail the question of when you can return a reference and when you can't:

```
class Rational {          // class for rational numbers
public:
  Rational(int numerator = 0, int denominator = 1);
  ~Rational();

  ...

private:
  int n, d;               // numerator and denominator

  // notice that operator* (incorrectly) returns a reference
  friend const Rational& operator*(const Rational& lhs,
                                   const Rational& rhs);
};

// an incorrect implementation of operator*
inline const Rational& operator*(const Rational& lhs,
                                 const Rational& rhs)
{
  Rational result(lhs.n * rhs.n, lhs.d * rhs.d);
  return result;
}
```

Here, the local object `result` is constructed upon entry into the body of `operator*`. However, local objects are automatically destroyed when they go out of scope. `result` will go out of scope after execution of the `return` statement, so when you write this,

```
Rational two = 2;

Rational four = two * two;    // same as
                              // operator*(two, two)
```

what happens during the function call is this:

1. The local object `result` is constructed.

2. A reference is initialized to be another name for `result`, and this reference is squirreled away as `operator*`'s return value.

3. The local object `result` is destroyed, and the space it used to occupy on the stack is made available for use by other parts of the program or by other programs.

4. The object `four` is initialized using the reference of step 2.

Everything is fine until step 4, at which point there occurs, as they say in the highest of high-tech circles, "a major lossage." The reference initialized in step 2 ceased to refer to a valid object as of the end of step 3,

so the outcome of the initialization of object four is completely undefined.

The lesson should be clear: don't return a reference to a local object.

"Okay," you say, "the problem is that the object I want to use goes out
of scope too soon. I can fix that. I'll just call new instead of using a local
object." Like this:

```
// another incorrect implementation of operator*
inline const Rational& operator*(const Rational& lhs,
                                 const Rational& rhs)
{
  // create a new object on the heap
  Rational *result =
    new Rational(lhs.n * rhs.n, lhs.d * rhs.d);

  // return it
  return *result;
}
```

This approach does indeed avoid the problem of the previous example,
but it introduces a new one in its place. To avoid a memory leak in your
software, you know you must ensure that delete is applied to every
pointer conjured up by new, but ay, there's the rub: who's to make the
matching call to delete for this function's use of new?

Clearly, the *caller* of operator* must see to it that delete is applied.
Clear, yes, and even easy to document, but nonetheless the cause is
hopeless. There are two reasons for this pessimistic assessment.

First, it's well-known that programmers, as a breed, are sloppy. That
doesn't mean that you're sloppy or that I'm sloppy, but rare is the programmer who doesn't work with someone who is — shall we say? — a
little on the flaky side. What are the odds that such programmers —
and we all know that they exist — will remember that whenever they
call operator*, they must *take the address of the result* and then use
delete on it? That is, they must use operator* like this:

```
const Rational& four = two * two;   // get dereferenced
                                    // pointer; store it in
                                    // a reference
  ...

delete &four;                       // retrieve pointer
                                    // and delete it
```

The odds are vanishingly small. Remember, if only a *single caller* of operator* fails to follow the rules, you have a memory leak.

Returning dereferenced pointers has a second, more serious, problem, because it persists even in the presence of the most conscientious of programmers. Often, the result of operator* is a temporary intermediate value, an object that exists only for the purposes of evaluating a larger expression. For example:

```
Rational one(1), two(2), three(3), four(4);
Rational product;

product = one * two * three * four;
```

Evaluation of the expression to be assigned to product requires three separate calls to operator*, a fact that becomes more evident when you rewrite the expression in its equivalent functional form:

```
product = operator*(operator*(operator*(one, two), three), four);
```

You know that each of the calls to operator* returns an object that needs to be deleted, but there is no possibility of applying delete, because none of the returned objects has been saved anywhere.

The only solution to this difficulty is to ask clients to code like this:

```
const Rational& temp1 = one * two;
const Rational& temp2 = temp1 * three;
const Rational& temp3 = temp2 * four;

delete &temp1;
delete &temp2;
delete &temp3;
```

Do that, and the best you can hope for is that people will ignore you. More realistically, you'd be skinned alive, or possibly sentenced to ten years hard labor writing microcode for waffle irons and toaster ovens.

Learn your lesson now, then: writing a function that returns a dereferenced pointer is a memory leak just waiting to happen.

By the way, if you think you've come up with a way to avoid the undefined behavior inherent in returning a reference to a local object and the memory leak haunting the return of a reference to a heap-allocated object, turn to Item 23 and read why returning a reference to a local static object also fails to work correctly. It may save you the trouble of seeking medical care for the arm you're likely to strain trying to pat yourself on the back.

Item 32: Postpone variable definitions as long as possible.

So you subscribe to the C philosophy that variables should be defined at the beginning of a block. Cancel that subscription! In C++, it's unnecessary, unnatural, and expensive.

Remember that when you define a variable of a type with a constructor or destructor, you incur the cost of construction when control reaches the variable's definition, and you incur the cost of destruction when the variable goes out of scope. This means there's a cost associated with unused variables, so you want to avoid them whenever you can.

Suave and sophisticated in the ways of programming as I know you to be, you're probably thinking you never define unused variables, so this Item's advice is inapplicable to your tight, lean coding style. You may need to think again. Consider the following function, which returns an encrypted version of a password, provided the password is long enough. If the password is too short, the function throws an exception of type logic_error, which is defined in the standard C++ library (see Item 49):

```
// this function defines the variable "encrypted" too soon
string encryptPassword(const string& password)
{
  string encrypted;

  if (password.length() < MINIMUM_PASSWORD_LENGTH) {
    throw logic_error("Password is too short");
  }

  do whatever is necessary to place an encrypted
  version of password in encrypted;

  return encrypted;
}
```

The object encrypted isn't *completely* unused in this function, but it's unused if an exception is thrown. That is, you'll pay for the construction and destruction of encrypted even if encryptPassword throws an exception. As a result, you're better off postponing encrypted's definition until you *know* you'll need it:

```
// this function postpones "encrypted"'s definition until
// it's truly necessary
string encryptPassword(const string& password)
{
  if (password.length() < MINIMUM_PASSWORD_LENGTH) {
    throw logic_error("Password is too short");
  }

  string encrypted;

  do whatever is necessary to place an encrypted
  version of password in encrypted;

  return encrypted;
}
```

This code still isn't as tight as it might be, because encrypted is defined without any initialization arguments. That means its default constructor will be used. In many cases, the first thing you'll do to an object is give it some value, often via an assignment. Item 12 explains why default-constructing an object and then assigning to it is a lot less efficient than initializing it with the value you really want it to have. That analysis applies here, too. For example, suppose the hard part of encryptPassword is performed in this function:

```
void encrypt(string& s);          // encrypts s in place
```

Then encryptPassword could be implemented like this, though it wouldn't be the best way to do it:

```
// this function postpones "encrypted"'s definition until
// it's necessary, but it's still needlessly inefficient
string encryptPassword(const string& password)
{
  ...                             // check length as above

  string encrypted;               // default-construct encrypted
  encrypted = password;           // assign to encrypted
  encrypt(encrypted);
  return encrypted;
}
```

A preferable approach is to initialize encrypted with password, thus skipping the (pointless) default construction:

```
// finally, the best way to define and initialize encrypted
string encryptPassword(const string& password)
{
  ...                             // check length

  string encrypted(password);     // define and initialize
                                  // via copy constructor

  encrypt(encrypted);
  return encrypted;
}
```

This suggests the real meaning of "as long as possible" in this Item's title. Not only should you postpone a variable's definition until right before you have to use the variable, you should try to postpone the definition until you have initialization arguments for it. By doing so, you avoid not only constructing and destructing unneeded objects, you also avoid pointless default constructions. Further, you help document the purpose of variables by initializing them in contexts in which their meaning is clear. Remember how in C you're encouraged to put a short comment after each variable definition to explain what the variable will eventually be used for? Well, combine decent variable names (see also Item 28) with contextually meaningful initialization arguments, and you have every programmer's dream: a solid argument for *eliminating* some comments.

By postponing variable definitions, you improve program efficiency, increase program clarity, and reduce the need to document variable meanings. It looks like it's time to kiss those block-opening variable definitions good-bye.

Item 33: Use inlining judiciously.

Inline functions — what a *wonderful* idea! They look like functions, they act like functions, they're ever so much better than macros (see Item 1), and you can call them without having to incur the overhead of a function call. What more could you possibly ask for?

You actually get more than you might think, because avoiding the cost of a function call is only half the story. Compiler optimization routines are typically designed to concentrate on stretches of code that lack function calls, so when you inline a function, you may enable compilers to perform context-specific optimizations on the body of the function. Such optimizations would be impossible for "normal" function calls.

However, let's not get carried away. In programming, as in life, there is no free lunch, and inline functions are no exception. The whole idea behind an inline function is to replace each call of that function with its code body, and it doesn't take a Ph.D. in statistics to see that this is likely to increase the overall size of your object code. On machines with limited memory, overzealous inlining can give rise to programs that are too big for the available space. Even with virtual memory, inline-induced code bloat can lead to pathological paging behavior (thrashing) that will slow your program to a crawl. (It will, however, provide your disk controller with a nice exercise regimen.) Too much inlining can also reduce your instruction cache hit rate, thus reducing the speed of instruction fetch from that of cache memory to that of primary memory.

On the other hand, if an inline function body is *very* short, the code generated for the function body may actually be smaller than the code generated for a function call. If that is the case, inlining the function may actually lead to *smaller* object code and a higher cache hit rate!

Bear in mind that the `inline` directive, like `register`, is a *hint* to compilers, not a command. That means compilers are free to ignore your inline directives whenever they want to, and it's not that hard to make them want to. For example, most compilers refuse to inline "complicated" functions (e.g., those that contain loops or are recursive), and all but the most trivial virtual function calls stop inlining routines dead in their tracks. (This shouldn't be much of a surprise. `virtual` means "wait until runtime to figure out which function to call," and `inline` means "during compilation, replace the call site with the called function." If compilers don't know which function will be called, you can hardly blame them for refusing to make an inline call to it.) It all adds up to this: whether a given inline function is actually inlined is dependent on the implementation of the compiler you're using. Fortunately, most compilers have a diagnostic level that will result in a warning (see Item 48) if they fail to inline a function you've asked them to.

Suppose you've written some function f and you've declared it `inline`. What happens if a compiler chooses, for whatever reason, not to inline that function? The obvious answer is that f will be treated like a non-inline function: code for f will be generated as if it were a normal "outlined" function, and calls to f will proceed as normal function calls.

In theory, this is precisely what will happen, but this is one of those occasions when theory and practice may go their separate ways. That's because this very tidy solution to the problem of what to do about "outlined inlines" was added to C++ relatively late in the standardization process. Earlier specifications for the language (such as the ARM — see Item 50) told compiler vendors to implement different behavior, and the older behavior is still common enough that you need to understand what it is.

Think about it for a minute, and you'll realize that inline function definitions are virtually always put in header files. This allows multiple translation units (source files) to include the same header files and reap the advantages of the inline functions that are defined within them. Here's an example, in which I adopt the convention that source files end in ".cpp"; this is probably the most prevalent of the file naming conventions in the world of C++:

```
// This is file example.h
inline void f() { ... }          // definition of f

...


// This is file source1.cpp
#include "example.h"              // includes definition of f

...                              // contains calls to f


// This is file source2.cpp
#include "example.h"              // also includes definition
                                 // of f

...                              // also calls f
```

Under the old "outlined inline" rules and the assumption that f is *not* being inlined, when source1.cpp is compiled, the resulting object file will contain a function called f, just as if f had never been declared inline. Similarly, when source2.cpp is compiled, its generated object file will also hold a function called f. When you try to link the two object files together, you can reasonably expect your linker to complain that your program contains two definitions of f, an error.

To prevent this problem, the old rules decreed that compilers treat an un-inlined inline function as if the function had been declared static — that is, local to the file currently being compiled. In the example you just saw, compilers following the old rules would treat f as if it were static in source1.cpp when that file was being compiled and as if it were static in source2.cpp when that file was being compiled. This strategy eliminates the link-time problem, but at a cost: each translation unit that includes the definition of f (and that calls f) contains its own static copy of f. If f itself defines local static variables, each copy of f gets its *own copy* of the variables, something sure to astonish programmers who believe that "static" inside a function means "only one copy."

This leads to a stunning realization. Under both new rules and old, if an inline function isn't inlined, you *still* pay for the cost of a function call at each call site, but under the old rules, you can *also* suffer an increase in code size, because each translation unit that includes and calls f gets its own copy of f's code and f's static variables! (To make matters worse, each copy of f and each copy of f's static variables tend to end up on different virtual memory pages, so two calls to different copies of f are likely to entail one or more page faults.)

There's more. Sometimes your poor, embattled compilers have to generate a function body for an inline function even when they are perfectly willing to inline the function. In particular, if your program ever takes the address of an inline function, compilers must generate a function body for it. How can they come up with a pointer to a function that doesn't exist?

```
inline void f() {...}              // as above
void (*pf)() = f;                  // pf points to f
int main()
{
  f();                             // an inline call to f
  pf();                            // a non-inline call to f
                                   // through pf
  ...
}
```

In this case, you end up in the seemingly paradoxical situation whereby calls to f are inlined, but — under the old rules — each translation unit that takes f's address still generates a static copy of the function. (Under the new rules, only a single out-of-line copy of f will be generated, regardless of the number of translation units involved.)

This aspect of un-inlined inline functions can affect you even if you never use function pointers, because programmers aren't necessarily the only ones asking for pointers to functions. Sometimes compilers do it. In particular, compilers sometimes generate out-of-line copies of constructors and destructors so that they can get pointers to those functions for use in constructing and destructing arrays of objects of a class.

In fact, constructors and destructors are often worse candidates for inlining than a casual examination would indicate. For example, consider the constructor for class Derived below:

```
class Base {
public:
  ...
private:
  string bm1, bm2;                 // base members 1 and 2
};
class Derived: public Base {
public:
  Derived() {}                     // Derived's ctor is
  ...                              // empty — or is it?
```

```
private:
  string dm1, dm2, dm3;          // derived members 1-3
};
```

This constructor certainly looks like an excellent candidate for inlining, since it contains no code. But looks can be deceiving. Just because it contains no code doesn't necessarily mean it contains no code. In fact, it may contain a fair amount of code.

C++ makes various guarantees about things that happen when objects are created and destroyed. Item 5 describes how when you use new, your dynamically created objects are automatically initialized by their constructors, and how when you use delete, the corresponding destructors are invoked. Item 13 explains that when you create an object, each base class of and each data member in that object is automatically constructed, and the reverse process regarding destruction automatically occurs when an object is destroyed. Those items describe what C++ says must happen, but C++ does not say *how* they happen. That's up to compiler implementers, but it should be clear that those things don't just happen by themselves. There has to be some code in your program to make those things happen, and that code — the code written by compiler implementers and inserted into your program during compilation — has to go somewhere. Sometimes, it ends up in your constructors and destructors, so some implementations will generate code equivalent to the following for the allegedly empty Derived constructor above:

```
// possible implementation of Derived constructor
 Derived::Derived()
{
  // allocate heap memory for this object if it's supposed
  // to be on the heap; see Item 8 for info on operator new
  if (this object is on the heap)
    this = ::operator new(sizeof(Derived));

  Base::Base();                    // initialize Base part

  dm1.string();                    // construct dm1
  dm2.string();                    // construct dm2
  dm3.string();                    // construct dm3
}
```

You could never hope to get code like this to compile, because it's not legal C++ — not for you, anyway. For one thing, you have no way of asking whether an object is on the heap from inside its constructor. For another, you're forbidden from assigning to this. And you can't invoke constructors via function calls, either. Your compilers, however, labor under no such constraints — they can do whatever they like. But the legality of the code is not the point. The point is that code to call operator new (if necessary), to construct base class parts, and to construct data members may be silently inserted into your constructors, and when it is, those constructors increase in size, thus making them less attractive candidates for inlining. Of course, the same reasoning applies to the Base constructor, so if it's inlined, all the code inserted into it is also inserted into the Derived constructor (via the Derived constructor's call to the Base constructor). And if the string constructor also happens to be inlined, the Derived constructor will gain *five copies* of that function's code, one for each of the five strings in a Derived object (the two it inherits plus the three it declares itself). Now do you see why it's not necessarily a no-brain decision whether to inline Derived's constructor? Of course, similar considerations apply to Derived's destructor, which, one way or another, must see to it that all the objects initialized by Derived's constructor are properly destroyed. It may also need to free the dynamically allocated memory formerly occupied by the just-destroyed Derived object.

Library designers must evaluate the impact of declaring functions inline, because inline functions make it impossible to provide binary upgrades to the inline functions in a library. In other words, if f is an inline function in a library, clients of the library compile the body of f into their applications. If a library implementer later decides to change f, all clients who've used f must recompile. This is often highly undesirable (see also Item 34). On the other hand, if f is a non-inline function, a modification to f requires only that clients relink. This is a substantially less onerous burden than recompiling and, if the library containing the function is dynamically linked, one that may be absorbed in a way that's completely transparent to clients.

For purposes of program development, it is important to keep all these considerations in mind, but from a purely practical point of view during coding, one fact dominates all others: most debuggers have trouble with inline functions.

This should be no great revelation. How do you set a breakpoint in a function that isn't there? How do you step through such a function? How do you trap calls to it? Without being unreasonably clever (or deviously underhanded), you simply can't. Happily, this leads to a logical strategy for determining which functions should be declared inline and which should not.

Initially, don't inline anything, or at least limit your inlining to those functions that are truly trivial, such as age below:

```
class Person {
public:
  int age() const { return personAge; }

  ...

private:
  int personAge;

  ...

};
```

By employing inlines cautiously, you facilitate your use of a debugger, but you also put inlining in its proper place: as a hand-applied optimization. Don't forget the empirically determined rule of 80-20, which states that a typical program spends 80 percent of its time executing only 20 percent of its code. It's an important rule, because it reminds you that your goal as a software developer is to identify the 20 percent of your code that is actually capable of increasing your program's overall performance. You can inline and otherwise tweak your functions until the cows come home, but it's all wasted effort unless you're focusing on the *right* functions.

Once you've identified the set of important functions in your application, the ones whose inlining will actually make a difference (a set that is itself dependent on the architecture on which you're running), don't hesitate to declare them inline. At the same time, however, be on the lookout for problems caused by code bloat, and watch out for compiler warnings (see Item 48) that indicate that your inline functions haven't been inlined.

Used judiciously, inline functions are an invaluable component of every C++ programmer's toolbox, but, as the foregoing discussion has revealed, they're not quite as simple and straightforward as you might have thought.

Item 34: Minimize compilation dependencies between files.

So you go into your C++ program and you make a minor change to the implementation of a class. Not the class interface, mind you, just the implementation; only the private stuff. Then you get set to rebuild the program, figuring that the compilation and linking should take only a few seconds. After all, only one class has been modified. You click on Rebuild or type make (or its moral equivalent), and you are astonished, then mortified, as you realize that the whole *world* is being recompiled and relinked!

Don't you just *hate* it when that happens?

The problem is that C++ doesn't do a very good job of separating interfaces from implementations. In particular, class definitions include not only the interface specification, but also a fair number of implementation details. For example:

```
class Person {
public:
  Person(const string& name, const Date& birthday,
         const Address& addr, const Country& country);
  virtual ~Person();

    ...                        // copy constructor and assignment
                               // operator omitted for simplicity
  string name() const;
  string birthDate() const;
  string address() const;
  string nationality() const;

private:
  string name_;              // implementation detail
  Date birthDate_;           // implementation detail
  Address address_;          // implementation detail
  Country citizenship_;      // implementation detail
};
```

This is hardly a Nobel Prize-winning class design, although it does illustrate an interesting naming convention for distinguishing private data from public functions when the same name makes sense for both: the former are tagged with a trailing underbar. The important thing to observe is that class Person can't be compiled unless the compiler also has access to definitions for the classes in terms of which Person is implemented, namely, string, Date, Address, and Country. Such definitions are typically provided through #include directives, so at the top of the file defining the Person class, you are likely to find something like this:

```
#include <string>         // for type string (see Item 49)
#include "date.h"
#include "address.h"
#include "country.h"
```

Unfortunately, this sets up a compilation dependency between the file defining Person and these include files. As a result, if any of these auxiliary classes changes its implementation, or if any of the classes on which it depends changes *its* implementation, the file containing the Person class must be recompiled, as must any files that use the Person class. For clients of Person, this can be more than annoying. It can be downright incapacitating.

You might wonder why C++ insists on putting the implementation details of a class in the class definition. For example, why can't you define Person this way,

```
class string;     // "conceptual" forward declaration for the
                  // string type. See Item 49 for details.

class Date;       // forward declaration
class Address;    // forward declaration
class Country;    // forward declaration

class Person {
public:
  Person(const string& name, const Date& birthday,
         const Address& addr, const Country& country);
  virtual ~Person();

  ...                             // copy ctor, operator=

  string name() const;
  string birthDate() const;
  string address() const;
  string nationality() const;
};
```

specifying the implementation details of the class separately? If that were possible, clients of Person would have to recompile only if the interface to the class changed. Because interfaces tend to stabilize before implementations do, such a separation of interface from implementation could save untold hours of recompilation and linking over the course of a large software effort.

Alas, the real world intrudes on this idyllic scenario, as you will appreciate when you consider something like this:

```
int main()
{
  int x;              // define an int

  Person p(...);      // define a Person
                      // (arguments omitted for
  ...                 // simplicity)

}
```

When compilers see the definition for x, they know they must allocate enough space to hold an int. No problem. Each compiler knows how big an int is. When compilers see the definition for p, however, they know they have to allocate enough space for a Person, but how are they supposed to know how big a Person object is? The only way they can get that information is to consult the class definition, but if it were legal for a class definition to omit the implementation details, how would compilers know how much space to allocate?

In principle, this is no insuperable problem. Languages such as Small-talk, Eiffel, and Java get around it all the time. The way they do it is by allocating only enough space for a *pointer* to an object when an object is defined. That is, they handle the code above as if it had been written like this:

```
int main()
{
  int x;                          // define an int

  Person *p;                      // define a pointer
                                  // to a Person

  ...
}
```

It may have occurred to you that this is in fact legal C++, and it turns out that you can play the "hide the object implementation behind a pointer" game yourself.

Here's how you employ the technique to decouple Person's interface from its implementation. First, you put only the following in the header file declaring the Person class:

```
// compilers still need to know about these type
// names for the Person constructor
class string;     // again, see Item 49 for information
                  // on why this isn't correct for string
class Date;
class Address;
class Country;

// class PersonImpl will contain the implementation
// details of a Person object; this is just a
// forward declaration of the class name
class PersonImpl;

class Person {
public:
  Person(const string& name, const Date& birthday,
         const Address& addr, const Country& country);
  virtual ~Person();

  ...                             // copy ctor, operator=

  string name() const;
  string birthDate() const;
  string address() const;
  string nationality() const;

private:
  PersonImpl *impl;               // pointer to implementation
};
```

Now clients of `Person` are completely divorced from the details of strings, dates, addresses, countries, and persons. Those classes can be modified at will, but `Person` clients may remain blissfully unaware. More to the point, they may remain blissfully un-recompiled. In addition, because they're unable to see the details of `Person`'s implementation, clients are unlikely to write code that somehow depends on those details. This is a true separation of interface and implementation.

The key to this separation is replacement of dependencies on class *definitions* with dependencies on class *declarations*. That's all you need to know about minimizing compilation dependencies: make your header files self-sufficient whenever it's practical, and when it's not practical, be dependent on class declarations, not class definitions. Everything else flows from this simple design strategy.

There are three immediate implications:

- **Avoid using objects when object references and pointers will do**. You may define references and pointers to a type with only a *declaration* for the type. Defining *objects* of a type necessitates the presence of the type's definition.

- **Use class declarations instead of class definitions whenever you can**. Note that you *never* need a class definition to declare a function using that class, not even if the function passes or returns the class type by value:

```
class Date;                    // class declaration

Date returnADate();            // fine — no definition
void takeADate(Date d);        // of Date is needed
```

Of course, pass-by-value is generally a bad idea (see Item 22), but if you find yourself forced to use it for some reason, there's still no justification for introducing unnecessary compilation dependencies.

If you're surprised that the declarations for `returnADate` and `takeADate` compile without a definition for `Date`, join the club; so was I. It's not as curious as it seems, however, because if anybody *calls* those functions, `Date`'s definition must be visible. Oh, I know what you're thinking: why bother to declare functions that nobody calls? Simple. It's not that *nobody* calls them, it's that *not everybody* calls them. For example, if you have a library containing hundreds of function declarations (possibly spread over several namespaces — see Item 28), it's unlikely that every client calls every function. By moving the onus of providing class definitions (via

#include directives) from your header file of function *declarations* to clients' files containing function *calls*, you eliminate artificial client dependencies on type definitions they don't really need.

- **Don't #include header files in your header files unless your headers won't compile without them**. Instead, manually declare the classes you need, and let clients of your header files #include the additional headers necessary to make *their* code compile. A few clients may grumble that this is inconvenient, but rest assured that you are saving them much more pain than you're inflicting. In fact, this technique is so well-regarded, it's enshrined in the standard C++ library (see Item 49); the header <iosfwd> contains declarations (and only declarations) for the types in the iostream library.

Classes like Person that contain only a pointer to an unspecified implementation are often called *Handle* classes or *Envelope* classes. (In the former case, the classes they point to are called *Body* classes; in latter case, the pointed-to classes are known as *Letter* classes.) Occasionally, you may hear people refer to such classes as *Cheshire Cat* classes, an allusion to the cat in *Alice in Wonderland* that could, when it chose, leave behind only its smile after the rest of it had vanished.

Lest you wonder how Handle classes actually do anything, the answer is simple: they forward all their function calls to the corresponding Body classes, and those classes do the real work. For example, here's how two of Person's member functions would be implemented:

```
#include "Person.h"        // because we're implementing
                           // the Person class, we must
                           // #include its class definition

#include "PersonImpl.h"    // we must also #include
                           // PersonImpl's class definition,
                           // otherwise we couldn't call
                           // its member functions. Note
                           // that PersonImpl has exactly
                           // the same member functions as
                           // Person — their interfaces
                           // are identical

Person::Person(const string& name, const Date& birthday,
               const Address& addr, const Country& country)
{
  impl = new PersonImpl(name, birthday, addr, country);
}
```

```
string Person::name() const
{
  return impl->name();
}
```

Note how the Person constructor calls the PersonImpl constructor (implicitly, by using new — see Item 5) and how Person::name calls PersonImpl::name. This is important. Making Person a handle class doesn't change what Person does, it just changes where it does it.

An alternative to the Handle class approach is to make Person a special kind of abstract base class called a *Protocol class*. By definition, a Protocol class has no implementation; its *raison d'être* is to specify an interface for derived classes (see Item 36). As a result, it typically has no data members, no constructors, a virtual destructor (see Item 14), and a set of pure virtual functions that specify the interface. A Protocol class for Person might look like this:

```
class Person {
public:
  virtual ~Person();

  virtual string name() const = 0;
  virtual string birthDate() const = 0;
  virtual string address() const = 0;
  virtual string nationality() const = 0;
};
```

Clients of this Person class must program in terms of Person pointers and references, because it's not possible to instantiate classes containing pure virtual functions. (It is, however, possible to instantiate classes *derived* from Person — see below.) Like clients of Handle classes, clients of Protocol classes need not recompile unless the Protocol class's interface is modified.

Of course, clients of a Protocol class must have *some* way of creating new objects. They typically do it by calling a function that plays the role of the constructor for the hidden (derived) classes that are actually instantiated. Such functions go by several names (among them *factory functions* and *virtual constructors*), but they all behave the same way: they return pointers to dynamically allocated objects that support the Protocol class's interface. Such a function might be declared like this,

```
// makePerson is a "virtual constructor" (aka, a "factory
// function") for objects supporting the Person interface
Person*
  makePerson( const string& name,       // return a ptr to
              const Date& birthday,     // a new Person
              const Address& addr,      // initialized with
              const Country& country);  // the given params
```

and used by clients like this:

```
string name;
Date dateOfBirth;
Address address;
Country nation;

...

// create an object supporting the Person interface
Person *pp = makePerson(name, dateOfBirth, address, nation);

...

cout << pp->name()              // use the object via the
     << " was born on "         // Person interface
     << pp->birthDate()
     << " and now lives at "
     << pp->address();

...

delete pp;                      // delete the object when
                                // it's no longer needed
```

Because functions like makePerson are closely associated with the Protocol class whose interface is supported by the objects they create, it's good style to declare them static inside the Protocol class:

```
class Person {
public:
  ...                           // as above

// makePerson is now a member of the class
static Person * makePerson( const  string& name,
                            const Date& birthday,
                            const Address& addr,
                            const Country& country);
};
```

This avoids cluttering the global namespace (or any other namespace) with lots of functions of this nature (see also Item 28).

At some point, of course, concrete classes supporting the Protocol class's interface must be defined and real constructors must be called. That all happens behind the scenes inside the implementation files for the virtual constructors. For example, the Protocol class Person might have a concrete derived class RealPerson that provides implementations for the virtual functions it inherits:

```
class RealPerson: public Person {
public:
  RealPerson(const string& name, const Date& birthday,
             const Address& addr, const Country& country)
  : name_(name), birthday_(birthday),
    address_(addr), country_(country)
  {}
```

```
    virtual ~RealPerson() {}
    string name() const;          // implementations of
    string birthDate() const;     // these functions are not
    string address() const;       // shown, but they are
    string nationality() const;   // easy to imagine
  private:
    string name_;
    Date birthday_;
    Address address_;
    Country country_;
  };
```

Given RealPerson, it is truly trivial to write Person::makePerson:

```
Person * Person::makePerson(const string& name,
                            const Date& birthday,
                            const Address& addr,
                            const Country& country)
{
  return new RealPerson(name, birthday, addr, country);
}
```

RealPerson demonstrates one of the two most common mechanisms for implementing a Protocol class: it inherits its interface specification from the Protocol class (Person), then it implements the functions in the interface. A second way to implement a Protocol class involves multiple inheritance, a topic explored in Item 43.

Okay, so Handle classes and Protocol classes decouple interfaces from implementations, thereby reducing compilation dependencies between files. Cynic that you are, I know you're waiting for the fine print. "What does all this hocus-pocus cost me?" you mutter. The answer is the usual one in Computer Science: it costs you some speed at runtime, plus some additional memory per object.

In the case of Handle classes, member functions have to go through the implementation pointer to get to the object's data. That adds one level of indirection per access. And you must add the size of this implementation pointer to the amount of memory required to store each object. Finally, the implementation pointer has to be initialized (in the Handle class's constructors) to point to a dynamically allocated implementation object, so you incur the overhead inherent in dynamic memory allocation (and subsequent deallocation) — see Item 10.

For Protocol classes, every function call is virtual, so you pay the cost of an indirect jump each time you make a function call (see Item 14). Also, objects derived from the Protocol class must contain a virtual table pointer (again, see Item 14). This pointer may increase the amount of memory needed to store an object, depending on whether the Protocol class is the exclusive source of virtual functions for the object.

Finally, neither Handle classes nor Protocol classes can get much use out of inline functions. All practical uses of inlines require access to implementation details, and that's the very thing that Handle classes and Protocol classes are designed to avoid in the first place.

It would be a serious mistake, however, to dismiss Handle classes and Protocol classes simply because they have a cost associated with them. So do virtual functions, and you wouldn't want to forgo those, would you? (If so, you're reading the wrong book.) Instead, consider using these techniques in an evolutionary manner. Use Handle classes and Protocol classes during development to minimize the impact on clients when implementations change. Replace Handle classes and Protocol classes with concrete classes for production use when it can be shown that the difference in speed and/or size is significant enough to justify the increased coupling between classes. Someday, we may hope, tools will be available to perform this kind of transformation automatically.

A skillful blending of Handle classes, Protocol classes, and concrete classes will allow you to develop software systems that execute efficiently and are easy to evolve, but there is a serious disadvantage: you may have to cut down on the long breaks you've been taking while your programs recompile.

Inheritance and Object-Oriented Design

Many people are of the opinion that inheritance is what object-oriented programming is all about. Whether that's so is debatable, but the number of Items in the other sections of this book should convince you that as far as effective C++ programming is concerned, you have a lot more tools at your disposal than simply specifying which classes inherit from which other classes.

Still, designing and implementing class hierarchies is fundamentally different from anything found in the world of C. Certainly it is in the area of inheritance and object-oriented design that you are most likely to radically rethink your approach to the construction of software systems. Furthermore, C++ provides a bewildering assortment of object-oriented building blocks, including public, protected, and private base classes; virtual and nonvirtual base classes; and virtual and nonvirtual member functions. Each of these features interacts not only with one another, but also with the other components of the language. As a result, trying to understand what each feature means, when it should be used, and how it is best combined with the non-object-oriented aspects of C++ can be a daunting endeavor.

Further complicating the matter is the fact that different features of the language appear to do more or less the same thing. Examples:

- You need a collection of classes with many shared characteristics. Should you use inheritance and have all the classes derived from a common base class, or should you use templates and have them all generated from a common code skeleton?

- Class A is to be implemented in terms of class B. Should A have a data member of type B, or should A privately inherit from B?

- You need to design a type-safe homogeneous container class, one not present in the standard library. (See Item 49 for a list of containers the library *does* provide.) Should you use templates, or would it be better to build type-safe interfaces around a class that is itself implemented using generic (void*) pointers?

In the Items in this section, I offer guidance on how to answer questions such as these. However, I cannot hope to address every aspect of object-oriented design. Instead, I concentrate on explaining what the different features in C++ really *mean*, on what you are really *saying* when you use a particular feature. For example, public inheritance means "isa" (see Item 35), and if you try to make it mean anything else, you will run into trouble. Similarly, a virtual function means "interface must be inherited," while a nonvirtual function means "both interface *and* implementation must be inherited." Failing to distinguish between these meanings has caused many a C++ programmer untold grief.

If you understand the meanings of C++'s varied features, you'll find that your outlook on object-oriented design shifts. Instead of it being an exercise in differentiating between language constructs, it will properly become a matter of figuring out what it is you want to say about your software system. Once you know what you want to say, you'll be able to translate that into the appropriate C++ features without too much difficulty.

The importance of saying what you mean and understanding what you're saying cannot be overestimated. The items that follow provide a detailed examination of how to do this effectively. Item 44 summarizes the correspondence between C++'s object-oriented constructs and what they mean. It serves as a nice capstone for this section, as well as a concise reference for future consultation.

Item 35: Make sure public inheritance models "isa."

In his book, *Some Must Watch While Some Must Sleep* (W. H. Freeman and Company, 1974), William Dement relates the story of his attempt to fix in the minds of his students the most important lessons of his course. It is claimed, he told his class, that the average British schoolchild remembers little more history than that the Battle of Hastings was in 1066. If a child remembers little else, Dement emphasized, he or she remembers the date 1066. For the students in *his* course, Dement went on, there were only a few central messages, including, interestingly enough, the fact that sleeping pills cause insomnia. He implored his students to remember these few critical facts even if they forgot everything else discussed in the course, and he returned to these fundamental precepts repeatedly during the term.

At the end of the course, the last question on the final exam was, "Write one thing from the course that you will surely remember for the rest of your life." When Dement graded the exams, he was stunned. Nearly everyone had written "1066."

It is thus with great trepidation that I proclaim to you now that the single most important rule in object-oriented programming with C++ is this: public inheritance means "isa." Commit this rule to memory.

If you write that class D ("Derived") publicly inherits from class B ("Base"), you are telling C++ compilers (as well as human readers of your code) that every object of type D is also an object of type B, but *not vice versa*. You are saying that B represents a more general concept than D, that D represents a more specialized concept than B. You are asserting that anywhere an object of type B can be used, an object of type D can be used just as well, because every object of type D *is* an object of type B. On the other hand, if you need an object of type D, an object of type B will not do: every D isa B, but not vice versa.

C++ enforces this interpretation of public inheritance. Consider this example:

```
class Person { ... };

class Student: public Person { ... };
```

We know from everyday experience that every student is a person, but not every person is a student. That is exactly what this hierarchy asserts. We expect that anything that is true of a person — for example, that he or she has a date of birth — is also true of a student, but we do not expect that everything that is true of a student — that he or she is enrolled in a particular school, for instance — is true of people in general. The notion of a person is more general than is that of a student; a student is a specialized type of person.

Within the realm of C++, any function that expects an argument of type Person (or pointer-to-Person or reference-to-Person) will instead take a Student object (or pointer-to-Student or reference-to-Student):

```
void dance(const Person& p);   // anyone can dance

void study(const Student& s);  // only students study

Person p;                      // p is a Person
Student s;                     // s is a Student

dance(p);                      // fine, p is a Person
```

```
dance(s);                    // fine, s is a Student,
                             // and a Student isa Person

study(s);                    // fine

study(p);                    // error! p isn't a Student
```

This is true only for *public* inheritance. C++ will behave as I've described only if Student is publicly derived from Person. Private inheritance means something entirely different (see Item 42), and no one seems to know what protected inheritance is supposed to mean.

The equivalence of public inheritance and isa sounds simple, but in practice, things aren't always so straightforward. Sometimes your intuition can mislead you. For example, it is a fact that a penguin is a bird, and it is a fact that birds can fly. If we naively try to express this in C++, our effort yields:

```
class Bird {
public:
  virtual void fly();          // birds can fly

  ...

};

class Penguin: public Bird {    // penguins are birds

  ...

};
```

Suddenly we are in trouble, because this hierarchy says that penguins can fly, which we know is not true. What happened?

In this case, we are the victims of an imprecise language (English). When we say that birds can fly, we don't really mean that *all* birds can fly, only that, in general, birds have the ability to fly. If we were more precise, we'd recognize that there are in fact several types of non-flying birds, and we would come up with the following hierarchy, which models reality much better:

```
class Bird {
  ...                          // no fly function is
};                             // declared
class FlyingBird: public Bird {
public:
  virtual void fly();
  ...
};
```

```
class NonFlyingBird: public Bird {

    ...                                // no fly function is
                                       // declared
};

class Penguin: public NonFlyingBird {

    ...                                // no fly function is
                                       // declared
};
```

This hierarchy is much more faithful to what we really know than was the original design.

Even now we're not entirely finished with these fowl matters, because for some software systems, it may be entirely appropriate to say that a penguin isa bird. In particular, if your application has much to do with beaks and wings and nothing to do with flying, the original hierarchy might work out just fine. Irritating though this may seem, it's a simple reflection of the fact that there is no one ideal design for all software. The best design depends on what the system is expected to do, both now and in the future. If your application has no knowledge of flying and isn't expected to ever have any, making Penguin a derived class of Bird may be a perfectly valid design decision. In fact, it may be preferable to a decision that makes a distinction between flying and non-flying birds, because such a distinction would be absent from the world you are trying to model. Adding superfluous classes to a hierarchy can be just as bad a design decision as having the wrong inheritance relationships between classes.

There is another school of thought on how to handle what I call the "All birds can fly, penguins are birds, penguins can't fly, uh oh" problem. That is to redefine the fly function for penguins so that it generates a runtime error:

```
void error(const string& msg); // defined elsewhere

class Penguin: public Bird {
public:
  virtual void fly() { error("Penguins can't fly!"); }

    ...

};
```

Interpreted languages such as Smalltalk tend to adopt this approach, but it's important to recognize that this says something entirely different from what you might think. This does *not* say, "Penguins can't fly." This says, "Penguins can fly, but it's an error for them to try to do so."

How can you tell the difference? From the time at which the error is detected. The injunction, "Penguins can't fly," can be enforced by compilers, but violations of the statement, "It's an error for penguins to try to fly," can be detected only at runtime.

To express the constraint, "Penguins can't fly," you make sure that no such function is defined for Penguin objects:

```
class Bird {

    ...                         // no fly function is
                                // declared
};

class NonFlyingBird: public Bird {

    ...                         // no fly function is
                                // declared
};

class Penguin: public NonFlyingBird {

    ...                         // no fly function is
                                // declared
};
```

If you try to make a penguin fly, compilers will reprimand you for your transgression:

```
Penguin p;

p.fly();                        // error!
```

This is very different from the behavior you get if you use the Smalltalk approach. With that methodology, compilers won't say a word.

The C++ philosophy is fundamentally different from the Smalltalk philosophy, so you're better off doing things the C++ way as long as you're programming in C++. In addition, there are certain technical advantages to detecting errors during compilation instead of at runtime — see Item 46.

Perhaps you'll concede that your ornithological intuition may be lacking, but you can rely on your mastery of elementary geometry, right? I mean, how complicated can rectangles and squares be?

Well, answer this simple question: should class Square publicly inherit from class Rectangle?

"Duh!" you say, "Of course it should! Everybody knows that a square is a rectangle, but generally not vice versa." True enough, at least in high school. But I don't think we're in high school anymore.

Consider this code:

```
class Rectangle {
public:
  virtual void setHeight(int newHeight);
  virtual void setWidth(int newWidth);

  virtual int height() const;        // return current
  virtual int width() const;         // values

  ...

};
  void makeBigger(Rectangle& r)      // function to
  {                                  // increase r's area
    int oldHeight = r.height();

    r.setWidth(r.width() + 10);      // add 10 to r's width

    assert(r.height() == oldHeight); // assert that r's
  }                                  // height is unchanged
```

Clearly, the assertion should never fail. makeBigger only changes r's width. Its height is never modified.

Now consider this code, which uses public inheritance to allow squares to be treated like rectangles:

```
class Square: public Rectangle { ... };

Square s;

...

assert(s.width() == s.height());     // this must be true
                                     // for all squares

makeBigger(s);                       // by inheritance, s
                                     // isa Rectangle, so
                                     // we can increase its
                                     // area

assert(s.width() == s.height());     // this must still be
                                     // true for all squares
```

It's just as clear here as it was above that this last assertion should also never fail. By definition, the width of a square is the same as its height.

But now we have a problem. How can we reconcile the following assertions?

- Before calling makeBigger, s's height is the same as its width;

- Inside makeBigger, s's width is changed, but its height is not;

- After returning from makeBigger, s's height is again the same as its width. (Note that s is passed to makeBigger by reference, so makeBigger modifies s itself, not a copy of s.)

Well?

Welcome to the wonderful world of public inheritance, where the instincts you've developed in other fields of study — including mathematics — may not serve you as well as you expect. The fundamental difficulty in this case is that something applicable to a rectangle (its width may be modified independently of its height) is not applicable to a square (its width and height are constrained to be the same). But public inheritance asserts that everything applicable to base class objects — *everything!* — is also applicable to derived class objects. In the case of rectangles and squares (and a similar example involving sets and lists in Item 40), that assertion fails to hold, so using public inheritance to model their relationship is just plain wrong. Compilers will let you do it, of course, but as we've just seen, that's no guarantee the code will behave properly. As every programmer must learn (some more often than others), just because the code compiles doesn't mean it will work.

Now, don't fret that the software intuition you've developed over the years will fail you as you approach object-oriented design. That knowledge is still valuable, but now that you've added inheritance to your arsenal of design alternatives, you'll have to augment your intuition with new insights to guide you in inheritance's proper application. In time, the notion of having Penguin inherit from Bird or Square inherit from Rectangle will give you the same funny feeling you probably get now when somebody shows you a function several pages long. It's *possible* that it's the right way to approach things, it's just not very likely.

Of course, the isa relationship is not the only one that can exist between classes. Two other common inter-class relationships are "has-a" and "is-implemented-in-terms-of." These relationships are considered in Items 40 and 42. It's not uncommon for C++ designs to go awry because one of these other important relationships was incorrectly modeled as isa, so you should make sure that you understand the differences between these relationships and that you know how they are best modeled in C++.

Item 36: Differentiate between inheritance of interface and inheritance of implementation.

The seemingly straightforward notion of (public) inheritance turns out, upon closer examination, to be composed of two separable parts: inheritance of function interfaces and inheritance of function implementations. The difference between these two kinds of inheritance corresponds exactly to the difference between function declarations and function definitions discussed in the Introduction to this book.

As a class designer, you sometimes want derived classes to inherit only the interface (declaration) of a member function; sometimes you want derived classes to inherit both the interface and the implementation for a function, but you want to allow them to override the implementation you provide; and sometimes you want them to inherit both interface and implementation without allowing them to override anything.

To get a better feel for the differences among these options, consider a class hierarchy for representing geometric shapes in a graphics application:

```
class Shape {
public:
  virtual void draw() const = 0;

  virtual void error(const string& msg);

  int objectID() const;

  ...

};

class Rectangle: public Shape { ... };

class Ellipse: public Shape { ... };
```

Shape is an abstract class; its pure virtual function draw marks it as such. As a result, clients cannot create instances of the Shape class, only of the classes derived from it. Nonetheless, Shape exerts a strong influence on all classes that (publicly) inherit from it, because

- Member function *interfaces are always inherited.* As explained in Item 35, public inheritance means isa, so anything that is true of a base class must also be true of its derived classes. Hence, if a function applies to a class, it must also apply to its subclasses.

Three functions are declared in the Shape class. The first, draw, draws the current object on an implicit display. The second, error, is called by member functions if they need to report an error. The third, objectID, returns a unique integer identifier for the current object; Item 17 gives an example of how such a function might be used. Each function is declared in a different way: draw is a pure virtual function; error is a simple (impure?) virtual function; and objectID is a nonvirtual function. What are the implications of these different declarations?

Consider first the pure virtual function draw. The two most salient features of pure virtual functions are that they *must* be redeclared by any concrete class that inherits them, and they typically have no definition in abstract classes. Put these two traits together, and you realize that

- The purpose of declaring a pure virtual function is to have derived classes inherit a function *interface only*.

This makes perfect sense for the Shape::draw function, because it is a reasonable demand that all Shape objects must be drawable, but the Shape class can provide no reasonable default implementation for that function. The algorithm for drawing an ellipse is very different from the algorithm for drawing a rectangle, for example. A good way to interpret the declaration of Shape::draw is as saying to designers of subclasses, "You must provide a draw function, but I have no idea how you're going to implement it."

Incidentally, it *is* possible to provide a definition for a pure virtual function. That is, you could provide an implementation for Shape::draw, and C++ wouldn't complain, but the only way to call it would be to fully specify the call with the class name:

```
Shape *ps = new Shape;              // error! Shape is abstract

Shape *ps1 = new Rectangle;         // fine
ps1->draw();                        // calls Rectangle::draw

Shape *ps2 = new Ellipse;           // fine
ps2->draw();                        // calls Ellipse::draw

ps1->Shape::draw();                 // calls Shape::draw

ps2->Shape::draw();                 // calls Shape::draw
```

Aside from helping impress fellow programmers at cocktail parties, knowledge of this feature is generally of limited utility. As you'll see below, however, it can be employed as a mechanism for providing a safer-than-usual default implementation for simple (impure) virtual functions.

Sometimes it's useful to declare a class containing *nothing* but pure virtual functions. Such a *Protocol class* can provide only function interfaces for derived classes, never implementations. Protocol classes are described in Item 34 and are mentioned again in Item 43.

The story behind simple virtual functions is a bit different from that behind pure virtuals. As usual, derived classes inherit the interface of the function, but simple virtual functions traditionally provide an implementation that derived classes may or may not choose to override. If you think about this for a minute, you'll realize that

- The purpose of declaring a simple virtual function is to have derived classes inherit a function *interface as well as a default implementation.*

In the case of Shape::error, the interface says that every class must support a function to be called when an error is encountered, but each class is free to handle errors in whatever way it sees fit. If a class doesn't want to do anything special, it can just fall back on the default error-handling provided in the Shape class. That is, the declaration of Shape::error says to designers of subclasses, "You've got to support an error function, but if you don't want to write your own, you can fall back on the default version in the Shape class."

It turns out that it can be dangerous to allow simple virtual functions to specify both a function declaration and a default implementation. To see why, consider a hierarchy of airplanes for XYZ Airlines. XYZ has only two kinds of planes, the Model A and the Model B, and both are flown in exactly the same way. Hence, XYZ designs the following hierarchy:

```
class Airport { ... };          // represents airports

class Airplane {
public:
  virtual void fly(const Airport& destination);

  ...

};

void Airplane::fly(const Airport& destination)
{
  default code for flying an airplane to
  the given destination
}

class ModelA: public Airplane { ... };

class ModelB: public Airplane { ... };
```

To express that all planes have to support a fly function, and in recognition of the fact that different models of plane could, in principle, require different implementations for fly, Airplane::fly is declared virtual. However, in order to avoid writing identical code in the ModelA and `ModelB` classes, the default flying behavior is provided as the body of `Airplane::fly`, which both `ModelA` and `ModelB` inherit.

This is a classic object-oriented design. Two classes share a common feature (the way they implement `fly`), so the common feature is moved into a base class, and the feature is inherited by the two classes. This design makes common features explicit, avoids code duplication, facilitates future enhancements, and eases long-term maintenance — all the things for which object-oriented technology is so highly touted. XYZ Airlines should be proud.

Now suppose that XYZ, its fortunes on the rise, decides to acquire a new type of airplane, the Model C. The Model C differs from the Model A and the Model B. In particular, it is flown differently.

XYZ's programmers add the class for Model C to the hierarchy, but in their haste to get the new model into service, they forget to redefine the `fly` function:

```
class ModelC: public Airplane {

    ...                             // no fly function is
                                    // declared
};
```

In their code, then, they have something akin to the following:

```
Airport JFK(...);               // JFK is an airport in
                                // New York City

Airplane *pa = new ModelC;

...

pa->fly(JFK);                   // calls Airplane::fly!
```

This is a disaster: an attempt is being made to fly a `ModelC` object as if it were a `ModelA` or a `ModelB`. That's not the kind of behavior that inspires confidence in the traveling public.

The problem here is not that `Airplane::fly` has default behavior, but that `ModelC` was allowed to inherit that behavior without explicitly saying that it wanted to. Fortunately, it's easy to offer default behavior to subclasses, but not give it to them unless they ask for it. The trick is to sever the connection between the *interface* of the virtual function and its default *implementation*. Here's one way to do it:

```
class Airplane {
public:
  virtual void fly(const Airport& destination) = 0;

  ...

protected:
  void defaultFly(const Airport& destination);
};
```

```
void Airplane::defaultFly(const Airport& destination)
{
  default code for flying an airplane to
  the given destination
}
```

Notice how `Airplane::fly` has been turned into a *pure* virtual function. That provides the interface for flying. The default implementation is also present in the `Airplane` class, but now it's in the form of an independent function, `defaultFly`. Classes like `ModelA` and `ModelB` that want to use the default behavior simply make an inline call to `defaultFly` inside their body of `fly` (but see Item 33 for information on the interaction of inlining and virtual functions):

```
class ModelA: public Airplane {
public:
  virtual void fly(const Airport& destination)
  { defaultFly(destination); }

  ...

};

class ModelB: public Airplane {
public:
  virtual void fly(const Airport& destination)
  { defaultFly(destination); }

  ...

};
```

For the `ModelC` class, there is no possibility of accidentally inheriting the incorrect implementation of `fly`, because the pure virtual in `Airplane` forces `ModelC` to provide its own version of `fly`.

```
class ModelC: public Airplane {
public:
  virtual void fly(const Airport& destination);

  ...

};

void ModelC::fly(const Airport& destination)
{
  code for flying a ModelC airplane to the given destination
}
```

This scheme isn't foolproof (programmers can still copy-and-paste themselves into trouble), but it's more reliable than the original design. As for `Airplane::defaultFly`, it's protected because it's truly an implementation detail of `Airplane` and its derived classes. Clients using airplanes should care only that they can be flown, not how the flying is implemented.

It's also important that `Airplane::defaultFly` is a *nonvirtual* function. This is because no subclass should redefine this function, a truth to which Item 37 is devoted. If `defaultFly` were virtual, you'd have a circular problem: what if some subclass forgets to redefine `default-Fly` when it's supposed to?

Some people object to the idea of having separate functions for providing interface and default implementation, such as `fly` and `default-Fly` above. For one thing, they note, it pollutes the class namespace with a proliferation of closely-related function names. Yet they still agree that interface and default implementation should be separated. How do they resolve this seeming contradiction? By taking advantage of the fact that pure virtual functions must be redeclared in subclasses, but they may also have implementations of their own. Here's how the `Airplane` hierarchy could take advantage of the ability to define a pure virtual function:

```
class Airplane {
public:
  virtual void fly(const Airport& destination) = 0;

  ...

};

void Airplane::fly(const Airport& destination)
{
  default code for flying an airplane to
  the given destination
}
class ModelA: public Airplane {
public:
  virtual void fly(const Airport& destination)
  { Airplane::fly(destination); }

  ...

};

class ModelB: public Airplane {
public:
  virtual void fly(const Airport& destination)
  { Airplane::fly(destination); }

  ...

};
```

```
class ModelC: public Airplane {
public:
  virtual void fly(const Airport& destination);

  ...

};

void ModelC::fly(const Airport& destination)
{
  code for flying a ModelC airplane to the given destination
}
```

This is almost exactly the same design as before, except that the body of the pure virtual function `Airplane::fly` takes the place of the independent function `Airplane::defaultFly`. In essence, `fly` has been broken into its two fundamental components. Its declaration specifies its interface (which derived classes *must* use), while its definition specifies its default behavior (which derived classes *may* use, but only if they explicitly request it). In merging `fly` and `defaultFly`, however, you've lost the ability to give the two functions different protection levels: the code that used to be `protected` (by being in `defaultFly`) is now `public` (because it's in `fly`).

Finally, we come to `Shape`'s nonvirtual function, `objectID`. When a member function is nonvirtual, it's not supposed to behave differently in derived classes. In fact, a nonvirtual member function specifies an *invariant over specialization*, because it identifies behavior that is not supposed to change, no matter how specialized a derived class becomes. As such,

- The purpose of declaring a nonvirtual function is to have derived classes inherit a function *interface as well as a mandatory implementation.*

You can think of the declaration for `Shape::objectID` as saying, "Every `Shape` object has a function that yields an object identifier, and that object identifier is always computed in the same way. That way is determined by the definition of `Shape::objectID`, and no derived class should try to change how it's done." Because a nonvirtual function identifies an *invariant* over specialization, it should never be redefined in a subclass, a point that is discussed in detail in Item 37.

The differences in declarations for pure virtual, simple virtual, and nonvirtual functions allow you to specify with precision what you want derived classes to inherit: interface only, interface and a default implementation, or interface and a mandatory implementation, respectively. Because these different types of declarations mean fundamentally different things, you must choose carefully among them when you declare your member functions. If you do, you should avoid the two most common mistakes made by inexperienced class designers.

The first mistake is to declare all functions nonvirtual. That leaves no room for specialization in derived classes; nonvirtual destructors are particularly problematic (see Item 14). Of course, it's perfectly reasonable to design a class that is not intended to be used as a base class. In that case, a set of exclusively nonvirtual member functions is appropriate. Too often, however, such classes are declared either out of ignorance of the differences between virtual and nonvirtual functions or as a result of an unsubstantiated concern over the performance cost of virtual functions. The fact of the matter is that almost any class that's to be used as a base class will have virtual functions (again, see Item 14).

If you're concerned about the cost of virtual functions, allow me to bring up the rule of 80-20 (see also Item 33), which states that in a typical program, 80 percent of the runtime will be spent executing just 20 percent of the code. This rule is important, because it means that, on average, 80 percent of your function calls can be virtual without having the slightest detectable impact on your program's overall performance. Before you go gray worrying about whether you can afford the cost of a virtual function, then, take the simple precaution of making sure that you're focusing on the 20 percent of your program where the decision might really make a difference.

The other common problem is to declare *all* member functions virtual. Sometimes this is the right thing to do — witness Protocol classes (see Item 34), for example. However, it can also be a sign of a class designer who lacks the backbone to take a firm stand. Some functions should *not* be redefinable in derived classes, and whenever that's the case, you've got to say so by making those functions nonvirtual. It serves no one to pretend that your class can be all things to all people if they'll just take the time to redefine all your functions. Remember that if you have a base class B, a derived class D, and a member function mf, then each of the following calls to mf *must* work properly:

```
D *pd = new D;
B *pb = pd;

pb->mf();                          // call mf through a
                                   // pointer-to-base

pd->mf();                          // call mf through a
                                   // pointer-to-derived
```

Sometimes, you must make mf a nonvirtual function to ensure that everything behaves the way it's supposed to (see Item 37). If you have an invariant over specialization, don't be afraid to say so!

Item 37: Never redefine an inherited nonvirtual function.

There are two ways of looking at this issue: the theoretical way and the pragmatic way. Let's start with the pragmatic way. After all, theoreticians are used to being patient.

Suppose I tell you that a class D is publicly derived from a class B and that there is a public member function mf defined in class B. The parameters and return type of mf are unimportant, so let's just assume they're both void. In other words, I say this:

```
class B {
public:
  void mf();
  ...
};

class D: public B { ... };
```

Even without knowing anything about B, D, or mf, given an object x of type D,

```
D x;                        // x is an object of type D
```

you would probably be quite surprised if this,

```
B *pB = &x;                 // get pointer to x

pB->mf();                   // call mf through pointer
```

behaved differently from this:

```
D *pD = &x;                 // get pointer to x

pD->mf();                   // call mf through pointer
```

That's because in both cases you're invoking the member function mf on the object x. Because it's the same function and the same object in both cases, it should behave the same way, right?

Right, it should. But it might not. In particular, it won't if mf is nonvirtual and D has defined its own version of mf:

```
class D: public B {
public:
  void mf();                // hides B::mf; see Item 50

  ...

};
```

```
pB->mf();                          // calls B::mf

pD->mf();                          // calls D::mf
```

The reason for this two-faced behavior is that *nonvirtual* functions like B::mf and D::mf are statically bound (see Item 38). That means that because pB is declared to be of type pointer-to-B, nonvirtual functions invoked through pB will *always* be those defined for class B, even if pB points to an object of a class derived from B, as it does in this example.

Virtual functions, on the other hand, are dynamically bound (again, see Item 38), so they don't suffer from this problem. If mf were a virtual function, a call to mf through either pB or pD would result in an invocation of D::mf, because what pB and pD *really* point to is an object of type D.

The bottom line, then, is that if you are writing class D and you redefine a nonvirtual function mf that you inherit from class B, D objects will likely exhibit schizophrenic behavior. In particular, any given D object may act like either a B or a D when mf is called, and the determining factor will have nothing to do with the object itself, but with the declared type of the pointer that points to it. References exhibit the same baffling behavior as do pointers.

So much for the pragmatic argument. What you want now, I know, is some kind of theoretical justification for not redefining inherited nonvirtual functions. I am pleased to oblige.

Item 35 explains that public inheritance means isa, and Item 36 describes why declaring a nonvirtual function in a class establishes an invariant over specialization for that class. If you apply these observations to the classes B and D and to the nonvirtual member function B::mf, then

- Everything that is applicable to B objects is also applicable to D objects, because every D object isa B object;

- Subclasses of B must inherit both the interface *and* the implementation of mf, because mf is nonvirtual in B.

Now, if D redefines mf, there is a contradiction in your design. If D *really* needs to implement mf differently from B, and if every B object — no matter how specialized — *really* has to use the B implementation for mf, then it's simply not true that every D isa B. In that case, D shouldn't publicly inherit from B. On the other hand, if D *really* has to publicly inherit from B, and if D *really* needs to implement mf differently from B, then it's just not true that mf reflects an invariant over specialization for B. In that case, mf should be virtual. Finally, if every D *really* isa B, and if mf really corresponds to an invariant over specialization for B, then D can't honestly need to redefine mf, and it shouldn't try to do so.

Regardless of which argument applies, something has to give, and under no conditions is it the prohibition on redefining an inherited nonvirtual function.

Item 38: Never redefine an inherited default parameter value.

Let's simplify this discussion right from the start. A default parameter can exist only as part of a function, and you can inherit only two kinds of functions: virtual and nonvirtual. Therefore, the only way to redefine a default parameter value is to redefine an inherited function. However, it's always a mistake to redefine an inherited nonvirtual function (see Item 37), so we can safely limit our discussion here to the situation in which you inherit a *virtual* function with a default parameter value.

That being the case, the justification for this Item becomes quite straightforward: virtual functions are dynamically bound, but default parameter values are statically bound.

What's that? You say you're not up on the latest object-oriented lingo, or perhaps the difference between static and dynamic binding has slipped your already overburdened mind? Let's review, then.

An object's *static type* is the type you declare it to have in the program text. Consider this class hierarchy:

```
enum ShapeColor { RED, GREEN, BLUE };

// a class for geometric shapes
class Shape {
public:
  // all shapes must offer a function to draw themselves
  virtual void draw(ShapeColor color = RED) const = 0;

  ...

};

class Rectangle: public Shape {
public:
  // notice the different default parameter value - bad!
  virtual void draw(ShapeColor color = GREEN) const;

  ...

};
```

```
class Circle: public Shape {
public:
  virtual void draw(ShapeColor color) const;

  ...

};
```

Graphically, it looks like this:

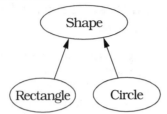

Now consider these pointers:

```
Shape *ps;                       // static type = Shape*

Shape *pc = new Circle;          // static type = Shape*

Shape *pr = new Rectangle;       // static type = Shape*
```

In this example, ps, pc, and pr are all declared to be of type pointer-to-Shape, so they all have that as their static type. Notice that it makes absolutely no difference what they're *really* pointing to — their static type is Shape* regardless.

An object's *dynamic type* is determined by the type of the object to which it currently refers. That is, its dynamic type indicates how it will behave. In the example above, pc's dynamic type is Circle*, and pr's dynamic type is Rectangle*. As for ps, it doesn't really have a dynamic type, because it doesn't refer to any object (yet).

Dynamic types, as their name suggests, can change as a program runs, typically through assignments:

```
ps = pc;                         // ps's dynamic type is
                                 // now Circle*

ps = pr;                         // ps's dynamic type is
                                 // now Rectangle*
```

Virtual functions are *dynamically bound*, meaning that the particular function called is determined by the dynamic type of the object through which it's invoked:

```
pc->draw(RED);                   // calls Circle::draw(RED)

pr->draw(RED);                   // calls Rectangle::draw(RED)
```

This is all old hat, I know; you surely understand virtual functions. The twist comes in when you consider virtual functions with default parameter values, because, as I said above, virtual functions are dynamically bound, but default parameters are statically bound. That means that you may end up invoking a virtual function defined in a *derived class* but using a default parameter value from a *base class*:

```
pr->draw();                        // calls Rectangle::draw(RED)!
```

In this case, pr's dynamic type is `Rectangle*`, so the `Rectangle` virtual function is called, just as you would expect. In `Rectangle::draw`, the default parameter value is GREEN. Because pr's static type is `Shape*`, however, the default parameter value for this function call is taken from the `Shape` class, not the `Rectangle` class! The result is a call consisting of a strange and almost certainly unanticipated combination of the declarations for draw in both the `Shape` and `Rectangle` classes. Trust me when I tell you that you don't want your software to behave this way, or at least believe me when I tell you that your *clients* won't want your software to behave this way.

Needless to say, the fact that ps, pc, and pr are pointers is of no consequence in this matter. Were they references, the problem would persist. The only important things are that draw is a virtual function, and one of its default parameter values is redefined in a subclass.

Why does C++ insist on acting in this perverse manner? The answer has to do with runtime efficiency. If default parameter values were dynamically bound, compilers would have to come up with a way of determining the appropriate default value(s) for parameters of virtual functions at runtime, which would be slower and more complicated than the current mechanism of determining them during compilation. The decision was made to err on the side of speed and simplicity of implementation, and the result is that you now enjoy execution behavior that is efficient, but, if you fail to heed the advice of this Item, confusing.

Item 39: Avoid casts down the inheritance hierarchy.

In these tumultuous economic times, it's a good idea to keep an eye on our financial institutions, so consider a Protocol class (see Item 34) for bank accounts:

```
class Person { ... };

class BankAccount {
public:
  BankAccount(const Person *primaryOwner,
              const Person *jointOwner);
  virtual ~BankAccount();

  virtual void makeDeposit(double amount) = 0;
  virtual void makeWithdrawal(double amount) = 0;

  virtual double balance() const = 0;

  ...

};
```

Many banks now offer a bewildering array of account types, but to keep things simple, let's assume there is only one type of bank account, namely, a savings account:

```
class SavingsAccount: public BankAccount {
public:
  SavingsAccount(const Person *primaryOwner,
              const Person *jointOwner);
  ~SavingsAccount();

  void creditInterest();          // add interest to account

  ...

};
```

This isn't much of a savings account, but then again, what *is* these days? At any rate, it's enough for our purposes.

A bank is likely to keep a list of all its accounts, perhaps implemented via the list class template from the standard library (see Item 49). Suppose this list is imaginatively named allAccounts:

```
list<BankAccount*> allAccounts;    // all accounts at the
                                   // bank
```

Like all standard containers, lists store *copies* of the things placed into them, so to avoid storing multiple copies of each BankAccount, the bank has decided to have allAccounts hold *pointers* to BankAccounts instead of BankAccounts themselves.

Now imagine you're supposed to write the code to iterate over all the accounts, crediting the interest due each one. You might try this,

```
// a loop that won't compile (see below if you've never
// seen code using "iterators" before)
for (list<BankAccount*>::iterator p = allAccounts.begin();
     p != allAccounts.end();
     ++p) {

  (*p)->creditInterest();          // error!

}
```

but your compilers would quickly bring you to your senses: allAccounts contains pointers to BankAccount objects, not to SavingsAccount objects, so each time around the loop, p points to a BankAccount. That makes the call to creditInterest invalid, because creditInterest is declared only for SavingsAccount objects, not BankAccounts.

If "list<BankAccount*>::iterator p = allAccounts.begin()" looks to you more like transmission line noise than C++, you've apparently never had the pleasure of meeting the container class templates in the standard library. This part of the library is usually known as the Standard Template Library (the "STL"), and you can get an overview of it in Item 49. For the time being, all you need to know is that the variable p acts like a pointer that loops through the elements of allAccounts from beginning to end. That is, p acts as if its type were BankAccount** and the list elements were stored in an array.

It's frustrating that the loop above won't compile. Sure, allAccounts is defined as holding BankAccount*s, but you *know* that it actually holds SavingsAccount*s in the loop above, because SavingsAccount is the only class that can be instantiated. Stupid compilers! You decide to tell them what you know to be obvious and what they are too dense to figure out on their own: allAccounts really contains SavingsAccount*s:

```
// a loop that will compile, but that is nonetheless evil
for (list<BankAccount*>::iterator p = allAccounts.begin();
     p != allAccounts.end();
     ++p) {

  static_cast<SavingsAccount*>(*p)->creditInterest();

}
```

All your problems are solved! Solved clearly, solved elegantly, solved concisely, all by the simple use of a cast. You know what type of pointer allAccounts really holds, your dopey compilers don't, so you use a cast to tell them. What could be more logical?

There is a biblical analogy I'd like to draw here. Casts are to C++ programmers what the apple was to Eve.

This kind of cast — from a base class pointer to a derived class pointer — is called a *downcast*, because you're casting down the inheritance hierarchy. In the example you just looked at, downcasting happens to work, but it leads to a maintenance nightmare, as you will soon see.

But back to the bank. Buoyed by the success of its savings accounts, let's suppose the bank decides to offer checking accounts, too. Furthermore, assume that checking accounts also bear interest, just like savings accounts:

```
class CheckingAccount: public BankAccount {
public:
  void creditInterest();        // add interest to account

  ...

};
```

Needless to say, allAccounts will now be a list containing pointers to both savings and checking accounts. Suddenly, the interest-crediting loop you wrote above is in serious trouble.

Your first problem is that it will continue to compile without your changing it to reflect the existence of CheckingAccount objects. This is because compilers will foolishly believe you when you tell them (through the static_cast) that *p really points to a SavingsAccount*. After all, you're the boss. That's Maintenance Nightmare Number One. Maintenance Nightmare Number Two is what you're tempted to do to fix the problem, which is typically to write code like this:

```
for (list<BankAccount*>::iterator p = allAccounts.begin();
     p != allAccounts.end();
     ++p) {

  if (*p points to a SavingsAccount)
    static_cast<SavingsAccount*>(*p)->creditInterest();
  else
    static_cast<CheckingAccount*>(*p)->creditInterest();

}
```

Anytime you find yourself writing code of the form, "if the object is of type T1, then do something, but if it's of type T2, then do something else," slap yourself. That isn't The C++ Way. Yes, it's a reasonable strategy in C or in Pascal, but not in C++. In C++, you use virtual functions.

Remember that with a virtual function, *compilers* are responsible for making sure that the right function is called, depending on the type of the object being used. Don't litter your code with conditionals or switch statements; let your compilers do the work for you. Here's how:

```
class BankAccount { ... };        // as above

// new class representing accounts that bear interest
class InterestBearingAccount: public BankAccount {
public:
  virtual void creditInterest() = 0;

  ...

};

class SavingsAccount: public InterestBearingAccount {

  ...                              // as above

};

class CheckingAccount: public InterestBearingAccount {

  ...                              // as above

};
```

Graphically, it looks like this:

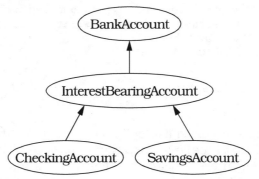

Because both savings and checking accounts earn interest, you'd naturally like to move that common behavior up into a common base class. However, under the assumption that not all accounts in the bank will necessarily bear interest (certainly a valid assumption in my experience), you can't move it into the BankAccount class. As a result, you've introduced a new subclass of BankAccount called Interest-BearingAccount, and you've made SavingsAccount and CheckingAccount inherit from it.

The fact that both savings and checking accounts bear interest is indicated by the InterestBearingAccount pure virtual function cred-

itInterest, which is presumably defined in its subclasses
SavingsAccount and CheckingAccount.

This new class hierarchy allows you to rewrite your loop as follows:

```
// better, but still not perfect
for (list<BankAccount*>::iterator p = allAccounts.begin();
     p != allAccounts.end();
     ++p) {

  static_cast<InterestBearingAccount*>(*p)->creditInterest();

}
```

Although this loop still contains a nasty little cast, it's much more ro-
bust than it used to be, because it will continue to work even if new
subclasses of InterestBearingAccount are added to your application.

To get rid of the cast entirely, you must make some additional changes
to your design. One approach is to tighten up the specification of your
list of accounts. If you could get a list of InterestBearingAccount
objects instead of BankAccount objects, everything would be peachy:

```
// all interest-bearing accounts in the bank
list<InterestBearingAccount*> allIBAccounts;

// a loop that compiles and works, both now and forever
for (list<InterestBearingAccount*>::iterator p =
       allIBAccounts.begin();
     p != allIBAccounts.end();
     ++p) {

  (*p)->creditInterest();

}
```

If getting a more specialized list isn't an option, it might make sense to
say that the creditInterest operation applies to *all* bank accounts,
but that for non-interest-bearing accounts, it's just a no-op. That
could be expressed this way:

```
class BankAccount {
public:
  virtual void creditInterest() {}

  ...

};

class SavingsAccount: public BankAccount { ... };

class CheckingAccount: public BankAccount { ... };

list<BankAccount*> allAccounts;
```

```
// look ma, no cast!
for (list<BankAccount*>::iterator p = allAccounts.begin();
     p != allAccounts.end();
     ++p) {

  (*p)->creditInterest();

}
```

Notice that the virtual function `BankAccount::creditInterest` provides an empty default implementation. This is a convenient way to specify that its behavior is a no-op by default, but it can lead to unforeseen difficulties in its own right. For the inside story on why, as well as how to eliminate the danger, consult Item 36. Notice also that `creditInterest` is (implicitly) an inline function. There's nothing wrong with that, but because it's also virtual, the inline directive will probably be ignored. Item 33 explains why.

As you have seen, downcasts can be eliminated in a number of ways. The best way is to replace such casts with calls to virtual functions, possibly also making each virtual function a no-op for any classes to which it doesn't truly apply. A second method is to tighten up the typing so that there is no ambiguity between the declared type of a pointer and the pointer type that you know is really there. Whatever the effort required to get rid of downcasts, it's effort well spent, because downcasts are ugly and error-prone, and they lead to code that's difficult to understand, enhance, and maintain.

What I've just written is the truth and nothing but the truth. It is not, however, the whole truth. There are occasions when you really *do* have to perform a downcast.

For example, suppose you faced the situation we considered at the outset of this Item, i.e., `allAccounts` holds `BankAccount` pointers, `creditInterest` is defined only for `SavingsAccount` objects, and you must write a loop to credit interest to every account. Further suppose that all those things are beyond your control; you can't change the definitions for `BankAccount`, `SavingsAccount`, or `allAccounts`. (This would happen if they were defined in a library to which you had read-only access.) If that were the case, you'd *have* to use downcasting, no matter how distasteful you found the idea.

Nevertheless, there is a better way to do it than through a raw cast such as we saw above. The better way is called "safe downcasting," and it's implemented via C++'s `dynamic_cast` operator. When you use `dynamic_cast` on a pointer, the cast is attempted, and if it succeeds (i.e., if the dynamic type of the pointer (see Item 38) is consistent with the type to which it's being cast), a valid pointer of the new type is returned. If the `dynamic_cast` fails, the null pointer is returned.

Here's the banking example with safe downcasting added:

```
class BankAccount { ... };          // as at the beginning of
                                    // this Item

class SavingsAccount:               // ditto
  public BankAccount { ... };

class CheckingAccount:              // ditto again
  public BankAccount { ... };

list<BankAccount*> allAccounts;     // this should look
                                    // familiar...

void error(const string& msg);      // error-handling function;
                                    // see below

// well, ma, at least the casts are safe...
for (list<BankAccount*>::iterator p = allAccounts.begin();
     p != allAccounts.end();
     ++p) {

  // try safe-downcasting *p to a SavingsAccount*; see
  // below for information on the definition of psa
  if (SavingsAccount *psa =
        dynamic_cast<SavingsAccount*>(*p)) {
    psa->creditInterest();
  }

  // try safe-downcasting it to a CheckingAccount
  else if (CheckingAccount *pca =
             dynamic_cast<CheckingAccount*>(*p)) {
    pca->creditInterest();
  }

  // uh oh — unknown account type
  else {
    error("Unknown account type!");
  }
}
```

This scheme is far from ideal, but at least you can detect when your downcasts fail, something that's impossible without the use of `dynamic_cast`. Note, however, that prudence dictates you also check for the case where *all* the downcasts fail. That's the purpose of the final `else` clause in the code above. With virtual functions, there'd be no need for such a test, because every virtual call must resolve to *some* function. When you start downcasting, however, all bets are off. If somebody added a new type of account to the hierarchy, for example, but failed to update the code above, all the downcasts would fail.

That's why it's important you handle that possibility. In all likelihood, it's not supposed to be the case that all the casts can fail, but when you allow downcasting, bad things start to happen to good programmers.

Did you check your glasses in a panic when you noticed what looks like variable definitions in the conditions of the if statements above? If so, worry not; your vision's fine. The ability to define such variables was added to the language at the same time as dynamic_cast. This feature lets you write neater code, because you don't really need psa or pca unless the dynamic_casts that initialize them succeed, and with the new syntax, you don't have to define those variables outside the conditionals containing the casts. (Item 32 explains why you generally want to avoid superfluous variable definitions, anyway.) If your compilers don't yet support this new way of defining variables, you can do it the old way:

```
for (list<BankAccount*>::iterator p = allAccounts.begin();
     p != allAccounts.end();
     ++p) {

  SavingsAccount *psa;          // traditional definition
  CheckingAccount *pca;         // traditional definition

  if (psa = dynamic_cast<SavingsAccount*>(*p)) {
    psa->creditInterest();
  }

  else if (pca = dynamic_cast<CheckingAccount*>(*p)) {
    pca->creditInterest();
  }

  else {
    error("Unknown account type!");
  }
}
```

In the grand scheme of things, of course, where you place your definitions for variables like psa and pca is of little consequence. The important thing is this: the if-then-else style of programming that downcasting invariably leads to is vastly inferior to the use of virtual functions, and you should reserve it for situations in which you truly have no alternative. With any luck, you will never face such a bleak and desolate programming landscape.

Item 40: Model "has-a" or "is-implemented-in-terms-of" through layering.

Layering is the process of building one class on top of another class by having the layering class contain an object of the layered class as a data member. For example:

```
class Address { ... };          // where someone lives

class PhoneNumber { ... };

class Person {
public:
  ...

private:
  string name;                  // layered object
  Address address;              // ditto
  PhoneNumber voiceNumber;      // ditto
  PhoneNumber faxNumber;        // ditto
};
```

In this example, the Person class is said to be layered on top of the string, Address, and PhoneNumber classes, because it contains data members of those types. The term *layering* has lots of synonyms. It's also known as *composition*, *containment*, and *embedding*.

Item 35 explains that public inheritance means "isa." In contrast, layering means either "has-a" or "is-implemented-in-terms-of."

The Person class above demonstrates the has-a relationship. A Person object has a name, an address, and telephone numbers for voice and FAX communication. You wouldn't say that a person *is* a name or that a person *is* an address. You would say that a person *has* a name and *has* an address, etc. Most people have little difficulty with this distinction, so confusion between the roles of isa and has-a is relatively rare.

Somewhat more troublesome is the difference between isa and is-implemented-in-terms-of. For example, suppose you need a template for classes representing sets of arbitrary objects, i.e., collections without duplicates. Because reuse is a wonderful thing, and because you wisely read Item 49's overview of the standard C++ library, your first instinct is to employ the library's set template. After all, why write a new template when you can use an established one written by somebody else?

As you delve into set's documentation, however, you discover a limitation your application can't live with: a set requires that the elements contained within it be *totally ordered*, i.e., for every pair of objects a and b in the set, it must be possible to determine whether a<b or b<a. For many types, this requirement is easy to satisfy, and having a total ordering among objects allows set to offer certain attractive guarantees regarding its performance. (See Item 49 for more on performance guarantees in the standard library.) Your need, however, is for something more general: a set-like class where objects need not be totally ordered, they need only be what the C++ standard colorfully terms "EqualityComparable": it's possible to determine whether a==b for objects a and b of the same type. This more modest requirement is better suited to types representing things like colors. Is red less than green or is green less than red? For your application, it seems you'll need to write your own template after all.

Still, reuse *is* a wonderful thing. Being the data structure maven you are, you know that of the nearly limitless choices for implementing sets, one particularly simple way is to employ linked lists. But guess what? The list template (which generates linked list classes) is just *sitting* there in the standard library! You decide to (re)use it.

In particular, you decide to have your nascent Set template inherit from list. That is, Set<T> will inherit from list<T>. After all, in your implementation, a Set object will in fact *be* a list object. You thus declare your Set template like this:

```
// the wrong way to use list for Set
template<class T>
class Set: public list<T> { ... };
```

Everything may seem fine and dandy at this point, but in fact there is something quite wrong. As Item 35 explains, if D isa B, everything true of B is also true of D. However, a list object may contain duplicates, so if the value 3051 is inserted into a list<int> twice, that list will contain two copies of 3051. In contrast, a Set may not contain duplicates, so if the value 3051 is inserted into a Set<int> twice, the set contains only one copy of the value. It is thus a vicious lie that a Set isa list, because some of the things that are true for list objects are not true for Set objects.

Because the relationship between these two classes isn't isa, public inheritance is the wrong way to model that relationship. The right way is to realize that a Set object can be *implemented in terms of* a list object:

```
// the right way to use list for Set
template<class T>
class Set {
public:
  bool member(const T& item) const;

  void insert(const T& item);
  void remove(const T& item);

  int cardinality() const;

private:
  list<T> rep;                    // representation for a set
};
```

Set's member functions can lean heavily on functionality already offered by list and other parts of the standard library, so the implementation is neither difficult to write nor thrilling to read:

```
template<class T>
bool Set<T>::member(const T& item) const
{ return find(rep.begin(), rep.end(), item) != rep.end(); }

template<class T>
void Set<T>::insert(const T& item)
{ if (!member(item)) rep.push_back(item); }

template<class T>
void Set<T>::remove(const T& item)
{
  list<T>::iterator it =
    find(rep.begin(), rep.end(), item);

  if (it != rep.end()) rep.erase(it);
}

template<class T>
int Set<T>::cardinality() const
{ return rep.size(); }
```

These functions are simple enough that they make reasonable candidates for inlining, though I know you'd want to review the discussion in Item 33 before making any firm inlining decisions. (In the code above, functions like find, begin, end, push_back, etc., are part of the standard library's framework for working with container templates like list. You'll find an overview of this framework in Item 49.)

It's worth remarking that the Set class interface fails the test of being complete and minimal (see Item 18). In terms of completeness, the primary omission is that of a way to iterate over the contents of a set, something that might well be necessary for many applications (and that is provided by all members of the standard library, including set). An additional drawback is that Set fails to follow the container class conventions embraced by the standard library (see Item 49), and that makes it more difficult to take advantage of other parts of the library when working with Sets.

Nits about Set's interface, however, shouldn't be allowed to overshadow what Set got indisputably right: the relationship between Set and list. That relationship is not isa (though it initially looked like it might be), it's "is-implemented-in-terms-of," and the use of layering to implement that relationship is something of which any class designer may be justly proud.

Incidentally, when you use layering to relate two classes, you create a compile-time dependency between those classes. For information on why this should concern you, as well as what you can do to allay your worries, turn to Item 34.

Item 41: Differentiate between inheritance and templates.

Consider the following two design problems:

- Being a devoted student of Computer Science, you want to create classes representing stacks of objects. You'll need several different classes, because each stack must be homogeneous, i.e., it must have only a single type of object in it. For example, you might have a class for stacks of ints, a second class for stacks of strings, a third for stacks of stacks of strings, etc. You're interested only in supporting a minimal interface to the class (see Item 18), so you'll limit your operations to stack creation, stack destruction, pushing objects onto the stack, popping objects off the stack, and determining whether the stack is empty. For this exercise, you'll ignore the classes in the standard library (including stack — see Item 49), because you crave the experience of writing the code yourself. Reuse is a wonderful thing, but when your goal is a deep understanding of how something works, there's nothing quite like diving in and getting your hands dirty.

- Being a devoted feline aficionado, you want to design classes representing cats. You'll need several different classes, because each breed of cat is a little different. Like all objects, cats can be created and destroyed, but, as any cat-lover knows, the only other things cats do are eat and sleep. However, each breed of cat eats and sleeps in its own endearing way.

These two problem specifications sound similar, yet they result in utterly different software designs. Why?

The answer has to do with the relationship between each class's behavior and the *type* of object being manipulated. With both stacks and cats, you're dealing with a variety of different types (stacks containing objects of type T, cats of breed T), but the question you must ask yourself is this: does the type T affect the *behavior* of the class? If T does *not* affect the behavior, you can use a template. If T *does* affect the behavior, you'll need virtual functions, and you'll therefore use inheritance.

Here's how you might define a linked-list implementation of a Stack class, assuming that the objects to be stacked are of type T:

```
class Stack {
public:
  Stack();
  ~Stack();

  void push(const T& object);
  T pop();

  bool empty() const;            // is stack empty?
private:
  struct StackNode {             // linked list node
    T data;                      // data at this node
    StackNode *next;             // next node in list

    // StackNode constructor initializes both fields
    StackNode(const T& newData, StackNode *nextNode)
    : data(newData), next(nextNode) {}
  };

  StackNode *top;                // top of stack

  Stack(const Stack& rhs);                  // prevent copying and
  Stack& operator=(const Stack& rhs); // assignment (see Item 27)
};
```

Stack objects would thus build data structures that look like this:

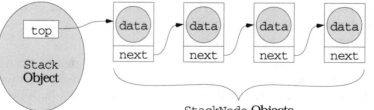

StackNode Objects

The linked list itself is made up of StackNode objects, but that's an implementation detail of the Stack class, so StackNode has been declared a private type of Stack. Notice that StackNode has a constructor to make sure all its fields are initialized properly. Just because you can write linked lists in your sleep is no reason to omit technological advances such as constructors.

Here's a reasonable first cut at how you might implement the Stack member functions. As with many prototype implementations (and far too much production software), there's no checking for errors, because in a prototypical world, nothing ever goes wrong.

```cpp
Stack::Stack(): top(0) {}          // initialize top to null

void Stack::push(const T& object)
{
  top = new StackNode(object, top);     // put new node at
}                                        // front of list

T Stack::pop()
{
  StackNode *topOfStack = top;  // remember top node
  top = top->next;

  T data = topOfStack->data;    // remember node data
  delete topOfStack;

  return data;
}

Stack::~Stack()                       // delete all in stack
{
  while (top) {
    StackNode *toDie = top;       // get ptr to top node
    top = top->next;              // move to next node
    delete toDie;                 // delete former top node
  }
}

bool Stack::empty() const
{ return top == 0; }
```

There's nothing riveting about these implementations. In fact, the only interesting thing about them is this: you are able to write each member function knowing essentially *nothing* about T. (You assume you can call T's copy constructor, but, as Item 45 explains, that's a pretty reasonable assumption.) The code you write for construction, destruction, pushing, popping, and determining whether the stack is empty is the same, no matter what T is. Except for the assumption that you can call T's copy constructor, the behavior of a stack does not depend on T in any way. That's the hallmark of a template class: the behavior doesn't depend on the type.

Turning your Stack class into a template, by the way, is so simple, even Dilbert's pointy-haired boss could do it:

```cpp
template<class T> class Stack {

  ...                             // exactly the same as above

};
```

But on to cats. Why won't templates work with cats?

Reread the specification and note the requirement that "each breed of cat eats and sleeps in its own endearing way." That means you're going to have to implement *different behavior* for each type of cat. You can't just write a single function to handle all cats, all you can do is *specify an interface* for a function that each type of cat must implement. Aha! The way to propagate a function *interface only* is to declare a pure virtual function (see Item 36):

```
class Cat {
public:
  virtual ~Cat();                    // see Item 14

  virtual void eat() = 0;            // all cats eat
  virtual void sleep() = 0;          // all cats sleep
};
```

Subclasses of Cat — say, Siamese and BritishShortHairedTabby — must of course redefine the eat and sleep function interfaces they inherit:

```
class Siamese: public Cat {
public:
  void eat();
  void sleep();

  . . .

};

class BritishShortHairedTabby: public Cat {
public:
  void eat();
  void sleep();

  . . .

};
```

Okay, you now know why templates work for the Stack class and why they won't work for the Cat class. You also know why inheritance works for the Cat class. The only remaining question is why inheritance won't work for the Stack class. To see why, try to declare the root class of a Stack hierarchy, the single class from which all other stack classes would inherit:

```
class Stack {                      // a stack of anything
public:
  virtual void push(const ??? object) = 0;
  virtual ??? pop() = 0;

  . . .

};
```

Now the difficulty becomes clear. What types are you going to declare for the pure virtual functions push and pop? Remember that each sub-class must redeclare the virtual functions it inherits with *exactly* the same parameter types and with return types consistent with the base class declarations. Unfortunately, a stack of ints will want to push and pop int objects, whereas a stack of, say, Cats, will want to push and pop Cat objects. How can the Stack class declare its pure virtual functions in such a way that clients can create both stacks of ints and stacks of Cats? The cold, hard truth is that it can't, and that's why inheritance is unsuitable for creating stacks.

But maybe you're the sneaky type. Maybe you think you can outsmart your compilers by using generic (void*) pointers. As it turns out, generic pointers don't help you here. You simply can't get around the requirement that a virtual function's declarations in derived classes must never contradict its declaration in the base class. However, generic pointers can help with a different problem, one related to the efficiency of classes generated from templates. For details, see Item 42.

Now that we've dispensed with stacks and cats, we can summarize the lessons of this Item as follows:

- A template should be used to generate a collection of classes when the type of the objects *does not* affect the behavior of the class's functions.

- Inheritance should be used for a collection of classes when the type of the objects *does* affect the behavior of the class's functions.

Internalize these two little bullet points, and you'll be well on your way to mastering the choice between inheritance and templates.

Item 42: Use private inheritance judiciously.

Item 35 demonstrates that C++ treats public inheritance as an isa relationship. It does this by showing that compilers, when given a hierarchy in which a class Student publicly inherits from a class Person, implicitly convert Students to Persons when that is necessary for a function call to succeed. It's worth repeating a portion of that example using private inheritance instead of public inheritance:

```
class Person { ... };

class Student:              // this time we use
  private Person { ... };   // private inheritance

void dance(const Person& p);  // anyone can dance

void study(const Student& s); // only students study
```

```
Person p;                    // p is a Person
Student s;                   // s is a Student

dance(p);                    // fine, p is a Person

dance(s);                    // error! a Student isn't
                             // a Person
```

Clearly, private inheritance doesn't mean isa. What does it mean then?

"Whoa!" you say. "Before we get to the meaning, let's cover the behavior. How does private inheritance behave?" Well, the first rule governing private inheritance you've just seen in action: in contrast to public inheritance, compilers will generally *not* convert a derived class object (such as Student) into a base class object (such as Person) if the inheritance relationship between the classes is private. That's why the call to dance fails for the object s. The second rule is that members inherited from a private base class become private members of the derived class, even if they were protected or public in the base class. So much for behavior.

That brings us to meaning. Private inheritance means is-implemented-in-terms-of. If you make a class D privately inherit from a class B, you do so because you are interested in taking advantage of some of the code that has already been written for class B, not because there is any conceptual relationship between objects of type B and objects of type D. As such, private inheritance is purely an implementation technique. Using the terms introduced in Item 36, private inheritance means that implementation *only* should be inherited; interface should be ignored. If D privately inherits from B, it means that D objects are implemented in terms of B objects, nothing more. Private inheritance means nothing during software *design*, only during software *implementation*.

The fact that private inheritance means is-implemented-in-terms-of is a little disturbing, because Item 40 points out that layering can mean the same thing. How are you supposed to choose between them? The answer is simple: use layering whenever you can, use private inheritance whenever you must. When must you? When protected members and/or virtual functions enter the picture — but more on that in a moment.

Item 41 shows a way to write a Stack template that generates classes holding objects of different types. You may wish to familiarize yourself with that Item now. Templates are one of the most useful features in C++, but once you start using them regularly, you'll discover that if you instantiate a template a dozen times, you are likely to instantiate the *code* for the template a dozen times. In the case of the Stack template, the code making up Stack<int>'s member functions will be completely separate from the code making up Stack<double>'s member functions. Sometimes this is unavoidable, but such code replication is likely to exist even if the template functions could in fact share code. There is a name for the resultant increase in object code size: template-induced *code bloat*. It is not a good thing.

For certain kinds of classes, you can use generic pointers to avoid it. The classes to which this approach is applicable store *pointers* instead of objects, and they are implemented by:

1. Creating a single class that stores void* pointers to objects.

2. Creating a set of additional classes whose only purpose is to enforce strong typing. These classes all use the generic class of step 1 for the actual work.

Here's an example using the non-template Stack class of Item 41, except here it stores generic pointers instead of objects:

```
class GenericStack {
public:
  GenericStack();
  ~GenericStack();

  void push(void *object);
  void * pop();

  bool empty() const;
private:
  struct StackNode {
    void *data;                   // data at this node
    StackNode *next;              // next node in list

    StackNode(void *newData, StackNode *nextNode)
    : data(newData), next(nextNode) {}
  };

  StackNode *top;                           // top of stack

  GenericStack(const GenericStack& rhs);    // prevent copying and
  GenericStack&                             // assignment (see
    operator=(const GenericStack& rhs);     // Item 27)
};
```

Because this class stores pointers instead of objects, it is possible that an object is pointed to by more than one stack (i.e., has been pushed onto multiple stacks). It is thus of critical importance that pop and the class destructor *not* delete the data pointer of any StackNode object they destroy, although they must continue to delete the StackNode object itself. After all, the StackNode objects are allocated inside the GenericStack class, so they must also be deallocated inside that class. As a result, the implementation of the Stack class in Item 41 suffices almost perfectly for the GenericStack class. The only changes you need to make involve substitutions of void* for T.

The GenericStack class by itself is of little utility — it's too easy to misuse. For example, a client could mistakenly push a pointer to a Cat object onto a stack meant to hold only pointers to ints, and compilers would merrily accept it. After all, a pointer's a pointer when it comes to void* parameters.

To regain the type safety to which you have become accustomed, you create *interface classes* to GenericStack, like this:

```
class IntStack {                    // interface class for ints
public:
  void push(int *intPtr) { s.push(intPtr); }
  int * pop() { return static_cast<int*>(s.pop()); }
  bool empty() const { return s.empty(); }

private:
  GenericStack s;                   // implementation
};
class CatStack {                    // interface class for cats
public:
  void push(Cat *catPtr) { s.push(catPtr); }
  Cat * pop() { return static_cast<Cat*>(s.pop()); }
  bool empty() const { return s.empty(); }

private:
  GenericStack s;                   // implementation
};
```

As you can see, the IntStack and CatStack classes serve only to enforce strong typing. Only int pointers can be pushed onto an IntStack or popped from it, and only Cat pointers can be pushed onto a CatStack or popped from it. Both IntStack and CatStack are implemented in terms of the class GenericStack, a relationship that is expressed through layering (see Item 40), and IntStack and CatStack will share the code for the functions in GenericStack that actually implement their behavior. Furthermore, the fact that all IntStack and CatStack member functions are (implicitly) inline means that the runtime cost of using these interface classes is zip, zero, nada, nil.

But what if potential clients don't realize that? What if they mistakenly believe that use of GenericStack is more efficient, or what if they're just wild and reckless and think only wimps need type-safety nets? What's to keep them from bypassing IntStack and CatStack and going straight to GenericStack, where they'll be free to make the kinds of type errors C++ was specifically designed to prevent?

Nothing. Nothing prevents that. But maybe something should.

I mentioned at the outset of this Item that an alternative way to assert an is-implemented-in-terms-of relationship between classes is through private inheritance. In this case, that technique offers an advantage over layering, because it allows you to express the idea that GenericStack is too unsafe for general use, that it should be used only to implement other classes. You say that by protecting Generic-Stack's member functions:

```
class GenericStack {
protected:
  GenericStack();
  ~GenericStack();

  void push(void *object);
  void * pop();

  bool empty() const;

private:
  ...                          // same as above
};

GenericStack s;                // error! constructor is
                               // protected


class IntStack: private GenericStack {
public:
  void push(int *intPtr) { GenericStack::push(intPtr); }
  int * pop() { return static_cast<int*>(GenericStack::pop()); }
  bool empty() const { return GenericStack::empty(); }
};
class CatStack: private GenericStack {
public:
  void push(Cat *catPtr) { GenericStack::push(catPtr); }
  Cat * pop() { return static_cast<Cat*>(GenericStack::pop()); }
  bool empty() const { return GenericStack::empty(); }
};

IntStack is;                   // fine

CatStack cs;                   // also fine
```

Like the layering approach, the implementation based on private inheritance avoids code duplication, because the type-safe interface classes consist of nothing but inline calls to the underlying Generic-Stack functions.

Building type-safe interfaces on top of the GenericStack class is a pretty slick maneuver, but it's awfully unpleasant to have to type in all those interface classes by hand. Fortunately, you don't have to. You can use templates to generate them automatically. Here's a template to generate type-safe stack interfaces using private inheritance:

```
template<class T>
class Stack: private GenericStack {
public:
  void push(T *objectPtr) { GenericStack::push(objectPtr); }
  T * pop() { return static_cast<T*>(GenericStack::pop()); }
  bool empty() const { return GenericStack::empty(); }
};
```

This is amazing code, though you may not realize it right away. Because of the template, compilers will automatically generate as many interface classes as you need. Because those classes are type-safe, client type errors are detected during compilation. Because Generic-Stack's member functions are protected and interface classes use it as a private base class, clients are unable to bypass the interface classes. Because each interface class member function is (implicitly) declared inline, no runtime cost is incurred by use of the type-safe classes; the generated code is exactly the same as if clients programmed with GenericStack directly (assuming compilers respect the inline request — see Item 33). And because GenericStack uses void* pointers, you pay for only one copy of the code for manipulating stacks, no matter how many different types of stack you use in your program. In short, this design gives you code that's both maximally efficient and maximally type safe. It's difficult to do better than that.

One of the precepts of this book is that C++'s features interact in remarkable ways. This example, I hope you'll agree, is pretty remarkable.

The insight to carry away from this example is that it could not have been achieved using layering. Only inheritance gives access to protected members, and only inheritance allows for virtual functions to be redefined. (For an example of how the existence of virtual functions can motivate the use of private inheritance, see Item 43.) Because virtual functions and protected members exist, private inheritance is sometimes the only practical way to express an is-implemented-in-terms-of relationship between classes. As a result, you shouldn't be afraid to use private inheritance when it's the most appropriate implementation technique at your disposal. At the same time, however, layering is the preferable technique in general, so you should employ it whenever you can.

Item 43: Use multiple inheritance judiciously.

Depending on who's doing the talking, multiple inheritance (MI) is either the product of divine inspiration or the manifest work of the devil.

Proponents hail it as essential to the natural modeling of real-world problems, while critics argue that it is slow, difficult to implement, and no more powerful than single inheritance. Disconcertingly, the world of object-oriented programming languages remains split on the issue: C++, Eiffel, and the Common LISP Object System (CLOS) offer MI; Smalltalk, Objective C, and Object Pascal do not; and Java supports only a restricted form of it. What's a poor, struggling programmer to believe?

Before you believe anything, you need to get your facts straight. The one indisputable fact about MI in C++ is that it opens up a Pandora's box of complexities that simply do not exist under single inheritance. Of these, the most basic is ambiguity (see Item 26). If a derived class inherits a member name from more than one base class, any reference to that name is ambiguous; you must explicitly say which member you mean. Here's an example that's based on a discussion in the ARM (see Item 50):

```
class Lottery {
public:
  virtual int draw();

  ...

};

class GraphicalObject {
public:
  virtual int draw();

  ...

};

class LotterySimulation: public Lottery,
                         public GraphicalObject {

  ...                                    // doesn't declare draw

};

LotterySimulation *pls = new LotterySimulation;

pls->draw();                     // error! − ambiguous
pls->Lottery::draw();            // fine
pls->GraphicalObject::draw();    // fine
```

This looks clumsy, but at least it works. Unfortunately, the clumsiness is difficult to eliminate. Even if one of the inherited draw functions were private and hence inaccessible, the ambiguity would remain. (There's a good reason for that, but a complete explanation of the situation is provided in Item 26, so I won't repeat it here.)

Explicitly qualifying members is more than clumsy, however, it's also limiting. When you explicitly qualify a virtual function with a class name, the function doesn't act virtual any longer. Instead, the function called is precisely the one you specify, even if the object on which it's invoked is of a derived class:

```cpp
class SpecialLotterySimulation: public LotterySimulation {
public:
  virtual int draw();

  ...

};

pls = new SpecialLotterySimulation;

pls->draw();                    // error! - still ambiguous
pls->Lottery::draw();           // calls Lottery::draw
pls->GraphicalObject::draw();   // calls GraphicalObject::draw
```

In this case, notice that even though pls points to a SpecialLotterySimulation object, there is no way (short of a downcast — see Item 39) to invoke the draw function defined in that class.

But wait, there's more. The draw functions in both Lottery and GraphicalObject are declared virtual so that subclasses can redefine them (see Item 36), but what if LotterySimulation would like to redefine *both* of them? The unpleasant truth is that it can't, because a class is allowed to have only a single function called draw that takes no arguments. (There is a special exception to this rule if one of the functions is const and one is not — see Item 21.)

At one point, this difficulty was considered a serious enough problem to justify a change in the language. The ARM discusses the possibility of allowing inherited virtual functions to be "renamed," but then it was discovered that the problem can be circumvented by the addition of a pair of new classes:

```cpp
class AuxLottery: public Lottery {
public:
  virtual int lotteryDraw() = 0;

  virtual int draw() { return lotteryDraw(); }
};

class AuxGraphicalObject: public GraphicalObject {
public:
  virtual int graphicalObjectDraw() = 0;

  virtual int draw() { return graphicalObjectDraw(); }
};
```

```
class LotterySimulation: public AuxLottery,
                         public AuxGraphicalObject {
public:
  virtual int lotteryDraw();
  virtual int graphicalObjectDraw();

  ...

};
```

Each of the two new classes, AuxLottery and AuxGraphicalObject, essentially declares a new name for the draw function that each inherits. This new name takes the form of a pure virtual function, in this case lotteryDraw and graphicalObjectDraw; the functions are pure virtual so that concrete subclasses must redefine them. Furthermore, each class redefines the draw that it inherits to itself invoke the new pure virtual function. The net effect is that within this class hierarchy, the single, ambiguous name draw has effectively been split into two unambiguous, but operationally equivalent, names: lotteryDraw and graphicalObjectDraw:

```
LotterySimulation *pls = new LotterySimulation;

Lottery *pl = pls;
GraphicalObject *pgo = pls;

// this calls LotterySimulation::lotteryDraw
pl->draw();

// this calls LotterySimulation::graphicalObjectDraw
pgo->draw();
```

This strategy, replete as it is with the clever application of pure virtual, simple virtual, and inline functions (see Item 33), should be committed to memory. In the first place, it solves a problem that you may encounter some day. In the second, it can serve to remind you of the complications that can arise in the presence of multiple inheritance. Yes, this tactic works, but do you really want to be forced to introduce new classes just so you can redefine a virtual function? The classes Aux-Lottery and AuxGraphicalObject are essential to the correct operation of this hierarchy, but they correspond neither to an abstraction in the problem domain nor to an abstraction in the implementation domain. They exist purely as an implementation device — nothing more. You already know that good software is "device independent." That rule of thumb applies here, too.

The ambiguity problem, interesting though it is, hardly begins to scratch the surface of the issues you'll confront when you flirt with MI. Another one grows out of the empirical observation that an inheritance hierarchy that starts out looking like this,

```
class B { ... };
class C { ... };
class D: public B, public C { ... };
```

has a distressing tendency to evolve into one that looks like this:

```
class A { ... };
class B: virtual public A { ... };
class C: virtual public A { ... };
class D: public B, public C { ... };
```

Now, it may or may not be true that diamonds are a girl's best friend, but it is certainly true that a diamond-shaped inheritance hierarchy such as this is *not* very friendly. If you create a hierarchy such as this, you are immediately confronted with the question of whether to make A a virtual base class, i.e., whether inheritance from A should be virtual. In practice, the answer is almost invariably that it should; only rarely will you want an object of type D to contain multiple copies of the data members of A. In recognition of this truth, B and C above declare A as a virtual base class.

Unfortunately, at the time you define B and C, you may not know whether any class will decide to inherit from both of them, and in fact you shouldn't need to know this in order to define them correctly. As a class designer, this puts you in a dreadful quandary. If you do *not* declare A as a virtual base of B and C, a later designer of D may need to modify the definitions of B and C in order to use them effectively. Frequently, this is unacceptable, often because the definitions of A, B, and C are read-only. This would be the case if A, B, and C were in a library, for example, and D was written by a library client.

On the other hand, if you *do* declare A as a virtual base of B and C, you typically impose an additional cost in both space and time on clients of those classes. That is because virtual base classes are often implemented as *pointers* to objects, rather than as objects themselves. It goes without saying that the layout of objects in memory is compiler-dependent, but the fact remains that the memory layout for an object of type D with A as a nonvirtual base is typically a contiguous series of memory locations, whereas the memory layout for an object of type D with A as a virtual base is sometimes a contiguous series of memory locations, two of which contain pointers to the memory locations containing the data members of the virtual base class:

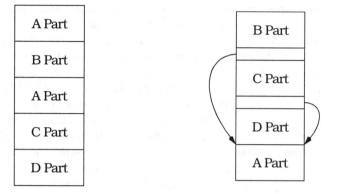

Common memory layout
of a D object where A is a
nonvirtual base class

Some compilers' memory
layout of a D object where
A is a virtual base class

Even compilers that don't use this particular implementation strategy generally impose some kind of space penalty for using virtual inheritance.

In view of these considerations, it would seem that effective class design in the presence of MI calls for clairvoyance on the part of library designers. Seeing as how run-of-the-mill common sense is an increasingly rare commodity these days, you would be ill-advised to rely too heavily on a language feature that calls for designers to be not only anticipatory of future needs, but downright prophetic.

Of course, this could also be said of the choice between virtual and nonvirtual functions in a base class, but there is a crucial difference. Item 36 explains that a virtual function has a well-defined high-level meaning that is distinct from the equally well-defined high-level meaning of a nonvirtual function, so it is possible to choose between the two based on what you want to communicate to writers of subclasses. However, the decision whether a base class should be virtual or nonvirtual lacks a well-defined high-level meaning. Rather, that decision is usually based on the structure of the entire inheritance hierarchy, and as such it cannot be made until the entire hierarchy is known. If you need to know exactly how your class is going to be used before you can define it correctly, it becomes very difficult to design effective classes.

Once you're past the problem of ambiguity and you've settled the question of whether inheritance from your base class(es) should be virtual, still more complications confront you. Rather than belaboring things, I'll simply mention two other issues you need to keep in mind:

- **Passing constructor arguments to virtual base classes**. Under nonvirtual inheritance, arguments for a base class constructor are specified in the member initialization lists of the classes that are immediately derived from the base class. Because single inheritance hierarchies need only nonvirtual bases, arguments are passed up the inheritance hierarchy in a very natural fashion: the classes at level *n* of the hierarchy pass arguments to the classes at level *n-1*. For constructors of a virtual base class, however, arguments are specified in the member initialization lists of the classes that are *most derived* from the base. As a result, the class initializing a virtual base may be arbitrarily far from it in the inheritance graph, and the class performing the initialization can change as new classes are added to the hierarchy. (A good way to avoid this problem is to eliminate the need to pass constructor arguments to virtual bases. The easiest way to do that is to avoid putting data members in such classes. This is the essence of the Java solution to the problem: virtual base classes in Java (i.e., "Interfaces") are prohibited from containing data.)

- **Dominance of virtual functions**. Just when you thought you had ambiguity all figured out, they change the rules on you. Consider again the diamond-shaped inheritance graph involving classes A, B, C, and D. Suppose that A defines a virtual member function mf, and C redefines it; B and D, however, do not redefine mf:

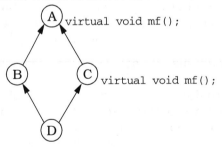

From our earlier discussion, you'd expect this to be ambiguous:

```
D *pd = new D;
pd->mf();                        // A::mf or C::mf?
```

Which mf should be called for a D object, the one directly inherited from C or the one indirectly inherited (via B) from A? The answer is that *it depends on how B and C inherit from A*. In particular, if A is a nonvirtual base of B or C, the call is ambiguous, but if A is a virtual base of both B and C, the redefinition of mf in C is said to *dominate* the original definition in A, and the call to mf through pd will resolve (unambiguously) to C::mf. If you sit down and work it all out, it emerges that this is the behavior you want, but it's kind of a pain to have to sit down and work it all out before it makes sense.

Perhaps by now you agree that MI can lead to complications. Perhaps you are convinced that no one in their right mind would ever use it. Perhaps you are prepared to propose to the international C++ standardization committee that multiple inheritance be removed from the language, or at least to propose to your manager that programmers at your company be physically barred from using it.

Perhaps you are being too hasty.

Bear in mind that the designer of C++ didn't set out to make multiple inheritance hard to use, it just turned out that making all the pieces work together in a more or less reasonable fashion inherently entailed the introduction of certain complexities. In the above discussion, you may have noticed that the bulk of these complexities arise in conjunction with the use of virtual base classes. If you can avoid the use of virtual bases — that is, if you can avoid the creation of the deadly diamond inheritance graph — things become much more manageable.

For example, Item 34 describes how a *Protocol class* exists only to specify an interface for derived classes; it has no data members, no constructors, a virtual destructor (see Item 14), and a set of pure virtual functions that specify the interface. A Protocol Person class might look like this:

```
class Person {
public:
  virtual ~Person();

  virtual string name() const = 0;
  virtual string birthDate() const = 0;
  virtual string address() const = 0;
  virtual string nationality() const = 0;
};
```

Clients of this class must program in terms of Person pointers and references, because abstract classes cannot be instantiated.

To create objects that can be manipulated as Person objects, clients of Person use *factory functions* (see Item 34) to instantiate concrete subclasses of that class:

```
// factory function to create a Person object from a
// unique database ID
Person * makePerson(DatabaseID personIdentifier);
```

```
DatabaseID askUserForDatabaseID();

DatabaseID pid = askUserForDatabaseID();
Person *pp = makePerson(pid);    // create object supporting
                                 // the Person interface

...                              // manipulate *pp via
                                 // Person's member functions

delete pp;                       // delete the object when
                                 // it's no longer needed
```

This just begs the question: how does makePerson create the objects to which it returns pointers? Clearly, there must be some concrete class derived from Person that makePerson can instantiate.

Suppose this class is called MyPerson. As a concrete class, MyPerson must provide implementations for the pure virtual functions it inherits from Person. It could write these from scratch, but it would be better software engineering to take advantage of existing components that already do most or all of what's necessary. For example, let's suppose a creaky old database-specific class PersonInfo already exists that provides the essence of what MyPerson needs:

```
class PersonInfo {
public:
  PersonInfo(DatabaseID pid);
  virtual ~PersonInfo();

  virtual const char * theName() const;
  virtual const char * theBirthDate() const;
  virtual const char * theAddress() const;
  virtual const char * theNationality() const;

  virtual const char * valueDelimOpen() const;     // see
  virtual const char * valueDelimClose() const;     // below

  ...

};
```

You can tell this is an old class, because the member functions return const char*s instead of string objects. Still, if the shoe fits, why not wear it? The names of this class's member functions suggest that the result is likely to be pretty comfortable.

You come to discover that PersonInfo, however, was designed to facilitate the process of printing database fields in various formats, with the beginning and end of each field value delimited by special strings. By default, the opening and closing delimiters for field values are square brackets, so the field value "Ring-tailed Lemur" would be formatted this way:

```
[Ring-tailed Lemur]
```

In recognition of the fact that square brackets are not universally desired by clients of PersonInfo, the virtual functions valueDelimOpen and valueDelimClose allow derived classes to specify their own opening and closing delimiter strings. The implementations of PersonInfo's theName, theBirthDate, theAddress, and theNationality call these virtual functions to add the appropriate delimiters to the values they return. Using PersonInfo::name as an example, the code looks like this:

```
const char * PersonInfo::valueDelimOpen() const
{
  return "[";                       // default opening delimiter
}

const char * PersonInfo::valueDelimClose() const
{
  return "]";                       // default closing delimiter
}

const char * PersonInfo::theName() const
{
  // reserve buffer for return value. Because this is
  // static, it's automatically initialized to all zeros
  static char value[MAX_FORMATTED_FIELD_VALUE_LENGTH];

  // write opening delimiter
  strcpy(value, valueDelimOpen());

  append to the string in value this object's name field

  // write closing delimiter
  strcat(value, valueDelimClose());

  return value;
}
```

One might quibble with the design of PersonInfo::theName (especially the use of a fixed-size static buffer — see Item 23), but set your quibbles aside and focus instead on this: theName calls valueDelimOpen to generate the opening delimiter of the string it will return, then it generates the name value itself, then it calls valueDelimClose. Because valueDelimOpen and valueDelimClose are virtual functions, the result returned by theName is dependent not only on PersonInfo, but also on the classes derived from PersonInfo.

As the implementer of MyPerson, that's good news, because while perusing the fine print in the Person documentation, you discover that name and its sister member functions are required to return unadorned values, i.e., no delimiters are allowed. That is, if a person is from Madagascar, a call to that person's `nationality` function should return "Madagascar", not "[Madagascar]".

The relationship between `MyPerson` and `PersonInfo` is that `Person-Info` happens to have some functions that make `MyPerson` easier to implement. That's all. There's no isa or has-a relationship anywhere in sight. Their relationship is thus is-implemented-in-terms-of, and we know that can be represented in two ways: via layering (see Item 40) and via private inheritance (see Item 42). Item 42 points out that layering is the generally preferred approach, but private inheritance is necessary if virtual functions are to be redefined. In this case, `MyPerson` needs to redefine `valueDelimOpen` and `valueDelimClose`, so layering won't do and private inheritance it must be: `MyPerson` must privately inherit from `PersonInfo`.

But `MyPerson` must also implement the `Person` interface, and that calls for public inheritance. This leads to one reasonable application of multiple inheritance: combine public inheritance of an interface with private inheritance of an implementation:

```
class Person {                 // this class specifies
public:                        // the interface to be
  virtual ~Person();           // implemented

  virtual string name() const = 0;
  virtual string birthDate() const = 0;
  virtual string address() const = 0;
  virtual string nationality() const = 0;
};

class DatabaseID { ... };      // used below; details
                               // are unimportant

class PersonInfo {             // this class has functions
public:                        // useful in implementing
  PersonInfo(DatabaseID pid);  // the Person interface
  virtual ~PersonInfo();

  virtual const char * theName() const;
  virtual const char * theBirthDate() const;
  virtual const char * theAddress() const;
  virtual const char * theNationality() const;

  virtual const char * valueDelimOpen() const;
  virtual const char * valueDelimClose() const;

  ...

};
```

```
class MyPerson: public Person,         // note use of
               private PersonInfo {    // multiple inheritance
public:
  MyPerson(DatabaseID pid): PersonInfo(pid) {}

  // redefinitions of inherited virtual delimiter functions
  const char * valueDelimOpen() const { return ""; }
  const char * valueDelimClose() const { return ""; }

  // implementations of the required Person member functions
  string name() const
  { return PersonInfo::theName(); }

  string birthDate() const
  { return PersonInfo::theBirthDate(); }

  string address() const
  { return PersonInfo::theAddress(); }

  string nationality() const
  { return PersonInfo::theNationality(); }
};
```

Graphically, it looks like this:

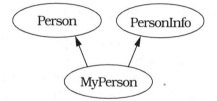

This kind of example demonstrates that MI can be both useful and comprehensible, although it's no accident that the dreaded diamond-shaped inheritance graph is conspicuously absent.

Still, you must guard against temptation. Sometimes you can fall into the trap of using MI to make a quick fix to an inheritance hierarchy that would be better served by a more fundamental redesign. For example, suppose you're working with a hierarchy for animated cartoon characters. At least conceptually, it makes sense for any kind of character to dance and sing, but the way in which each type of character performs these activities differs. Furthermore, the default behavior for singing and dancing is to do nothing.

The way to say all that in C++ is like this:

```
class CartoonCharacter {
public:
  virtual void dance() {}
  virtual void sing() {}
};
```

Virtual functions naturally model the constraint that dancing and singing make sense for all CartoonCharacter objects. Do-nothing default behavior is expressed by the empty definitions of those functions in the class (see Item 36).

Suppose a particular type of cartoon character is a grasshopper, which dances and sings in its own particular way:

```
class Grasshopper: public CartoonCharacter {
public:
  virtual void dance();          // definition is elsewhere
  virtual void sing();           // definition is elsewhere
};
```

Now suppose that after implementing the Grasshopper class, you decide you also need a class for crickets:

```
class Cricket: public CartoonCharacter {
public:
  virtual void dance();
  virtual void sing();
};
```

As you sit down to implement the Cricket class, you realize that a lot of the code you wrote for the Grasshopper class can be reused. However, it needs to be tweaked a bit here and there to account for the differences in singing and dancing between grasshoppers and crickets. You are suddenly struck by a clever way to reuse your existing code: you'll implement the Cricket class *in terms of* the Grasshopper class, and you'll use virtual functions to allow the Cricket class to customize Grasshopper behavior!

You immediately recognize that these twin requirements — an is-implemented-in-terms-of relationship and the ability to redefine virtual functions — mean that Cricket will have to privately inherit from Grasshopper, but of course a cricket is still a cartoon character, so you redefine Cricket to inherit from both Grasshopper and CartoonCharacter:

```
class Cricket: public CartoonCharacter,
               private Grasshopper {
public:
  virtual void dance();
  virtual void sing();
};
```

You then set out to make the necessary modifications to the Grasshopper class. In particular, you need to declare some new virtual functions for Cricket to redefine:

```
class Grasshopper: public CartoonCharacter {
public:
  virtual void dance();
  virtual void sing();

protected:
  virtual void danceCustomization1();
  virtual void danceCustomization2();

  virtual void singCustomization();
};
```

Dancing for grasshoppers is now defined like this:

```
void Grasshopper::dance()
{
  perform common dancing actions;

  danceCustomization1();

  perform more common dancing actions;

  danceCustomization2();

  perform final common dancing actions;
}
```

Grasshopper singing is similarly orchestrated.

Clearly, the Cricket class must be updated to take into account the new virtual functions it must redefine:

```
class Cricket: public CartoonCharacter,
               private Grasshopper {
public:
  virtual void dance() { Grasshopper::dance(); }
  virtual void sing() { Grasshopper::sing(); }

protected:
  virtual void danceCustomization1();
  virtual void danceCustomization2();

  virtual void singCustomization();
};
```

This seems to work fine. When a Cricket object is told to dance, it will execute the common dance code in the Grasshopper class, then execute the dance customization code in the Cricket class, then continue with the code in Grasshopper::dance, etc.

There is a serious flaw in your design, however, and that is that you have run headlong into Occam's razor, a bad idea with a razor of any kind, and especially so when it belongs to William of Occam. Occamism preaches that entities should not be multiplied beyond necessity, and in this case, the entities in question are inheritance relationships. If you believe that multiple inheritance is more complicated than single inheritance (and I hope that you do), then the design of the Cricket class is needlessly complex.

Fundamentally, the problem is that it is *not* true that the Cricket class is-implemented-in-terms-of the Grasshopper class. Rather, the Cricket class and the Grasshopper class *share common code*. In particular, they share the code that determines the dancing and singing behavior that grasshoppers and crickets have in common.

The way to say that two classes have something in common is *not* to have one class inherit from the other, but to have *both* of them inherit from a common base class. The common code for grasshoppers and crickets doesn't belong in the Grasshopper class, nor does it belong in the Cricket class. It belongs in a new class from which they both inherit, say, Insect:

```
class CartoonCharacter { ... };

class Insect: public CartoonCharacter {
public:
  virtual void dance();        // common code for both
  virtual void sing();         // grasshoppers and crickets

protected:
  virtual void danceCustomization1() = 0;
  virtual void danceCustomization2() = 0;

  virtual void singCustomization() = 0;
};

class Grasshopper: public Insect {
protected:
  virtual void danceCustomization1();
  virtual void danceCustomization2();

  virtual void singCustomization();
};

class Cricket: public Insect {
protected:
  virtual void danceCustomization1();
  virtual void danceCustomization2();

  virtual void singCustomization();
};
```

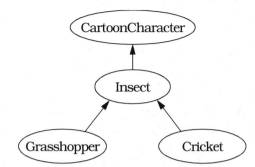

Notice how much cleaner this design is. Only single inheritance is involved, and furthermore, only *public* inheritance is used. Grasshopper and Cricket define only customization functions; they inherit the dance and sing functions unchanged from Insect. William of Occam would be proud.

Although this design is cleaner than the one involving MI, it may initially have appeared to be inferior. After all, compared to the MI approach, this single-inheritance architecture calls for the introduction of a brand new class, a class unnecessary if MI is used. Why introduce an extra class if you don't have to?

This brings you face to face with the seductive nature of multiple inheritance. On the surface, MI seems to be the easier course of action. It adds no new classes, and though it calls for the addition of some new virtual functions to the Grasshopper class, those functions have to be added somewhere in any case.

Imagine now a programmer maintaining a large C++ class library, one in which a new class has to be added, much as the Cricket class had to be added to the existing CartoonCharacter/Grasshopper hierarchy. The programmer knows that a large number of clients use the existing hierarchy, so the bigger the change to the library, the greater the disruption to clients. The programmer is determined to minimize that kind of disruption. Mulling over the options, the programmer realizes that if a single private inheritance link from Grasshopper to Cricket is added, no other change to the hierarchy will be needed. The programmer smiles at the thought, pleased with the prospect of a large increase in functionality at the cost of only a slight increase in complexity.

Imagine now that that maintenance programmer is you. Resist the seduction.

Item 44: Say what you mean; understand what you're saying.

In the introduction to this section on inheritance and object-oriented design, I emphasized the importance of understanding what different object-oriented constructs in C++ *mean*. This is quite different from just knowing the rules of the language. For example, the rules of C++ say that if class D publicly inherits from class B, there is a standard conversion from a D pointer to a B pointer; that the public member functions of B are inherited as public member functions of D, etc. That's all true, but it's close to useless if you're trying to translate your design into C++. Instead, you need to understand that public inheritance means isa, that if D publicly inherits from B, every object of type D isa object of type B, too. Thus, if you mean isa in your design, you know you have to use public inheritance.

Saying what you mean is only half the battle. The flip side of the coin is understanding what you're saying, and it's just as important. For example, it's irresponsible, if not downright immoral, to run around declaring member functions nonvirtual without recognizing that in so doing you are imposing constraints on subclasses. In declaring a non-virtual member function, what you're really saying is that the function represents an invariant over specialization, and it would be disastrous if you didn't know that.

The equivalence of public inheritance and isa, and of nonvirtual member functions and invariance over specialization, are examples of how certain C++ constructs correspond to design-level ideas. The list below summarizes the most important of these mappings.

- **A common base class means common traits**. If class D1 and class D2 both declare class B as a base, D1 and D2 inherit common data members and/or common member functions from B. See Item 43.

- **Public inheritance means isa**. If class D publicly inherits from class B, every object of type D is also an object of type B, but not vice versa. See Item 35.

- **Private inheritance means is-implemented-in-terms-of**. If class D privately inherits from class B, objects of type D are simply implemented in terms of objects of type B; no conceptual relationship exists between objects of types B and D. See Item 42.

- **Layering means has-a or is-implemented-in-terms-of.** If class A contains a data member of type B, objects of type A either have a component of type B or are implemented in terms of objects of type B. See Item 40.

The following mappings apply only when public inheritance is involved:

- **A pure virtual function means that only the function's interface is inherited.** If a class C declares a pure virtual member function mf, subclasses of C must inherit the interface for mf, and concrete subclasses of C must supply their own implementations for it. See Item 36.

- **A simple virtual function means that the function's interface plus a default implementation is inherited.** If a class C declares a simple (not pure) virtual function mf, subclasses of C must inherit the interface for mf, and they may also inherit a default implementation, if they choose. See Item 36.

- **A nonvirtual function means that the function's interface plus a mandatory implementation is inherited.** If a class C declares a nonvirtual member function mf, subclasses of C must inherit both the interface for mf and its implementation. In effect, mf defines an invariant over specialization of C. See Item 36.

Miscellany

Some guidelines for effective C++ programming defy convenient categorization. This section is where such guidelines come to roost. Not that that diminishes their importance. If you are to write effective software, you must understand what compilers are doing for you (to you?) behind your back, how to ensure that non-local static objects are initialized before they are used, what you can expect from the standard library, and where to go for insights into the language's underlying design philosophy. In this final section of the book, I expound on these issues, and more.

Item 45: Know what functions C++ silently writes and calls.

When is an empty class not an empty class? When C++ gets through with it. If you don't declare them yourself, your thoughtful compilers will declare their own versions of a copy constructor, an assignment operator, a destructor, and a pair of address-of operators. Furthermore, if you don't declare any constructors, they will declare a default constructor for you, too. All these functions will be public. In other words, if you write this,

```
class Empty{};
```

it's the same as if you'd written this:

```
class Empty {
public:
  Empty();                      // default constructor
  Empty(const Empty& rhs);      // copy constructor

  ~Empty();                     // destructor — see
                                // below for whether
                                // it's virtual

  Empty&
  operator=(const Empty& rhs);  // assignment operator

  Empty* operator&();           // address-of operators
  const Empty* operator&() const;
};
```

Now these functions are generated only if they are needed, but it doesn't take much to need them. The following code will cause each function to be generated:

```
const Empty e1;                 // default constructor;
                                // destructor

Empty e2(e1);                   // copy constructor

e2 = e1;                        // assignment operator

Empty *pe2 = &e2;               // address-of
                                // operator (non-const)

const Empty *pe1 = &e1;         // address-of
                                // operator (const)
```

Given that compilers are writing functions for you, what do the functions do? Well, the default constructor and the destructor don't really do anything. They just enable you to create and destroy objects of the class. (They also provide a convenient place for implementers to place code whose execution takes care of "behind the scenes" behavior — see Item 33.) Note that the generated destructor is nonvirtual (see Item 14) unless it's for a class inheriting from a base class that itself declares a virtual destructor. The default address-of operators just return the address of the object. These functions are effectively defined like this:

```
inline Empty::Empty() {}

inline Empty::~Empty() {}

inline Empty * Empty::operator&() { return this; }

inline const Empty * Empty::operator&() const
{ return this; }
```

As for the copy constructor and the assignment operator, the official rule is this: the default copy constructor (assignment operator) performs memberwise copy construction (assignment) of the nonstatic data members of the class. That is, if m is a nonstatic data member of type T in a class C and C declares no copy constructor (assignment operator), m will be copy constructed (assigned) using the copy constructor (assignment operator) defined for T, if there is one. If there isn't, this rule will be recursively applied to m's data members until a copy constructor (assignment operator) or built-in type (e.g., int, double, pointer, etc.) is found. By default, objects of built-in types are copy constructed (assigned) using bitwise copy from the source object to the destination object. For classes that inherit from other classes, this rule is applied to each level of the inheritance hierarchy, so user-defined copy constructors and assignment operators are called at whatever level they are declared.

I hope that's crystal clear.

But just in case it's not, here's an example. Consider the definition of a NamedObject template, whose instances are classes allowing you to associate names with objects:

```
template<class T>
class NamedObject {
public:
  NamedObject(const char *name, const T& value);
  NamedObject(const string& name, const T& value);

  ...

private:
  string nameValue;
  T objectValue;
};
```

Because the NamedObject classes declare at least one constructor, compilers won't generate default constructors, but because the classes fail to declare copy constructors or assignment operators, compilers will generate those functions (if they are needed).

Consider the following call to a copy constructor:

```
NamedObject<int> no1("Smallest Prime Number", 2);

NamedObject<int> no2(no1);      // calls copy constructor
```

The copy constructor generated by your compilers must initialize no2.nameValue and no2.objectValue using no1.nameValue and no1.objectValue, respectively. The type of nameValue is string, and string has a copy constructor (which you can verify by examining string in the standard library — see Item 49), so no2.nameValue will be initialized by calling the string copy constructor with no1.name-Value as its argument. On the other hand, the type of NamedObject<int>::objectValue is int (because T is int for this template instantiation), and no copy constructor is defined for ints, so no2.objectValue will be initialized by copying the bits over from no1.objectValue.

The compiler-generated assignment operator for NamedObject<int> would behave the same way, but in general, compiler-generated assignment operators behave as I've described only when the resulting code is both legal and has a reasonable chance of making sense. If either of these tests fails, compilers will refuse to generate an operator= for your class, and you'll receive some lovely diagnostic during compilation.

For example, suppose NamedObject were defined like this, where nameValue is a *reference* to a string and objectValue is a *const* T:

```
template<class T>
class NamedObject {
public:
    // this ctor no longer takes a const name, because name-
    // Value is now a reference-to-non-const string. The char*
    // ctor is gone, because we must have a string to refer to
    NamedObject(string& name, const T& value);

    ...                                 // as above, assume no
                                        // operator= is declared
private:
    string& nameValue;                  // this is now a reference
    const T objectValue;                // this is now const
};
```

Now consider what should happen here:

```
string newDog("Persephone");
string oldDog("Satch");

NamedObject<int> p(newDog, 2);      // as I write this, our dog
                                    // Persephone is about to
                                    // have her second birthday

NamedObject<int> s(oldDog, 29);     // the family dog Satch
                                    // (from my childhood)
                                    // would be 29 if she were
                                    // still alive

p = s;                              // what should happen to
                                    // the data members in p?
```

Before the assignment, p.nameValue refers to some string object and s.nameValue also refers to a string, though not the same one. How should the assignment affect p.nameValue? After the assignment, should p.nameValue refer to the string referred to by s.nameValue, i.e., should the reference itself be modified? If so, that breaks new ground, because C++ doesn't provide a way to make a reference refer to a different object. Alternatively, should the string object to which p.nameValue refers be modified, thus affecting other objects that hold pointers or references to that string, i.e., objects not directly involved in the assignment? Is that what the compiler-generated assignment operator should do?

Faced with such a conundrum, C++ refuses to compile the code. If you want to support assignment in a class containing a reference member, you must define the assignment operator yourself. Compilers behave similarly for classes containing const members (such as objectValue in the modified class above); it's not legal to modify const members, so compilers are unsure how to treat them during an implicitly generated assignment function. Finally, compilers refuse to generate assignment operators for derived classes that inherit from base classes declaring the standard assignment operator private. After all, compiler-generated assignment operators for derived classes are supposed to handle base class parts, too (see Item 16), but in doing so, they certainly shouldn't invoke member functions the derived class has no right to call.

All this talk of compiler-generated functions gives rise to the question, what do you do if you want to disallow use of those functions? That is, what if you deliberately don't declare, for example, an `operator=` because you never *ever* want to allow assignment of objects in your class? The solution to that little teaser is the subject of Item 27. For a discussion of the often-overlooked interactions between pointer members and compiler-generated copy constructors and assignment operators, check out Item 11.

Item 46: Prefer compile-time and link-time errors to runtime errors.

Other than in the few situations that cause C++ to throw exceptions (e.g., running out of memory — see Item 7), the notion of a runtime error is as foreign to C++ as it is to C. There's no detection of underflow, overflow, division by zero, no checking for array bounds violations, etc. Once your program gets past a compiler and linker, you're on your own — there's no safety net of any consequence. Much as with skydiving, some people are exhilarated by this state of affairs, others are paralyzed with fear. The motivation behind the philosophy, of course, is efficiency: without runtime checks, programs are smaller and faster.

There is a different way to approach things. Languages like Smalltalk and LISP generally detect fewer kinds of errors during compilation and linking, but they provide hefty runtime systems that catch errors during execution. Unlike C++, these languages are almost always interpreted, and you pay a performance penalty for the extra flexibility they offer.

Never forget that you are programming in C++. Even if you find the Smalltalk/LISP philosophy appealing, put it out of your mind. There's a lot to be said for adhering to the party line, and in this case, that means eschewing runtime errors. Whenever you can, push the detection of an error back from runtime to link-time, or, ideally, to compile-time.

Such a methodology pays dividends not only in terms of program size and speed, but also in terms of reliability. If your program gets through compilers and a linker without eliciting error messages, you may be confident there aren't any compiler- or linker-detectable errors in your program, period. (The other possibility, of course, is that there are bugs in your compilers or linkers, but let us not depress ourselves by admitting to such possibilities.)

With runtime errors, the situation is very different. Just because your program doesn't generate any runtime errors during a particular run, how can you be sure it won't generate errors during a different run, when you do things in a different order, use different data, or run for a longer or shorter period of time? You can test your program until you're blue in the face, but you'll still never cover all the possibilities. As a result, detecting errors at runtime is simply less secure than is catching them during compilation or linking.

Often, by making relatively minor changes to your design, you can catch during compilation what might otherwise be a runtime error. This frequently involves the addition of new types to the program. For example, suppose you are writing a class to represent dates in time. Your first cut might look like this:

```
class Date {
public:
  Date(int day, int month, int year);

  ...

};
```

If you were to implement this constructor, one of the problems you'd face would be that of sanity checking on the values for the day and the month. Let's see how you can eliminate the need to validate the value passed in for the month.

One obvious approach is to employ an enumerated type instead of an integer:

```
enum Month { Jan = 1, Feb = 2, ... , Nov = 11, Dec = 12 };

class Date {
public:
  Date(int day, Month month, int year);

  ...

};
```

Unfortunately, this doesn't buy you that much, because enums don't have to be initialized:

```
Month m;
Date d(22, m, 1857);          // m is undefined
```

As a result, the Date constructor would still have to validate the value
of the month parameter.

To achieve enough security to dispense with runtime checks, you've
got to use a class to represent months, and you must ensure that only
valid months are created:

```
class Month {
public:
  static const Month Jan() { return 1; }
  static const Month Feb() { return 2; }
  ...
  static const Month Dec() { return 12; }

  int asInt() const              // for convenience, make
  { return monthNumber; }        // it possible to convert
                                 // a Month to an int
private:
  Month(int number) : monthNumber(number) {}

  const int monthNumber;
};

class Date {
public:
  Date(int day, const Month& month, int year);
  ...
};
```

Several aspects of this design combine to make it work the way it does.
First, the Month constructor is private. This prevents clients from creating new months. The only ones available are those returned by
Month's static member functions, plus copies thereof. Second, each
predefined Month object is const, so it can't be changed. (Otherwise
the temptation to transform January into June might sometimes prove
overwhelming, at least in northern latitudes.) Finally, the only way to
get a Month object is by calling a function or by copying an existing
Month (via the implicit Month copy constructor — see Item 45). This
makes it possible to use Month objects anywhere and anytime; there's
no need to worry about accidently using one before it's been initialized.
(Item 47 explains why this might otherwise be a problem.)

Given these classes, it is all but impossible for a client to specify an invalid month. It would be completely impossible were it not for the following abomination:

```
Month *pm;                          // define uninitialized ptr
Date d(1, *pm, 1997);               // arghhh! use it!
```

However, this involves dereferencing an uninitialized pointer, the results of which are undefined. (See Item 3 for my feelings about undefined behavior.) Unfortunately, I know of no way to prevent or detect this kind of heresy. However, if we assume this never happens, or if we don't care how our software behaves if it does, the Date constructor can dispense with sanity checking on its Month parameter. On the other hand, the constructor must still check the day parameter for validity — how many days hath September, April, June, and November?

This Date example replaces runtime checks with compile-time checks. You may be wondering when it is possible to use link-time checks. In truth, not very often. C++ uses the linker to ensure that needed functions are defined exactly once (see Item 45 for a description of what it takes to "need" a function). It also uses the linker to ensure that static objects (see Item 47) are defined exactly once. You'll tend to use the linker in the same way. For example, Item 27 describes how the linker's checks can make it useful to deliberately avoid defining a function you explicitly declare.

Now don't get carried away. It's impractical to eliminate the need for *all* runtime checking. Any program that accepts interactive input, for example, is likely to have to validate that input. Similarly, a class implementing arrays that perform bounds checking (see Item 18) is usually going to have to validate the array index against the bounds every time an array access is made. Nonetheless, shifting checks from runtime to compile- or link-time is always a worthwhile goal, and you should pursue that goal whenever it is practical. Your reward for doing so is programs that are smaller, faster, and more reliable.

Item 47: Ensure that non-local static objects are initialized before they're used.

You're an adult now, so you don't need me to tell you it's foolhardy to use an object before it's been initialized. In fact, the whole notion may strike you as absurd; constructors make sure objects are initialized when they're created, *n'est-ce pas?*

Well, yes and no. Within a particular translation unit (i.e., source file), everything works fine, but things get trickier when the initialization of an object in one translation unit depends on the value of another object in a different translation unit *and* that second object itself requires initialization.

For example, suppose you've authored a library offering an abstraction of a file system, possibly including such capabilities as making files on the Internet look like they're local. Since your library makes the world look like a single file system, you might create a special object, the-FileSystem, within your library's namespace (see Item 28) for clients to use whenever they need to interact with the file system abstraction your library provides:

```
class FileSystem { ... };       // this class is in your
                                // library

FileSystem theFileSystem;       // this is the object
                                // with which library
                                // clients interact
```

Because theFileSystem represents something complicated, it's no surprise that its construction is both nontrivial and essential; use of theFileSystem before it had been constructed would yield *very* undefined behavior.

Now suppose some client of your library creates a class for directories in a file system. Naturally, their class uses theFileSystem:

```
class Directory {               // created by library client
public:
  Directory();
  ...
};

Directory::Directory()
{
  create a Directory object by invoking member
  functions on theFileSystem;
}
```

Further suppose this client decides to create a distinguished global Directory object for temporary files:

```
Directory tempDir;              // directory for temporary
                                // files
```

Now the problem of initialization order becomes apparent: unless the-FileSystem is initialized before tempDir, tempDir's constructor will attempt to use theFileSystem before it's been initialized. But the-FileSystem and tempDir were created by different people at different times in different files. How can you be sure that theFileSystem will be created before tempDir?

This kind of question arises anytime you have *non-local static objects* that are defined in different translation units and whose correct behavior is dependent on their being initialized in a particular order. Non-local static objects are objects that are

- defined at global or namespace scope (e.g., theFileSystem and tempDir),

- declared static in a class, or

- defined static at file scope.

Regrettably, there is no shorthand term for "non-local static objects," so you should accustom yourself to this somewhat awkward phrase.

You do not want the behavior of your software to be dependent on the initialization order of non-local static objects in different translation units, because you have no control over that order. Let me repeat that. *You have absolutely no control over the order in which non-local static objects in different translation units are initialized.*

It is reasonable to wonder why this is the case.

It is the case because determining the "proper" order in which to initialize non-local static objects is hard. Very hard. Halting-Problem hard. In its most general form — with multiple translation units and non-local static objects generated through implicit template instantiations (which may themselves arise via implicit template instantiations) — it's not only impossible to determine the right order of initialization, it's typically not even worth looking for special cases where it *is* possible to determine the right order.

In the field of Chaos Theory, there is a principle known as the "Butterfly Effect." This principle asserts that the tiny atmospheric disturbance caused by the beating of a butterfly's wings in one part of the world can lead to profound changes in weather patterns in places far distant. Somewhat more rigorously, it asserts that for some types of systems, minute perturbations in inputs can lead to radical changes in outputs.

The development of software systems can exhibit a Butterfly Effect of its own. Some systems are highly sensitive to the particulars of their requirements, and small changes in requirements can significantly affect the ease with which a system can be implemented. For example, Item 29 describes how changing the specification for an implicit conversion from String-to-char* to String-to-*const*-char* makes it possible to replace a slow or error-prone function with a fast, safe one.

The problem of ensuring that non-local static objects are initialized before use is similarly sensitive to the details of what you want to achieve. If, instead of demanding access to non-local static objects, you're willing to settle for access to objects that *act* like non-local static objects (except for the initialization headaches), the hard problem vanishes. In its stead is left a problem so easy to solve, it's hardly worth calling a problem any longer.

The technique — sometimes known as the *Singleton pattern* — is simplicity itself. First, you move each non-local static object into its own function, where you declare it static. Next, you have the function return a reference to the object it contains. Clients call the function instead of referring to the object. In other words, you replace non-local static objects with objects that are static inside functions.

The basis of this approach is the observation that although C++ says next to nothing about when a non-local static object is initialized, it specifies quite precisely when a static object inside a function (i.e. a *local* static object) is initialized: it's when the object's definition is first encountered during a call to that function. So if you replace direct accesses to non-local static objects with calls to functions that return references to local static objects inside them, you're guaranteed that the references you get back from the functions will refer to initialized objects. As a bonus, if you never call a function emulating a non-local static object, you never incur the cost of constructing and destructing the object, something that can't be said for true non-local static objects.

Here's the technique applied to both theFileSystem and tempDir:

```
class FileSystem { ... };        // same as before

FileSystem& theFileSystem()      // this function replaces
{                                // the theFileSystem object

  static FileSystem tfs;         // define and initialize
                                 // a local static object
                                 // (tfs = "the file system")

  return tfs;                    // return a reference to it
}

class Directory { ... };         // same as before
```

```
Directory::Directory()
{
  same as before, except references to theFileSystem are
  replaced by references to theFileSystem();
}

Directory& tempDir()              // this function replaces
{                                 // the tempDir object

  static Directory td;            // define/initialize local
                                  // static object

  return td;                      // return reference to it
}
```

Clients of this modified system program exactly as they used to, except they now refer to theFileSystem() and tempDir() instead of theFileSystem and tempDir. That is, they refer only to functions returning references to those objects, never to the objects themselves.

The reference-returning functions dictated by this scheme are always simple: define and initialize a local static object on line 1, return it on line 2. That's it. Because they're so simple, you may be tempted to declare them inline. Item 33 explains that late-breaking revisions to the C++ language specification make this a perfectly valid implementation strategy, but it also explains why you'll want to confirm your compilers' conformance with this aspect of the standard before putting it to use. If you try it with a compiler not yet in accord with the relevant parts of the standard, you risk getting multiple copies of both the access function and the static object defined within it. That's enough to make a grown programmer cry.

Now, there's no magic going on here. For this technique to be effective, it must be possible to come up with a reasonable initialization order for your objects. If you set things up such that object A must be initialized before object B, and you also make A's initialization dependent on B's having already been initialized, you are going to get in trouble, and frankly, you deserve it. If you steer shy of such pathological situations, however, the scheme described in this Item should serve you quite nicely.

Item 48: Pay attention to compiler warnings.

Many programmers routinely ignore compiler warnings. After all, if the problem were serious, it'd be an error, right? This kind of thinking may be relatively harmless in other languages, but in C++, it's a good bet compiler writers have a better grasp of what's going on than you do. For example, here's an error everybody makes at one time or another:

```
class B {
public:
  virtual void f() const;
};

class D: public B {
public:
  virtual void f();
};
```

The idea is for D::f to redefine the virtual function B::f, but there's a mistake: in B, f is a const member function, but in D it's not declared const. One compiler I know says this about that:

```
warning: D::f() hides virtual B::f()
```

Too many inexperienced programmers respond to this message by saying to themselves, "Of *course* D::f hides B::f — that's what it's *supposed* to do!" Wrong. What this compiler is trying to tell you is that the f declared in B has not been redeclared in D, it's been hidden entirely (see Item 50 for a description of why this is so). Ignoring this compiler warning will almost certainly lead to erroneous program behavior, followed by a lot of debugging to find out about something that this compiler detected in the first place.

After you gain experience with the warning messages from a particular compiler, of course, you'll learn to understand what the different messages mean (which is often very different from what they *seem* to mean, alas). Once you have that experience, there may be a whole range of warnings you'll choose to ignore. That's fine, but it's important to make sure that before you dismiss a warning, you understand exactly what it's trying to tell you.

As long as we're on the topic of warnings, recall that warnings are inherently implementation-dependent, so it's not a good idea to get sloppy in your programming, relying on compilers to spot your mistakes for you. The function-hiding code above, for instance, goes through a different (but widely used) compiler with nary a squawk. Compilers are supposed to translate C++ into an executable format, not act as your personal safety net. You want that kind of safety? Program in Ada.

Item 49: Familiarize yourself with the standard library.

C++'s standard library is big. Very big. Incredibly big. How big? Let me put it this way: the specification takes over 300 closely-packed pages in the C++ standard, and that all but excludes the standard C library, which is included in the C++ library "by reference." (That's the term they use, honest.)

Bigger isn't always better, of course, but in this case, bigger *is* better, because a big library contains lots of functionality. The more functionality in the standard library, the more functionality you can lean on as you develop your applications. The C++ library doesn't offer *everything* (support for concurrency and for graphical user interfaces is notably absent), but it does offer a lot. You can lean almost anything against it.

Before summarizing what's in the library, I need to tell you a bit about how it's organized. Because the library has so much in it, there's a reasonable chance you (or someone like you) may choose a class or function name that's the same as a name in the standard library. To shield you from the name conflicts that would result, virtually everything in the standard library is nestled in the namespace std (see Item 28). But that leads to a new problem. Gazillions of lines of existing C++ rely on functionality in the pseudo-standard library that's been in use for years, e.g., functionality declared in the headers <iostream.h>, <complex.h>, <limits.h>, etc. That existing software isn't designed to use namespaces, and it would be a shame if wrapping the standard library by std caused the existing code to break. (Authors of the broken code would likely use somewhat harsher language than "shame" to describe their feelings about having the library rug pulled out from underneath them.)

Mindful of the destructive power of rioting bands of incensed programmers, the standardization committee decided to create new header names for the std-wrapped components. The algorithm they chose for generating the new header names is as trivial as the results it produces are jarring: the .h on the existing C++ headers was simply dropped. So <iostream.h> became <iostream>, <complex.h> became <complex>, etc. For C headers, the same algorithm was applied, but a c was prepended to each result. Hence C's <string.h> became <cstring>, <stdio.h> became <cstdio>, etc. For a final twist, the old C++ headers were officially *deprecated* (i.e., listed as no longer supported), but the old C headers were not (to maintain C compatibility). In practice, compiler vendors have no incentive to disavow their customers' legacy software, so you can expect the old C++ headers to be supported for many years.

Practically speaking, then, this is the C++ header situation:

- Old C++ header names like <iostream.h> are likely to continue to be supported, even though they aren't in the official standard. The contents of such headers are in the global namespace but are *not* in namespace std.

- New C++ header names like `<iostream>` contain the same basic functionality as the corresponding old headers, but the contents of the headers are in namespace `std` only. (During standardization, the details of some of the library components were modified, so there isn't necessarily an exact match between the entities in an old C++ header and those in a new one.)

- Standard C headers like `<stdio.h>` continue to be supported. The contents of such headers are in namespace `std` and are *also* in the global namespace.

- New C++ headers for the functionality in the C library have names like `<cstdio>`. They offer the same contents as the corresponding old C headers, but the contents are in `std` only.

All this seems a little weird at first, but it's really not that hard to get used to. The biggest challenge is keeping all the string headers straight: `<string.h>` is the old C header for `char*`-based string manipulation functions, `<string>` is the `std`-wrapped C++ header for the new string classes (see below), and `<cstring>` is the `std`-wrapped version of the old C header. If you can master that (and I know you can), the rest of the library is easy.

The next thing you need to know about the standard library is that almost everything in it is a template. Consider your old friend iostreams. (If you and iostreams aren't friends, turn to Item 2 to find out why you should cultivate a relationship.) Iostreams help you manipulate streams of characters, but what's a character? Is it a `char`? A `wchar_t`? A Unicode character? Some other multi-byte character? There's no obviously right answer, so the library lets you choose. All the stream classes are really class templates, and you specify the character type when you instantiate a stream class. For example, the standard library defines the type of `cout` to be `ostream`, but `ostream` is really a typedef for `basic_ostream<char>`.

Similar considerations apply to most of the other classes in the standard library. `string` isn't a class, it's a class template: a type parameter defines the type of characters in each `string` class. `complex` isn't a class, it's a class template: a type parameter defines the type of the real and imaginary components in each `complex` class. `vector` isn't a class, it's a class template. On and on it goes.

You can't escape the templates in the standard library, but if you're used to working with only streams and strings of `char`s, you can mostly ignore them. That's because the library defines typedefs for `char` instantiations for these components of the library, thus letting you continue to program in terms of the objects `cin`, `cout`, `cerr`, etc., and the types `istream`, `ostream`, `string`, etc., without having to worry about the fact that cin's real type is basic_istream<char> and string's is basic_string<char>.

Many components in the standard library are templatized much more than this suggests. Consider again the seemingly straightforward notion of a string. Sure, it can be parameterized based on the type of characters it holds, but different character sets differ in details, e.g., special end-of-file characters, most efficient way of copying arrays of them, etc. Such characteristics are known in the standard as *traits*, and they are specified for string instantiations by an additional template parameter. In addition, string objects are likely to perform dynamic memory allocation and deallocation, but there are lots of different ways to approach that task (see Item 10). Which is best? You get to choose: the string template takes an Allocator parameter, and objects of type Allocator are used to allocate and deallocate the memory used by string objects.

Here's a full-blown declaration for the basic_string template and the string typedef that builds on it; you can find this (or something equivalent to it) in the header <string>:

```
namespace std {

  template<class charT,
          class traits = char_traits<charT>,
          class Allocator = allocator<charT> >
    class basic_string;

  typedef basic_string<char> string;

}
```

Notice how basic_string has default values for its traits and Allocator parameters. This is typical of the standard library. It offers flexibility to those who need it, but "typical" clients who just want to do the "normal" thing can ignore the complexity that makes possible the flexibility. In other words, if you just want string objects that act more or less like C strings, you can use string objects and remain merrily ignorant of the fact that you're really using objects of type basic_string<char, char_traits<char>, allocator<char> >.

Well, usually you can. Sometimes you have to peek under the hood a bit. For example, Item 34 discusses the advantages of declaring a class without providing its definition, and it remarks that the following is the wrong way to declare the string type:

```
class string;                      // this will compile, but
                                   // you don't want to do it
```

Setting aside namespace considerations for a moment, the real problem here is that string isn't a class, it's a typedef. It would be nice if you could solve the problem this way,

```
typedef basic_string<char> string;
```

but that won't compile. "What is this basic_string of which you speak?," your compilers will wonder, though they'll probably phrase the question rather differently. No, to declare string, you would first have to declare all the templates on which it depends. If you could do it, it would look something like this:

```
template<class charT> struct char_traits;

template<class T> class allocator;

template<class charT,
         class traits = char_traits<charT>,
         class Allocator = allocator<charT> >
  class basic_string;

typedef basic_string<char> string;
```

However, you can't declare string. At least you shouldn't. That's because library implementers are allowed to declare string (or anything else in the std namespace) differently from what's specified in the standard as long as the result offers standard-conforming behavior. For example, a basic_string implementation could add a fourth template parameter, but that parameter's default value would have to yield code that acts as the standard says an unadorned basic_string must.

End result? Don't try to manually declare string (or any other part of the standard library). Instead, just include the appropriate header, e.g. <string>.

With this background on headers and templates under our belts, we're in a position to survey the primary components of the standard C++ library:

- **The standard C library**. It's still there, and you can still use it. A few minor things have been tweaked here and there, but for all intents and purposes, it's the same C library that's been around for years.

- **Iostreams**. Compared to "traditional" iostream implementations, it's been templatized, its inheritance hierarchy has been modified, it's been augmented with the ability to throw exceptions, and it's been updated to support strings (via the stringstream classes) and internationalization (via locales — see below). Still, most everything you've come to expect from the iostream library continues to exist. In particular, it still supports stream buffers, formatters, manipulators, and files, plus the objects cin, cout, cerr, and clog. That means you can treat strings and files as streams, and you have extensive control over stream behavior, including buffering and formatting.

- **Strings**. string objects were designed to eliminate the need to use char* pointers in most applications. They support the operations you'd expect (e.g., concatenation, constant-time access to individual characters via operator[], etc.), they're convertible to char*s for compatibility with legacy code, and they handle memory management automatically. Some string implementations employ reference counting, which can lead to *better* performance (in both time and space) than char*-based strings.

- **Containers**. Stop writing your own basic container classes! The library offers efficient implementations of vectors (they act like dynamically extensible arrays), lists (doubly-linked), queues, stacks, deques, maps, sets, and bitsets. Alas, there are no hash tables in the library (though many vendors offer them as extensions), but compensating somewhat is the fact that strings are containers. That's important, because it means anything you can do to a container (see below), you can also do to a string.

  What's that? You want to know how I *know* the library implementations are efficient? Easy: the library specifies each class's interface, and part of each interface specification is a set of performance guarantees. So, for example, no matter how vector is implemented, it's not enough to offer just *access* to its elements, it must offer *constant-time* access. If it doesn't, it's not a valid vector implementation.

  In many C++ programs, dynamically allocated strings and arrays account for most uses of new and delete, and new/delete errors — especially leaks caused by failure to delete newed memory — are distressingly common. If you use string and vector objects (both of which perform their own memory management) instead of char*s and pointers to dynamically allocated arrays, many of your news and deletes will vanish, and so will the difficulties that frequently accompany their use (e.g., Items 6 and 11).

- **Algorithms**. Having standard containers is nice, but it's even nicer when there's an easy way to do things with them. The standard library offers over two dozen easy ways (i.e., predefined functions, officially known as *algorithms* — they're really function templates), most of which work with *all* the containers in the library — as well as with built-in arrays!.

Algorithms treat the contents of a container as a sequence, and each algorithm may be applied to either the sequence corresponding to all the values in a container or to a subsequence. Among the standard algorithms are `for_each` (apply a function to each element of a sequence), `find` (find the first location in a sequence holding a given value), `count_if` (count the number of elements in a sequence for which a given predicate is true), `equal` (determine whether two sequences hold equal-valued elements), `search` (find the first position in one sequence where a second sequence occurs as a subsequence), `copy` (copy one sequence into another), `unique` (remove duplicate values from a sequence), `rotate` (rotate the values in a sequence) and `sort` (sort the values in a sequence). Note that this is just a *sampling* of the algorithms available; the library contains many others.

Just as container operations come with performance guarantees, so do algorithms. For example, the `stable_sort` algorithm is required to perform no more than O(N log N) comparisons. (If the "Big O" notation in the previous sentence is foreign to you, don't sweat it. What it really means is that, broadly speaking, `stable_sort` must offer performance at the same level as the most efficient general-purpose serial sorting algorithms.)

- **Support for internationalization**. Different cultures do things in different ways. Like the C library, the C++ library offers features to facilitate the production of internationalized software, but the C++ approach, though conceptually akin to that of C, is different. It should not surprise you, for example, to learn that C++'s support for internationalization makes extensive use of templates, and it takes advantage of inheritance and virtual functions, too.

The primary library components supporting internationalization are *facets* and *locales*. Facets describe how particular characteristics of a culture should be handled, including collation rules (i.e., how strings in the local character set should be sorted), how dates and times should be expressed, how numeric and monetary values should be presented, how to map from message identifiers to (natural) language-specific messages, etc. Locales bundle together sets of facets. For example, a locale for the United States would include facets describing how to sort strings in American English, read and write dates and times, read and write monetary and numeric values, etc., in a way appropriate for people in the USA. A locale for France, on the other hand, would describe how to perform these tasks in a manner to which the French are accustomed. C++ allows multiple locales to be active within a single program, so different parts of an application may employ different conventions.

- **Support for numeric processing**. The end for FORTRAN may finally be near. The C++ library offers a template for complex number classes (the precision of the real and imaginary parts may be float, double, or long double) as well as for special array types specifically designed to facilitate numeric programming. Objects of type valarray, for example, are defined to hold elements that are free from aliasing. This allows compilers to be much more aggressive in their optimizations, especially for vector machines. The library also offers support for two different types of array slices, as well as providing algorithms to compute inner products, partial sums, adjacent differences, and more.

- **Diagnostic support**. The standard library offers support for three ways to report errors: via C's assertions (see Item 7), via error numbers, and via exceptions. To help provide some structure to exception types, the library defines the following hierarchy of exception classes:

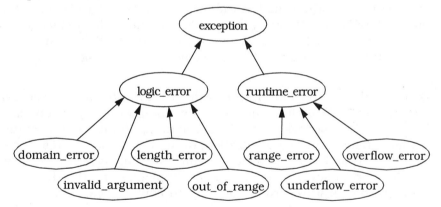

Exceptions of type logic_error (or its subclasses) represent errors in the logic of software. In theory, such errors could have been prevented by more careful programming. Exceptions of type runtime_error (or its derived classes) represent errors detectable only at runtime.

You may use these classes as is, you may inherit from them to create your own exception classes, or you may ignore them. Their use is not mandatory.

This list doesn't describe everything in the standard library. Remember, the specification runs over 300 pages. Still, it should give you the basic lay of the land.

The part of the library pertaining to containers and algorithms is commonly known as *Standard Template Library* (the *STL*). There is actually a third component to the STL — Iterators — that I haven't described. Iterators are pointer-like objects that allow STL algorithms and containers to work together. You need not understand iterators for the high-level description of the standard library I give here. If you're interested in them, however, you can find examples of their use in Item 39.

The STL is the most revolutionary part of the standard library, not because of the containers and algorithms it offers (though they are undeniably useful), but because of its architecture. Simply put, the architecture is extensible: you can *add* to the STL. Of course, the components of the standard library itself are fixed, but if you follow the conventions on which the STL is built, you can write your own containers, algorithms, and iterators that work as well with the standard STL components as the STL components work with one another. You can also take advantage of STL-compliant containers, algorithms, and iterators written by others, just as they can take advantage of yours. What makes the STL revolutionary is that it's not really software, it's a set of *conventions*. The STL components in the standard library are simply manifestations of the good that can come from following those conventions.

By using the components in the standard library, you can generally dispense with designing your own from-the-ground-up mechanisms for stream I/O, strings, containers (including iteration and common manipulations), internationalization, numeric data structures, and diagnostics. That leaves you a lot more time and energy for the really important part of software development: implementing the things that distinguish your wares from those of your competitors.

Item 50: Improve your understanding of C++.

There's a lot of *stuff* in C++. C stuff. Overloading stuff. Object-oriented stuff. Template stuff. Exception stuff. Namespace stuff. Stuff, stuff, stuff! Sometimes it can be overwhelming. How do you make sense of all that stuff?

It's not that hard once you understand the design goals that forged C++ into what it is. Foremost amongst those goals are the following:

- **Compatibility with C**. Lots and lots of C exists, as do lots and lots of C programmers. C++ takes advantage of and builds on — er, I mean it "leverages" — that base.

- **Efficiency**. Bjarne Stroustrup, the designer and first implementer of C++, knew from the outset that the C programmers he hoped to win over wouldn't look twice if they had to pay a performance penalty for switching languages. As a result, he made sure C++ was competitive with C when it came to efficiency — like within 5%.

- **Compatibility with traditional tools and environments**. Fancy development environments run here and there, but compilers, linkers, and editors run almost everywhere. C++ is designed to work in environments from mice to mainframes, so it brings along as little baggage as possible. You want to port C++? You port a *language* and take advantage of existing tools on the target platform. (However, it is often possible to provide a better implementation if, for example, the linker can be modified to address some of the more demanding aspects of inlining and templates.)

- **Applicability to real problems**. C++ wasn't designed to be a nice, pure language, good for teaching students how to program, it was designed to be a powerful tool for professional programmers solving real problems in diverse domains. The real world has some rough edges, so it's no surprise there's the occasional scratch marring the finish of the tools on which the pros rely.

These goals explain a multitude of language details that might otherwise merely chafe. Why do implicitly-generated copy constructors and assignment operators behave the way they do, especially for pointers (see Items 11 and 45)? Because that's how C copies and assigns `struct`s, and compatibility with C is important. Why aren't destructors automatically virtual (see Item 14), and why must implementation details appear in class definitions (see Item 34)? Because doing otherwise would impose a performance penalty, and efficiency is important. Why can't C++ detect initialization dependencies between non-local static objects (see Item 47)? Because C++ supports separate translation (i.e., the ability to compile source modules separately, then link several object files together to form an executable), relies on existing linkers, and doesn't mandate the existence of program databases. As a result, C++ compilers almost never know everything about an entire program. Finally, why doesn't C++ free programmers from tiresome duties like memory management (see Items 5–10) and low-level pointer manipulations? Because some programmers need those capabilities, and the needs of real programmers are of paramount importance.

This barely hints at how the design goals behind C++ shape the behavior of the language. To cover everything would take an entire book, so it's convenient that Stroustrup wrote one. That book is *The Design and Evolution of C++* (Addison-Wesley, 1994), sometimes known as simply "D&E." Read it, and you'll see what features were added to C++, in what order, and why. You'll also learn about features that were rejected, and why. You'll even get the inside story on how the `dynamic_cast` feature (see Item 39) was considered, rejected, reconsidered, then accepted — and why. If you're having trouble making sense of C++, D&E should dispel much of your confusion.

The Design and Evolution of C++ offers a wealth of insights into how C++ came to be what it is, but it's nothing like a formal specification for the language. For that you must turn to the international standard for C++, an impressive exercise in formalese running some 700 pages. There can read such riveting prose as this:

> A virtual function call uses the default arguments in the declaration of the virtual function determined by the static type of the pointer or reference denoting the object. An overriding function in a derived class does not acquire default arguments from the function it overrides.

This paragraph is the basis for Item 38 ("Never redefine an inherited default parameter value"), but I hope my treatment of the topic is somewhat more accessible than the text above.

The standard is hardly bedtime reading, but it's your best recourse — your *standard* recourse — if you and someone else (a compiler vendor, say, or a developer of some other tool that processes source code) disagree on what is and isn't C++. The whole purpose of a standard is to provide definitive information that settles arguments like that.

The standard's official title is a mouthful, but if you need to know it, you need to know it. Here it is: *International Standard for Information Systems—Programming Language C++*. It's published by Working Group 21 of the International Organization for Standardization (ISO). (If you insist on being picky about it, it's really published by — I am not making this up — ISO/IEC JTC1/SC22/WG21.) You can order a copy of the official standard from your national standards body (in the United States, that's ANSI, the American National Standards Institute), but copies of late drafts of the standard — which are quite similar (though not identical) to the final document — are freely available on the World Wide Web. A good place to look for a copy is `http://www.cygnus.com/misc/wp/`, but given the pace of change in cyberspace, don't be surprised if this link is broken by the time you try it. If it is, your favorite Web search engine will doubtless turn up a URL that works.

As I said, *The Design and Evolution of C++* is fine for insights into the language's design, and the standard is great for nailing down language details, but it would be nice if there were a comfortable middle ground between D&E's view from 10,000 meters and the standard's micron-level examination. Textbooks are supposed to fill this niche, but they generally drift toward the standard's perspective, whereby *what* the language is receives a lot more attention than *why* it's that way.

Enter the ARM. The ARM is another book, *The Annotated C++ Reference Manual*, by Margaret Ellis and Bjarne Stroustrup (Addison-Wesley, 1990). Upon its publication, it became *the* authority on C++, and the international standard started with the ARM (along with the existing C standard) as its basis. In the intervening years, the language specified by the standard has in some ways parted company with that described by the ARM, so the ARM is no longer the authority it once was. It's still a useful reference, however, because most of what it says is still true, and it's not uncommon for vendors to adhere to the ARM specification in areas of C++ where the standard has only recently settled down.

What makes the ARM really useful, however, isn't the RM part (the Reference Manual), it's the A part: the annotations. The ARM provides extensive commentary on *why* many features of C++ behave the way they do. Some of this information is in D&E, but much of it isn't, and you *do* want to know it. For instance, here's something that drives most people crazy when they first encounter it:

```
class Base {
public:
  virtual void f(int x);
};

class Derived: public Base {
public:
  virtual void f(double *pd);
};

Derived *pd = new Derived;
pd->f(10);                              // error!
```

The problem is that `Derived::f` hides `Base::f`, even though they take different parameter types, so compilers demand that the call to `f` take a `double*`, which the literal `10` most certainly is not.

This is inconvenient, but the ARM provides an explanation for this behavior. Suppose that when you called `f`, you really did want to call the version in `Derived`, but you accidentally used the wrong parameter type. Further suppose that `Derived` is way down in an inheritance hierarchy and that you were unaware that Derived indirectly inherits from some base class BaseClass, and that BaseClass declares a virtual function f that takes an int. In that case, you would have inadvertently called BaseClass::f, a function you didn't even know existed! This kind of error could occur frequently where large class hierarchies are used, so Stroustrup decided to nip it in the bud by having derived class members hide base class members on a per-name basis.

Note, by the way, that if the writer of Derived wants to allow clients to access Base::f, this is easily accomplished via a simple using declaration:

```
class Derived: public Base {
public:
  using Base::f;                   // import Base::f into
                                   // Derived's scope
  virtual void f(double *pd);
};

Derived *pd = new Derived;
pd->f(10);                         // fine, calls Base::f
```

For compilers not yet supporting using declarations, an alternative is to employ an inline function:

```
class Derived: public Base {
public:
  virtual void f(int x) { Base::f(x); }
  virtual void f(double *pd);
};

Derived *pd = new Derived;
pd->f(10);                         // fine, calls Derived::f(int),
                                   // which calls Base::f(int)
```

Between D&E and the ARM, you'll gain insights into the design and implementation of C++ that make it possible to appreciate the sound, no-nonsense architecture behind a sometimes baroque-looking facade. Fortify those insights with the detailed information in the standard, and you've got a foundation for software development that leads to truly *effective* C++.

Afterword

If, having digested 50 ways to improve your programs and designs, you still find yourself hungry for C++ guidelines, you may be interested in my second book on the subject, *More Effective C++: 35 New Ways to Improve Your Programs and Design*. Like *Effective C++*, *More Effective C++* covers material that's essential for effective C++ software development, but *Effective C++* focuses more on fundamentals, while *More Effective C++* also spends time on newer language features and on advanced programming techniques.

You can find detailed information on *More Effective C++* — including four complete Items, the book's list of recommended reading, and more — at the *More Effective C++* web site: `http://www.awl.com/cp/mec++.html`. In case you can't wait, the contents of *More Effective C++* are summarized below.

Basics

Item 1:   Distinguish between pointers and references
Item 2:   Prefer C++-style casts
Item 3:   Never treat arrays polymorphically
Item 4:   Avoid gratuitous default constructors

Operators

Item 5:   Be wary of user-defined conversion functions
Item 6:   Distinguish between prefix and postfix forms of increment and decrement operators
Item 7:   Never overload &&, ||, or ,
Item 8:   Understand the different meanings of `new` and `delete`

Exceptions

Item 9:   Use destructors to prevent resource leaks

Index

It is an unfortunate fact of life that the term *definition* means different things in C++ and in English. In this index, the term *definition* refers to a C++ definition. English definitions — definitions of terms — are labeled "definition (English)" and are summarized under "English definitions."

Operators are listed under *operator*. That is, operator<< is listed under operator<<, not under <<, etc. The exceptions to this rule are the operators new, delete, and sizeof, which are listed, oddly enough, under new, delete, and sizeof, respectively.

The example classes and class templates used in this book are indexed under *example classes/templates*, and the example function and function templates are indexed under *example functions/templates*.

Before A

.cpp files 138
0, see zero
1066 154
80-20 rule 143, 168

A

abort 26
  violated exception specifications
    and 28
abstract classes 161, 201
  definition (English) 63
abstraction, functional 89–90
accessibility
  control over data members' 89
  restrictions
    handles and 124
    inheritance and 115

Ada 57, 224
address equality 75
addresses, of inline functions 140
address-of operator, see operator&
adjacent differences 231
*Advanced C++: Programming Styles and
  Idioms* xvii, xviii
algorithms, in standard C++ library 229
aliasing 52, 53, 75–76, 101
  definition (English) 72
Alice's Restaurant, allusion to 43
allocation
  see memory management and opera-
    tor new
allocators 227
ambiguity
  deliberately introducing 111
  diamonds and 200
  libraries and 114
  MI and 114–115, 195, 200
  potential 113–116

J

K

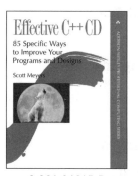

Register
Your Book
at www.aw.com/cseng/register

You may be eligible to receive:

- Advance notice of forthcoming editions of the book
- Related book recommendations
- Chapter excerpts and supplements of forthcoming titles
- Information about special contests and promotions throughout the year
- Notices and reminders about author appearances, tradeshows, and online chats with special guests

Contact us

If you are interested in writing a book or reviewing manuscripts prior to publication, please write to us at:

Editorial Department
Addison-Wesley Professional
75 Arlington Street, Suite 300
Boston, MA 02116 USA
Email: AWPro@aw.com

Addison-Wesley

Visit us on the Web: http://www.aw.com/cseng